x chakhy lubroed 1050 miles

x 1/2 year - check car

x oil change every 2500 - 3000
3000 miles change TIRES

DRAIN cooling system without gas

renew oil filter 3000 miles 1/2 year

Reverse
2nd
18-20

Lubercation 10,000

Lubenty peak ancel, inerenl 20,000

greece rear axil and universal pont

put your clutch down except in third
in before you Brake.

1. put key in Ign
2. depress clutch   (car in neu.)
3. press gas down 1/3 or 1/4 way
4. push or turn starter
5. put right foot on break peddl (rais gas pedel and
6. place lever in first
7. releace hand break
8 check trofact and give segnals
9. excelerate a little.

Stop

X RAIL ROAD

WORNING

US Highway

YES
Tues & Wed = 6th

MAN AND THE MOTOR CAR

MAN AND THE

fifth edition •

MOTOR CAR

by *The Center for Safety Education*
New York University

Prentice-Hall, Inc.

L. C. Cat. Card No.: 54-11805

First printing.........August, 1954
Second printing.........April, 1955
Third printing.....September, 1955
Fourth printing.....December, 1955
Fifth printing...........June, 1956
Sixth printing.........August, 1957

The work of the Center for Safety Education
is made possible through an annual grant from
the Accident Prevention Department of the
Association of Casualty and Surety Companies.

Printed in the United States of America
5 5 1 2 9

In its original form, *Man and the Motor Car* was published in 1936. The first text of its kind, it was widely used in schools that, prior to World War II, were pioneering in providing instruction in driver education. Since that time, four editions have been published, and *Man and the Motor Car* has become one of the most widely used books of its kind.

The first edition was revised and made available to schools in 1941. The popularity and widespread use of that revised edition is attested to by the fact that, in the period 1941 to 1949, *Man and the Motor Car* had 130 printings and was used in several thousand high schools. A number of states distributed the text as their official driver education book on a state-adoption plan. The 1941 revised edition, as well as the original edition in 1936, was prepared by a committee of driver education authorities under the leadership of Albert W. Whitney, then Consulting Director of the National Conservation Bureau, which is now called the Accident Prevention Department of the Association of Casualty and Surety Companies.

Man and the Motor Car was again revised in 1949. This edition included the basic content, approaches, and treatment of the 1936 and 1941 editions, and was fortified with appropriate new materials. Revised under the leadership of Milton D. Kramer, then Assistant Director of the Center for Safety Education, New York University, with the assistance of the staff of the Accident Prevention Department of the Association of Casualty and Surety Companies, the 1949 edition included a significant increase in illustrations and special topics, and a wide range of projects for the student.

Since the publication of the last edition, however, the driver education program has experienced unprecedented expansion and development. Therefore, the need for a revision of the Fourth Edition, to provide leadership in this growth, became apparent.

This new edition of *Man and the Motor Car* is a completely revised and rewritten text. In keeping with the high standards and traditions established by the previous editions, it is again the first book to reflect those principles and practices that have most recently been proved effective by research and reported experience. This textbook is organized on a unit basis, to facilitate the operation of a variety of enriched, correlated plans of classroom and practice driving instruction through a learning-by-doing approach. It is also the first to outline a complete, systematic, step-by-step procedure for learning fundamental skills in both standard shift and automatic transmission vehicles. The comprehensive contents include such current topics as superhighway driving, emergency situations, human relations in traffic, and a clear-cut outline of the role each individual can play in working toward a solution to the traffic problem. In general, this book provides a dynamic guide to experiences in safety for greater driving adventures.

Prepared for the Center for Safety Education, New York University, under the leadership of Edward W. Pepyne, Driver Education Consultant, the Fifth Edition of *Man and the Motor Car* provides the best approach to driver education known today. If this text is used properly, it *will* make you a better driver, it *can* help you to live more abundantly, and it *may* save your life!

EDITORIAL REVISION COMMITTEE

Edward W. Pepyne, Center for Safety Education, New York University—*Chairman*

Leon Brody, Center for Safety Education, New York University

J. Duke Elkow, Brooklyn College, New York

T. A. Seals, Association of Casualty and Surety Companies, New York

Herbert J. Stack, Director, Center for Safety Education, New York University

ACKNOWLEDGMENTS

The Editorial Revision Committee expresses appreciation to the following reviewers and contributors and to all others who directly or indirectly have aided in the production of this volume.

INDIVIDUAL CONTRIBUTORS AND REVIEWERS

Robert Allen, Association of Casualty and Surety Companies • Calvin R. Ashe, Baltimore Public Schools, Maryland • Frank Bennett, Baltimore Public Schools, Maryland • R. W. Bishop, State Teachers College, Millersville, Pennsylvania • Thomas Boate, Association of Casualty and Surety Companies, New York • Edward Bonessi, West Haven Public Schools, Connecticut • William Brewster, National Bureau of Casualty Underwriters, New York • Eugene S. Burke, Georgia Trucking Association • T. A. Carmichael, State Department of Education, Georgia • Price Clark, Association of Casualty and Surety Companies, New York • William Corgill, Association of Casualty and Surety Companies, New York • Walter A. Cutter, Center for Safety Education, New York University • Harold R. Danford, Dunedin Public Schools, Florida • Charles Dunbar, Milton Public Schools, Massachusetts • J. Frank Duryea, Automotive Inventor, Madison, Connecticut • Walter Eaton, Michigan Inter-Industry Highway Safety Committee • Eugene J. Fanning, Registry of Motor Vehicles, Massachusetts • Louis Fontaine, Palmer Public Schools, Massachusetts • Robert Grainger, Chester Public Schools, Pennsylvania • Clemens Gretter, Artist, New York • Devona Griffith, Center for Safety Education, New York University • John T. Haack, Davenport Public Schools, Iowa • Earl D. Heath, Center for Safety Education, New York University • J. Edgar Hoover, Federal Bureau of Investigation • Edith W. Klemens, Center for Safety Education, New York University • John Kowalski, Oswego State Teachers College, New York • John Larson, Center for Safety Education, New York University • Douglas Leake, Commercial Driving School Association, Massachusetts • Franklyn E. Learned, Supervisor of Safety Education, Connecticut • Edward Leonard, State Department of Motor Vehicles, New York • Charles Lemmell, State Department of Public Instruction, Dover, Delaware • William Leydig, Coraopolis, Pennsylvania • Robert K. Mattern, Public Schools, Pennsylvania • Delbert Means, Wichita Public Schools, Kansas • Richard O'Connor, New York City Board of Education • Wilber O'Donnell, Holyoke Public Schools and Springfield College, Massachusetts • Les Palmer, Agricultural and Mechanical College of Texas • Ronald Patterson, Michigan State College • Andrew Payton, Kent State University, Ohio • Nathaniel O. Schneider, New Jersey Safety Council • James Schrock, Teaneck Public Schools, New Jersey • Ernest I. Schrot, Lock Haven State Teachers College, Pennsylvania • Richard L. Sheppard, Porto-Clinic Instruments Inc., New York • William Sherman, Automobile Manufacturers Association, Detroit, Michigan • Harry Stevenson, Third Avenue Transit Company, New York • Marland K. Strasser, Association of Casualty and Surety Companies, San Francisco • William J. Toth, Center for Safety Education, New York University • Eugene Ungar, Bergenfield, New Jersey • Raymond Wahl, Northampton Public Schools, Pennsylvania • Leo R. Welch, Bureau of Traffic Safety, New Jersey • Theodore Williams, Boston Red Sox Baseball Club, Massachusetts • Raymond Winans, *West Springfield Record*, Massachusetts •

ORGANIZATIONAL REVIEWERS AND CONTRIBUTORS

Aetna Life Insurance Company • American Airlines • American Association of Motor Vehicle Administrators • American Oil Company • Associated Transport, Inc. • Association of Casualty and Surety Companies • Automobile Old Timers • Automobile Manufacturers Association • Baltimore and Ohio Railroad • Boston Red Sox Baseball Club • *Call-Chronicle* Newspapers, Allentown, Pennsylvania • Chrysler Corporation • Floyd Clymer Publications • Federal Bureau of Investigation • Ford Motor Company • General Motors Corporation • Grumman Aircraft Engineering Corporation • Hudson Motor Car Company • Byron G. Moon Company • National Association for the Prevention of Blindness • National Association of Secondary School Principals • National Commission on Safety Education • National Safety Council • New Jersey Turnpike Authority • Porto-Clinic Instruments, Inc. • Port of New York Authority • *Scholastic* Magazines • Smithsonian Institute • St. Louis Transit Company • Studebaker Corporation • Travelers Insurance Company • *West Springfield Record* • *Your Car* magazine • Educational Device Company •

• Color photograph on the cover by H. M. Perry from Shostal • Photographs on the title page are used through the courtesy of Ewing Galloway •

ACKNOWLEDGMENTS

Unit One: The Traffic Problem–A Challenge to Young Drivers

Problem 1: What is the traffic problem—and how are you concerned?   3

Its significance for young people   4
Preparing to drive   6

Problem 2: How is our nation concerned?   15

The traffic toll   15
Benefits and advantages   19
Power—servant or master   26

Problem 3: How did the problem develop?   29

From horseless carriages to streamlined horsepower   33
Early faith in the motor car   40
Obstacles to adequate traffic control   42
Do you accept the challenge?   48

Unit Two: Learning Fundamental Driving Skills

Problem 1: How can the instruments, switches, and controls help you?   53

Information instruments   53
Regulating switches   58
Driving controls   62
At the controls   66

Problem 2: How is good form in driving developed? 69

Forming habits 69
Fundamental drills 70
Preparing to drive 73
Moving the car 80
Driving in lower gears 86
Adjusting driving speed 89
Right and left turns 95
The Y turn 99
Maneuvering on grades 101
Parking—angle and parallel 106

Unit Three: The Driver

Problem 1: How does physical condition affect driving performance? 117

General physical condition 117

Problem 2: How do personality traits affect driving performance? 137

Problem drivers 138
What do these drivers mean to you? 143

Unit Four: Understanding Your Car— Its Construction, Operation, and Maintenance

Problem 1: What makes a car go? 151

The engine 152
The power train 164
The chassis and running gear 170
The body 174

Problem 2: How can you get your money's worth from your car?   177

Lubrication   177
Inspection, adjustment, and repairs   179
Periodic check-up   187
Driving economically   188
Protection against unforeseen loss   189
Buying a used car   190

Unit Five: Traffic Laws–Natural and Man-Made

Problem 1: How do the laws of motion and energy affect the car and the driver?   199

Friction   199
Centrifugal force   205
Momentum   208
Gravity   213
The influence of speed on traffic safety   214

Problem 2: What are the basic man-made traffic rules?   221

Basic rules   222

Problem 3: How does engineering affect traffic and its laws?   235

Traffic engineering   237
Effective use of existing facilities   238
Traffic control measures   238
Significance to drivers   245

Problem 4: What are the laws concerning licensing and liability?   247

Responsibility in case of accident   248
Liability   248
Insurance   250
In case of an accident   252

Problem 5: How are traffic laws enforced?   257

Co-operation with traffic officers   257
Enforcement agencies   258

Unit Six: The Art of Driving

Problem 1: What are the problems involved in city driving?   267

Driving hazards multiplied   268
Driving in traffic   268

Problem 2: What are the problems involved in highway driving?   279

Driving on highways   279
Route numbers and maps   291

Problem 3: What special problems are encountered on superhighways?   295

Reasons for turnpike accidents   296
Techniques for turnpike driving   298
Advantages of turnpike driving   300

Problem 4: What abilities are needed to meet driving emergencies successfully?   303

Emergency driving situations   304
Learning techniques   307

Problem 5: What are the fundamentals of the art of good driving?   317

The privilege of driving   318
Controlled power   319
Self-enforcement   319
Defensive driving   320
Inefficiency breeds accidents   323
Evaluating your performance   323

Unit Seven: Co-operation Among Highway Users

Problem 1: How can drivers and pedestrians co-operate more effectively?   333

Drivers must think for the pedestrian   334
Tactics for safe walking   336

Problem 2: What is the role of the cyclist in traffic?   341

The three streams of traffic   341

Unit Eight: Meeting the Challenge— It Can Be Done

How can you help?   351

Take an active interest   351
Co-operation and support   353

Index   359

MAN AND THE MOTOR CAR

PROBLEM ONE

What is the traffic problem — and how are you concerned?

PROBLEM TWO

How is our nation concerned?

PROBLEM THREE

How did the problem develop?

Fig. 1-1. Traffic—a life or death activity—in which, willing or not, we all must play.

THE TRAFFIC PROBLEM

What Is the Traffic Problem—and How Are You Concerned?

Highway traffic is the lifeblood of the United States' transportation system. When traffic fails to flow smoothly and efficiently, destruction, disfigurement, and death result—which affect the lives of every American. The driver is the key to the solution of our traffic problems. Unfortunately, drivers are not as good as they should be. This is especially true of young drivers. Lack of training is the reason that many motor vehicle operators do not drive efficiently and safely. Driver Education, then, is essential for making beginners good drivers and experienced drivers more competent. Efficient driving performance will bring about broad social advances and many personal benefits to each of us. It is obvious, therefore, that we all should become actively concerned with traffic safety.

America's traffic scene is a complex one. It is composed of some 70 million drivers of widely varying abilities . . . more than twice as many pedestrians, from toddlers to octogenarians . . . 60 million motor cars, including sleek new models and rattling relics . . . and 3½ million miles of roadways differing in design, construction, and condition. The problem of keeping pedestrian and vehicular traffic flowing smoothly and safely has, in recent years, mushroomed in complexity and difficulty.

The motor car, a relatively new factor in the American scene, has produced revolutionary changes in our pattern of daily living. It has made it possible for us to travel rapidly to many places and to transport all kinds of products much more efficiently. But these benefits have not come without serious complications. The cost of traffic accidents, from the humanitarian, social, and economic viewpoint, is staggering. It presents a critical challenge to every American.

Fig. 1-2. Driver Education classroom sessions are quite similar to skull practice sessions in athletics. (*Courtesy: State Board of Education, Dover, Delaware, and New York University.*)

The time has come for each of us to recognize the seriousness of the problem and our personal relationship to it. Every pedestrian, driver, and citizen is vitally concerned. There is no good reason why we should not be able to enjoy the benefits of modern transportation without paying dearly with life, limb, and property. Through individual concern and co-operative effort, this goal can be achieved.

ITS SIGNIFICANCE FOR YOUNG PEOPLE

The problem of traffic safety has special significance for youth of high school and college age. Many have questioned whether they possess the maturity and sense of social responsibility needed for proper (not just skillful) operation of a motor car. Critics point to the accident records, which indicate that drivers under twenty-five are involved in much more than their proportionate share of fatal accidents; they point to records of juvenile delinquency involving the use of cars; and they decry repeated violations by "grandstanders," whose reckless and irresponsible driving is a serious danger to society. It is a shame, these people say indignantly—something ought to be done about it. And, if young drivers will not do something themselves, others may take action.

Fig. 1-3. Learning to drive is very much like learning to fly. (*Courtesy: Grumman Aircraft Engineering Corporation.*)

Undoubtedly, there are many excellent young drivers. However, a small percentage repeatedly violate the rules of the road and are involved in numerous serious accidents. That these lack driving experience, exhibit poor judgment, or possess bad attitudes is obvious. Unfortunately, their performance creates an unfavorable reputation for the entire teen-age group.

Young drivers should rate among the best in the nation. They are usually in fine physical condition, have smooth, quick coordination, and possess keen, alert minds. Physically and mentally, they are prepared to develop the qualities that make good drivers —efficient performance, sound judgment, and co-operative attitudes—the same qualities that make good athletes, good neighbors, and good citizens.

THE STORY OF ALL RECKLESS DRIVERS

THE PLOT OFTEN VARIES BUT THE
RESULT IS USUALLY THE SAME

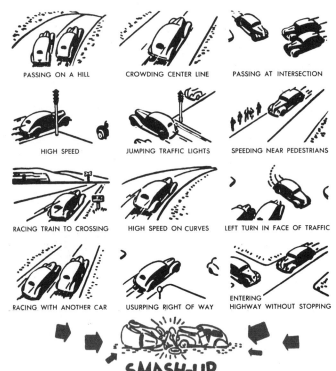

PASSING ON A HILL   CROWDING CENTER LINE   PASSING AT INTERSECTION

HIGH SPEED   JUMPING TRAFFIC LIGHTS   SPEEDING NEAR PEDESTRIANS

RACING TRAIN TO CROSSING   HIGH SPEED ON CURVES   LEFT TURN IN FACE OF TRAFFIC

RACING WITH ANOTHER CAR   USURPING RIGHT OF WAY   ENTERING HIGHWAY WITHOUT STOPPING

SMASH-UP

Fig. 1-4. All of the dangerous practices shown here lead to one end: damage, death, disaster.

PREPARING TO DRIVE

Education in the art of driving should start before you actually take the wheel. You can learn a great deal by observing the correct and incorrect procedures of other drivers before you begin to manipulate the controls. It is like learning to play tennis or basketball: although much of the knowledge and skill is gained through actual play, a great deal can and should be learned through study and observation of others.

In addition to observation, the learner will derive a great deal of value from participation in classroom discussions and projects dealing with traffic problems and driving performance. Such classroom activities are comparable to "skull practice" sessions employed by coaches of athletic teams and to procedures followed in aviation "ground school" prior to actual flying instruction.

A BLUEPRINT FOR TRAFFIC SAFETY EDUCATION

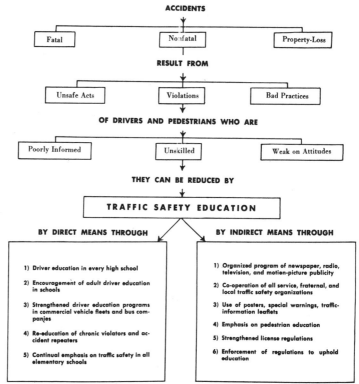

ACCIDENTS

| Fatal | Nonfatal | Property-Loss |

RESULT FROM

| Unsafe Acts | Violations | Bad Practices |

OF DRIVERS AND PEDESTRIANS WHO ARE

| Poorly Informed | Unskilled | Weak on Attitudes |

THEY CAN BE REDUCED BY

TRAFFIC SAFETY EDUCATION

BY DIRECT MEANS THROUGH

1) Driver education in every high school
2) Encouragement of adult driver education in schools
3) Strengthened driver education programs in commercial vehicle fleets and bus companies
4) Re-education of chronic violators and accident repeaters
5) Continual emphasis on traffic safety in all elementary schools

BY INDIRECT MEANS THROUGH

1) Organized program of newspaper, radio, television, and motion-picture publicity
2) Co-operation of all service, fraternal, and local traffic safety organizations
3) Use of posters, special warnings, traffic-information leaflets
4) Emphasis on pedestrian education
5) Strengthened license regulations
6) Enforcement of regulations to uphold education

Fig. 1-5. Accidents do not just happen; they are caused, and the causes can be eliminated. (*Courtesy: Center for Safety Education, New York University.*)

Practice Makes Perfect Drivers

As in learning to swim, to fly a plane, to operate a typewriter, or to play football, individual practice is essential in learning to drive an automobile. What you learn in the classroom is necessary and valuable, but you cannot develop the neuromuscular co-ordination that makes for skillful performance merely by watching, listening, or reading. You learn to do a thing by actually doing it. Furthermore, you learn to do just what you practice. The manner in which you practice, therefore, is very important.

Practice without guidance and direction is a type of trial-and-error learning—a "hit-or-miss" process of trying first one method and then another until finally, by elimination or luck, a technique that seems to work is found. Learning of this type wastes time and gives no assurance that the learning will ever be of high

"Don't be silly—no one gives signals anymore."

"The road looks clear, let's pass him."

Fig. 1-6. The "grandstander" on the highway, like the grandstander in sports, is as easy to recognize by his words as by his actions. *(Courtesy: Aetna Casualty and Surety Company.)*

quality. It is a method likely to produce second-rate or incorrect performance. In driving it can be highly dangerous.

Learning to drive under expert guidance is more rapid and produces a higher degree of skill. Just as the expert coaching received by big league athletes is revealed in the ease and efficiency they display in their performance, so practice driving under a competent instructor will help you develop the good form that characterizes the expert driver. In fact, the expert driver controls his car so skillfully and co-operates with other road users so well that he blends into the normal flow of traffic as if he were a member of an outstanding team of players. And on the road, as on the playing field, the emphasis *should* be on teamwork rather than on "grandstand" plays that characterize "show-offs."

In the final analysis, therefore, *the type of driver you will become depends on your desire to become a top-notch performer and on your willingness to follow directions and work hard.*

Even Experienced Drivers Are Going to "School"

People who have been driving for years often find that they do not know as much about good driving as they once thought they did, and that there is room for improvement in their performance. Many are enrolling in driver refresher courses offered by evening schools. Most professional drivers are being required by their employers to take special advanced courses. Increasing numbers of accident repeaters and chronic traffic violators are being given the opportunity to get remedial help in traffic court schools.

The problem of correcting chronic violators is a difficult one, but it can be done. It is important to remember, however, that be-

Fig. 1-7. When you drive a car, safety and sportsmanship pay off in popularity and greater adventures. (*Courtesy: Studebaker Corporation.*)

havior patterns established early in life are not easily changed, and that a large part of today's traffic problem is actually the result of inadequate learning by yesterday's youth. In the long run, a good start in learning to drive will be beneficial both to the learner and to those with whom he will eventually share the road.

HOW YOU ARE CONCERNED 9

Fig. 1-8. The end of a fool-hardy adventure. The driver of this car was operating too fast and on the wrong side of the road. (*Courtesy: Allentown* (*Pa.*) *"Call-Chronicle."*)

A Twofold Challenge to You!

It is up to you, therefore, to help demonstrate that the confidence expressed by permitting teen-agers to drive has not been misplaced. The laws of most states still support the belief that youth of high school age are mature enough to become good drivers.

It is also up to you to render a service to your community. You can help to raise the driving standards in your community by setting a good example of driving performance that may well shame older drivers into mending their ways. Within a few years, groups of young, trained drivers could accomplish a great deal toward changing the complexion of our accident-ridden traffic pattern. Young people can do this by mastering the finer techniques of driving, by observing the laws of the traffic game, and by exemplifying the spirit of sportsmanship and co-operation that makes for good citizenship on the road.

For Selfish Reasons, Too

Needless to say, as you work toward these objectives you will also get greater personal satisfaction out of driving and avoid the risk of poor performance that usually results in an interruption of fun and adventure.

As a skillful driver, you can enjoy countless recreational opportunities. You can go to beaches, ball games, and dances, undertake hunting, fishing, and camping trips, and derive pleasure from scores of other experiences. Also, through good driving you can get your money's worth from your automobile. Efficient mastery of your vehicle nets considerable savings through increased gasoline mileage, fewer repair bills, and better trade-in allowances. Moreover, by becoming a good driver, you will receive the respect that excellent performance merits. Your record, unmarred by accidents or violations, will be a source of justifiable pride.

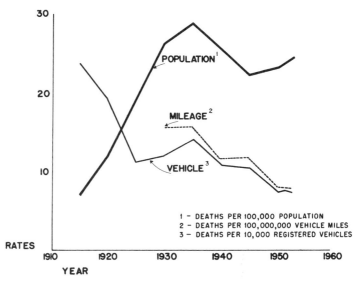

Fig. 1-9. Trends: Motor Vehicle Death Rate. (From Brody and Stack, "Highway Safety and Driver Education," Prentice-Hall.)

1 – DEATHS PER 100,000 POPULATION
2 – DEATHS PER 100,000,000 VEHICLE MILES
3 – DEATHS PER 10,000 REGISTERED VEHICLES

Safety for Greater Adventures

Danger seems to be a by-product of certain modern inventions. But we need these inventions and we must seek to control them. This involves learning to avoid unnecessary risks and to meet successfully those that cannot be avoided.

The good driver, then, will steer clear of unnecessary hazards and refrain from taking unnecessary chances. For example, by driving at reasonable speeds and keeping his car under control, he will not be faced by the dangers that go with excessive speeds. By going without his car for a day or two while it is undergoing repair, he will not be earmarked for an accident because of faulty brakes. By being extra alert in congested residential areas, he will avoid the risk of hitting a child who may chase a ball into the street. By yielding the right of way to a car that exhibits marks of frequent accident involvement, he will protect himself and his car from the threat of injury and damage by a "terror of the road." By doing these things, he substitutes a good adventure for a bad one. By playing it smart and avoiding unnecessary risks, he shows himself to be a mature, responsible driver who can take care of himself, his passengers, and his car under any circumstances.

Yes, safety is the way to more and better adventures. Accidents do not "just happen." They are caused by unsafe acts and unsafe conditions that can be eliminated. The fatalistic attitude that "accidents are going to happen—there is nothing we can do about it" is a product of the same kind of thinking that a short time ago regarded diptheria and smallpox epidemics as unavoidable plagues. Accidents happen to people who lack knowledge and skill or have bad attitudes. Safety depends on skill, intelligence, and efficiency; safe driving is skillful, intelligent, and efficient driving. Safe driving is a means by which you, your family, and your friends can have more and better driving adventures!

DISCUSSION TOPICS

1. How has the traffic problem affected you? Explain.
2. What general suggestions do you have for improving traffic conditions in your community?
3. What can driver education do to help the beginning driver? The experienced driver? The professional driver? The accident and violation repeater?
4. What is a "grandstander"? Can you give any specific examples?
5. What are five major advantages of being a good driver? What are some of the disadvantages of poor driving?
6. What can teen-agers do to raise driving standards? What should adults do? Give details.
7. What is meant by the phrase, "Safety for greater adventures"?
8. Give some examples of unnecessary risks from your own experience. Discuss the possible consequences in each case.
9. "Accidents will happen; there is nothing we can do about it." Criticize this statement.
10. "Safe driving is sissy driving." Evaluate this statement, supporting your argument with facts.
11. Can you see any relationship between good citizenship, good sportsmanship and good driving? What roles do co-operation, teamwork, and competition play in good driving?

PROJECTS AND PROBLEMS

1. Investigate the truth of this statement, "Teen-age drivers have the poorest driving records." Prepare a chart showing the total number of drivers and the total number of traffic accidents in your state last year. What percentages of the drivers are in the following age groups: under 20; 20-24; 25-29; 30-34; 35-39; 40-44. What percentages of the accidents involve drivers from each of these age groups? On the basis of these findings, what conclusions could you draw regarding the relationships of age to driving performance? Regarding the need for driver education?

2. Debate the proposition that, "No person should be granted a driver's license unless he has successfully completed a driver-education course."

3. Write a 500-word essay outlining the part teen-agers should play in the solution of the traffic problem.

4. Prepare an exhibit contrasting the advantages of good driving and the disadvantages of irresponsible driving.

5. Draw a series of posters dealing with the following themes: Practice makes perfect drivers; The grandstanders; Safety for greater adventures; Good sportsmanship, good citizenship, and good driving.

6. Interview 25 people in your community and record their answers to this question, "What is your general opinion of teen-age drivers?" Make a report of your findings. What significance does this community opinion have for young drivers?

THE TRAFFIC PROBLEM

How Is Our Nation Concerned?

America is a "nation on wheels." These wheels have helped to give us the highest standard of living in the world. But, although they have been productive and useful, they also have been destructive and deadly. The disfigurement and death they have wrought surpasses even the fury of war. Technology and manufacturing genius have given us the wheeled power to annihilate the problems of distance and time. Now we must turn to the social sciences, psychology and sociology, so that in the use of these vehicles we will not be in constant danger of annihilating one another.

Many Americans have come to think of their car as a fourth necessity along with food, clothing, and housing. In fact, hard times have proved, to the astonishment of many, that some families prefer losing their houses to parting with their cars. For the automobile has multiplied our efficiency and expanded our horizons. It has given us the freedom to live anywhere—miles from our jobs. Our countryside, our cities, and our pattern of daily living have undergone rapid and unprecedented changes. We have become a "nation on wheels."

THE TRAFFIC TOLL

Within the past half century, traffic accidents have killed or injured over 32 million Americans—a total greater than the combined populations of New York, Texas, Massachusetts, and Wisconsin. Each year the traffic toll amounts to nearly 40 thousand

LARGELY BECAUSE OF HIGHWAY TRANSPORTATION
AMERICAN CITIES HAVE 'EXPLODED'

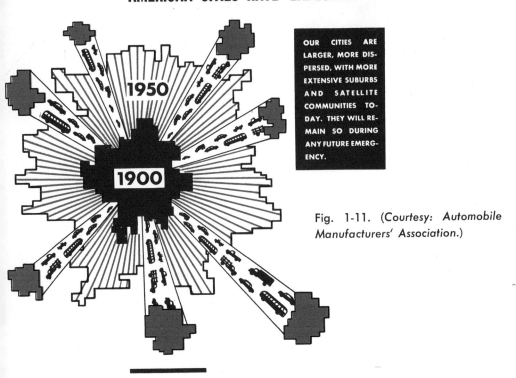

OUR CITIES ARE LARGER, MORE DISPERSED, WITH MORE EXTENSIVE SUBURBS AND SATELLITE COMMUNITIES TODAY. THEY WILL REMAIN SO DURING ANY FUTURE EMERGENCY.

Fig. 1-11. (*Courtesy: Automobile Manufacturers' Association.*)

WITHIN THE CITY THE AUTOMOBILE ACCOUNTS FOR NEARLY THREE-QUARTERS OF URBAN VEHICULAR TRAVEL

PRIVATE CARS   74%

TRANSIT   26%

2,074 U. S. CITIES HAVE NO PUBLIC TRANSIT SYSTEMS

people killed, about 2 million injured (of whom an estimated 100 thousand are permanently crippled or disfigured), and over four billions of dollars in financial losses. What a waste of human and material resources!

Worse Than War

The people of our nation, who had been quick to regard the locomotive and airplane as dangerous, were startled to discover that "horseless carriages" were killing people. By the time our eyes were fully opened the problem had reached appalling proportions. In the four years of our participation in World War II, 1,070,000 American servicemen were killed or wounded in com-

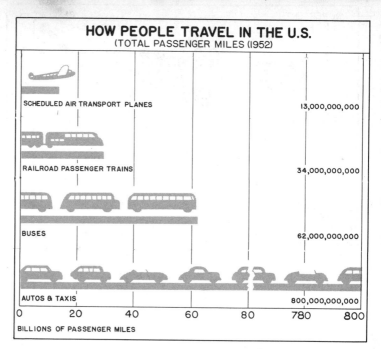

Fig. 1-12. More people travel by motor vehicle than all other forms of transportation combined. (Courtesy: "Scholastic Magazines.")

HOW PEOPLE TRAVEL IN THE U.S.
(TOTAL PASSENGER MILES (1952)

SCHEDULED AIR TRANSPORT PLANES   13,000,000,000

RAILROAD PASSENGER TRAINS   34,000,000,000

BUSES   62,000,000,000

AUTOS & TAXIS   800,000,000,000

0   20   40   60   80   780   800

BILLIONS OF PASSENGER MILES

bat; during the same period, 3,394,000 people were killed or injured in traffic accidents on the home front. In fact, more people have been killed or injured on our highways than have been slain or wounded on the battlefields of *all* the wars in which the United States has been involved. These facts are presented, not to detract from the horror and suffering due to war, but to give perspective to the magnitude and seriousness of the traffic problem.

The death and suffering of soldiers in war is tragic, but our sorrow is somewhat tempered by the knowledge that they died for a great cause. There is no such consolation in the case of the many thousands who die or are maimed every year because they or others were reckless, thoughtless, or unskillful in traffic.

A Common Concern

The full seriousness of the problem still goes unrecognized by many because of this lack of interest in accidents that do not involve them personally. There is a common error in thinking that "accidents happen to the other fellow—not to me." This error will become readily apparent if the present accident rate continues, for unless the rate diminishes, half of your present acquaintances may be hurt or killed as the result of a traffic accident some time in the future. In the average family with two children, it is

HOW OUR NATION IS CONCERNED

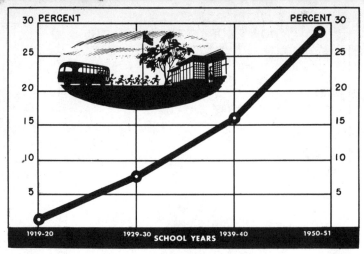

Fig. 1-13. Approximately 28 per cent of American pupils travel to school on special busses. (Courtesy: Automobile Manufacturers' Association.)

probable that one may be injured or killed by a motor car. Yes, there are many tragic possibilities to prove that accidents do not happen only to "the other fellow." These possibilities include yourself and those close to you.

In the long run, whether or not we are directly involved, we are all seriously affected. Tomorrow's traffic fatalities could include a scientist on the verge of discovering a cure for some killing or disabling disease to which most of us may be subject—or a military leader whose abilities are vitally needed for the nation's defense—or a musician whose talents have cheered the hearts of millions. Scientists, military leaders, and musicians, among many others, *have* been killed in traffic accidents. And in any case, our nation can ill afford this waste of human and material resources, as well as the traffic delays and congestion, that make this country's traffic problem such a serious one.

The problem must be solved—not only to prevent these losses, but also to assure America of the continued benefits and advantages that the motor car has made possible.

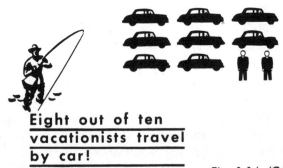

Eight out of ten vacationists travel by car!

Fig. 1-14. (Courtesy: National Highway Users Conference.)

THE TRAFFIC PROBLEM

HIGHWAY TRANSPORTATION'S CONTRIBUTION TO CIVILIAN DEFENSE

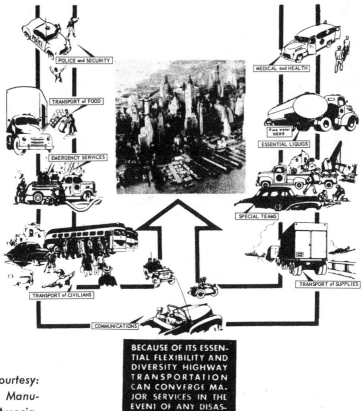

POLICE and SECURITY

TRANSPORT of FOOD

EMERGENCY SERVICES

TRANSPORT of CIVILIANS

COMMUNICATIONS

MEDICAL and HEALTH

Pure water HERE

ESSENTIAL LIQUIDS

SPECIAL TEAMS

TRANSPORT of SUPPLIES

BECAUSE OF ITS ESSENTIAL FLEXIBILITY AND DIVERSITY HIGHWAY TRANSPORTATION CAN CONVERGE MAJOR SERVICES IN THE EVENT OF ANY DISASTER TO OUR CIVILIAN POPULATION

Fig. 1-15. (Courtesy: Automobile Manufacturers' Association.)

BENEFITS AND ADVANTAGES

Recreational Advantages to Be Maintained

The automobile enables people in rural areas to enjoy the various advantages of the city. In like manner, city dwellers can experience the beauty and recreational advantages of the country. America's highways are an irresistible magnet to millions of traveling motorists. Eight out of ten vacationists travel by car; over half of our total population takes to the open highways annually on weekend trips or seasonal tours. This extensive traveling has helped to break down provincialism, and has developed a better understanding among our people of the folkways and ideas

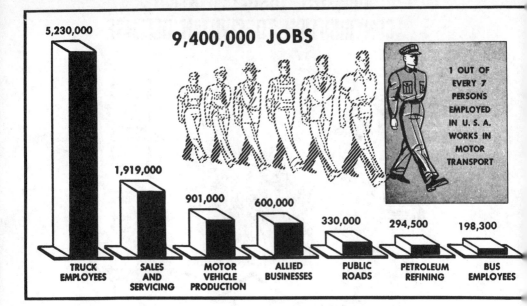

Fig. 1-16. The automobile has provided more jobs for more people than any other single element in American life. The combined adult populations of Colorado, Wyoming, Idaho, the six New England states, Montana, Arizona, and New Mexico equal the numbers of workers in highway transportation. (Courtesy: Automobile Manufacturers' Association.)

of various parts of the country—an understanding that is vital in a democratic society.

Extended Educational Opportunities

The motor vehicle has become important in expanding our educational horizons. Where good schools cannot be brought to pupils, the school bus brings pupils to the school. At least one out of every four American pupils travels to school in this manner. With the school bus has come the growth of the modern, consolidated school with its improved physical facilities and enriched curriculum. Likewise, mobile libraries now bring books within the reach of millions of people in both rural and metropolitan areas. Motorized transportation his indeed accomplished a great deal toward the extension of educational opportunities for all.

The Motor Car as a Job Maker

The automobile has become a dominant factor in our economic life. From a cluster of blacksmith shops and alley sheds at the turn of the century, the industry has grown to the largest job-

Fig. 1-17. The ability of trucks to deliver goods anywhere is an important feature of motor transportation. Trucks carry about two-thirds of the nation's freight to key cities and remote farm communities alike. (*Courtesy: Associated Transport, Inc.*)

maker in world history. About one in every seven persons employed in the United States works at a job resulting directly from the production or use of motor vehicles. In addition, untold numbers of enterprises depend indirectly upon the use of the automobile for income: hotels, motor courts, tourist homes, restaurants, roadside stands, golf courses, vacation resorts, drive-in theatres, and hundreds of others. *The automobile has provided more jobs for more people than any other single element in American life.*

1900 If in 1900 a policeman could protect this number of citizens . . .

NOW With radio and motor vehicles he can now protect about twice as many.

Fig. 1-18. The motor vehicle has expanded the efficiency of police protection. (*Courtesy: National Highway Users Conference.*)

Fig. 1-19. The success of a military operation depends on getting men and materiel to the right place at the right time. Owing to its flexibility, motor transportation plays an important role in military activities.

THE TRAFFIC PROBLEM

Economic Influence of Trucking

The motor vehicle has had other effects on our economic life. Trucks, for example, have a vital and unique role in the distribution of both manufactured and agricultural products. A truck can carry goods between almost any two geographical points, follow almost any desired route, or easily change its schedule to provide quick, effective service, regardless of whether a short or long haul is involved.

Bus Transportation

What the truck has accomplished in revolutionizing the delivery of freight and produce has been equalled by the bus in the field of human transportation. Its flexibility and speedy service have made the bus a popular vehicle for city or local transit, as well as for interurban or cross-country travel, thus bridging what would otherwise be a serious gap in passenger transportation. The total number of persons utilizing busses now exceeds the passenger traffic of railroads. Countless people use busses to travel to jobs that otherwise would be inaccessible for them.

National Defense

Motor transportation is a vital part of our nation's program of defense. Success in modern military maneuvers necessitates moving a sufficient amount of men and materials to the right place at the right time. About two in every five servicemen operate military vehicles as part of their regular service duties. In time of national emergency, untold numbers of civilians use motor vehicles to carry on the work of civilian defense. Of course, the services of trucks and busses assume added significance on the home front during an emergency.

General Furtherance of the Public Welfare

Highway transportation has had a tremendous impact on our society. The safety of each individual and of the general public— from death by illness or accident, from crime, from fire, from disaster—has been made more secure by ambulances, patrol cars, fire engines, and other emergency vehicles. How many lives have been saved by doctors because their automobiles have enabled them to arrive in time! Motorized rural free delivery has not only brought the mail to millions of farmers; it has become a "post office on wheels," providing complete postal service daily. High-

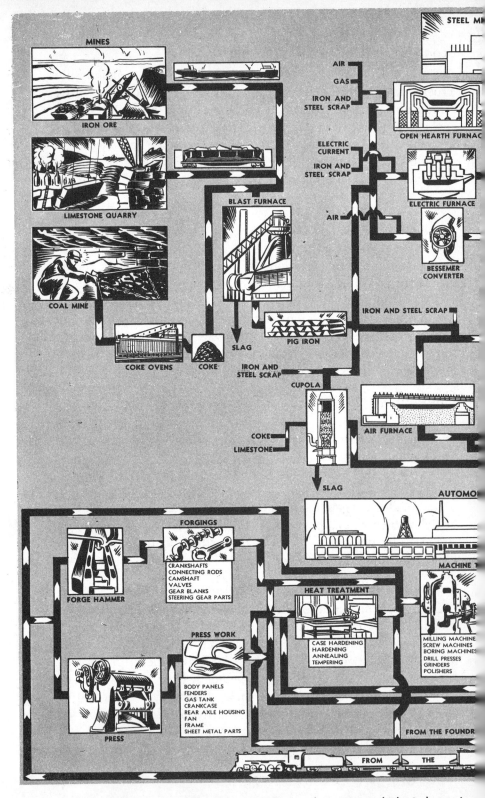

Fig. 1-20. Because of the scope of its operations, the motor vehicle industry is

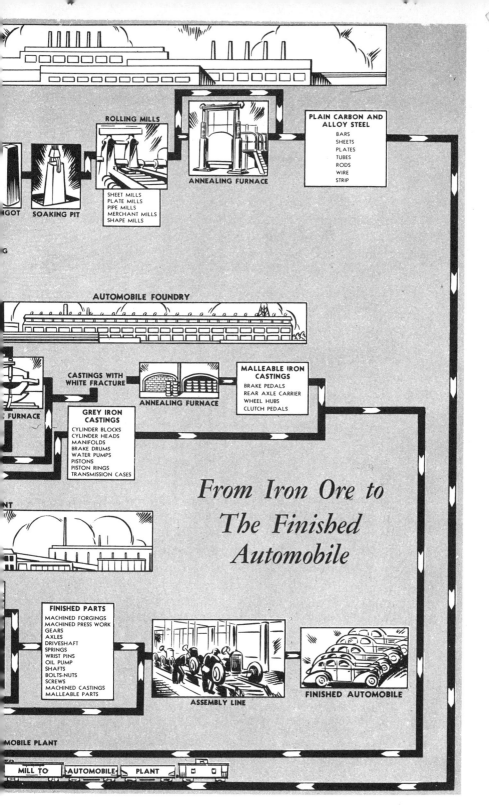

From Iron Ore to The Finished Automobile

ROLLING MILLS

SHEET MILLS
PLATE MILLS
PIPE MILLS
MERCHANT MILLS
SHAPE MILLS

INGOT

SOAKING PIT

ANNEALING FURNACE

PLAIN CARBON AND
ALLOY STEEL
BARS
SHEETS
PLATES
TUBES
RODS
WIRE
STRIP

AUTOMOBILE FOUNDRY

CASTINGS WITH
WHITE FRACTURE

ANNEALING FURNACE

MALLEABLE IRON
CASTINGS
BRAKE PEDALS
REAR AXLE CARRIER
WHEEL HUBS
CLUTCH PEDALS

FURNACE

GREY IRON
CASTINGS
CYLINDER BLOCKS
CYLINDER HEADS
MANIFOLDS
BRAKE DRUMS
WATER PUMPS
PISTONS
PISTON RINGS
TRANSMISSION CASES

FINISHED PARTS
MACHINED FORGINGS
MACHINED PRESS WORK
GEARS
AXLES
DRIVESHAFT
SPRINGS
WRIST PINS
OIL PUMP
SHAFTS
BOLTS-NUTS
SCREWS
MACHINED CASTINGS
MALLEABLE PARTS

ASSEMBLY LINE

FINISHED AUTOMOBILE

MOBILE PLANT

MILL TO   AUTOMOBILE   PLANT

red a key factor in the American economy. (Courtesy: *General Motors Corporation*.)

way transportation has given the nation's contractors the ability even to move mountains and rivers—and to build a better America at prices that would not be possible without the specialized vehicles that reduce construction costs. All in all, motor vehicles have greatly furthered the welfare of us all.

POWER—SERVANT OR MASTER

The explosions of the atomic and hydrogen bombs dramatize one of civilized man's major social problems—the control of power. Basically, this problem involves man's intelligent control of the forms of power that he has learned to produce. Power machines have no moral sense or conscience of their own; they produce results that are good or bad, destructive or creative, depending on the skill, understanding, and judgment of the people who use them. This is equally true whether the power is generated by atomic fission or by the combustion of a gasoline-air mixture.

The motor car has proved itself to be an invaluable machine for pleasure and service; it has also been demonstrated to be a weapon of death more destructive than a loaded gun. The driver makes the difference. He directs its action from the time he backs out of the driveway until he parks at his destination. Whether the trip ends in satisfaction and service or in destruction and disaster hinges on the driver's ability, maturity, and intelligence.

The Need

In general, the crucial need of our civilization seems to be to develop our social attitudes to keep pace with our material progress. So far as our nation's traffic problem is concerned, the general public must cultivate an understanding of the elements of traffic safety and the desire to perform accordingly. Research studies show that faulty attitudes of drivers are major factors in the causation of traffic accidents. The automobile has become a vital part of our society almost overnight, but we must learn to live with it. We already know that the solution of our traffic problem lies essentially in an intelligent, courteous, sportsmanlike pattern of driving behavior comparable to our standards in other social aspects of everyday life.

The issue today is less technological than psychological and sociological. The old challenge involving the conquest of time and distance in transportation has given way to a new one involving basic human relations among drivers.

26   THE TRAFFIC PROBLEM

DISCUSSION TOPICS

1. What difficulties would confront your community if all motor vehicles were taken away for one day?
2. In what specific ways has the motor vehicle most influenced and changed our way of life?
3. What is the traffic problem? Explain.
4. Can you see any similarity between the problem of atomic energy control and the problem of highway traffic control? Could they both be aspects of a larger problem? Explain.
5. What is meant by the phrase "Caveman thinking in modern traffic"?
6. How does the traffic situation today differ from the traffic situation 60 years ago?

PROJECTS AND PROBLEMS

1. Prepare a diagram or chart that indicates the number of Americans that have been killed or injured in wars and in traffic accidents. Also, compare the financial cost of traffic accidents with the cost of public education. What conclusions might be drawn from these charts?
2. Make a survey to determine the number of people you or your family know who hold jobs directly or indirectly because of the use of motor vehicles.
3. Assuming that the average person drives his car 10,000 miles a year at an average speed of 30 miles per hour, how much time does he actually spend behind the wheel? Compare this with the time spent in other activities such as eating, sleeping, reading, and so on.
4. Collect some pictures of your community as it was 50 years ago. Talk to some older folks who lived in the community at that time. What changes have taken place? How many of these changes are attributable to the motor car?
5. Draw a graph showing the number of people killed or injured in traffic accidents in your community during the last five years. What trends are indicated? How could such trends be explained? If the present trend continues, approximately how many people will be killed this year?
6. Survey the members of your group to determine how many of their acquaintances, friends, or relatives were involved in traffic accidents within the last five years. How many were injured or killed?

Fig. 1-21. The Model T Ford was one of the most important cars in the history of the automotive industry. The experimental model below shows how far modern automobile design has progressed. (*Courtesy: Ford Motor Company.*)

THE TRAFFIC PROBLEM

How Did the Problem Develop?

Within the last 60 years the motor car has developed from a mere circus curiosity to man's most popular machine for land transportation. The tremendous increase in the number, speed, and power of vehicles has resulted in many perplexing problems. Roads designed for a "horse and buggy" or "tin lizzie" era are now jammed with powerful, streamlined cars. Diverse local traffic ordinances are confusing and inadequate for today's widespread motor vehicle travel. Mutual understanding between enforcement officials and drivers has been slow to develop. Most drivers have never received any formal driving instruction, yet the complexity of today's traffic pattern requires it. The time has come for each of us to accept the challenge, overcome these obstacles, and pave the way for greater transportation progress in the future.

Just 50 years ago, "Thanks for the buggy ride," was not a wisecrack; it was an expression of genuine gratitude. During that era men moved about this vast continent in a variety of interesting but uncomfortable ways: on horseback; in coaches, wagons, and shays; on slow, smoky railroads; on river steamers, rafts, and canal boats. A ride in a buggy was a luxury. The fastest vehicle for the casual traveler was the bicycle, itself a new, awkward, and somewhat hazardous contraption.

Fig. 1-22. Photo of a model of Oliver Evans' "Orukter Amphibolos." The original machine was made in 1805, and not in 1804 as is so often stated in error. This model was made by Mr. Greville Bathe of Philadelphia. (*Courtesy: Smithsonian Institution.*)

Fig. 1-23. Simon Stevin's sailing chariot, Holland, about 1600. (*Courtesy: General Motors Corporation.*)

Fig. 1-24. Cugnot's vehicle of 1770, now preserved in the Conservatoire Nationale des Arts et Metiers at Paris. This is a photograph of the original vehicle, and not of a model. (*Courtesy: Smithsonian Institution.*)

PETER COOPER'S "TOM THUMB" 1829-30 BALTIMORE & OHIO R. R.

Fig. 1-26. The "Tom Thumb," the first locomotive built in America, made its
first trip from Baltimore to Ellicott's Mills, a distance of 13 miles, on August
28, 1830, pushing a small open car with 18 passengers at a speed varying
from 5 to 18 miles per hour. (Courtesy: Baltimore and Ohio Railroad.)

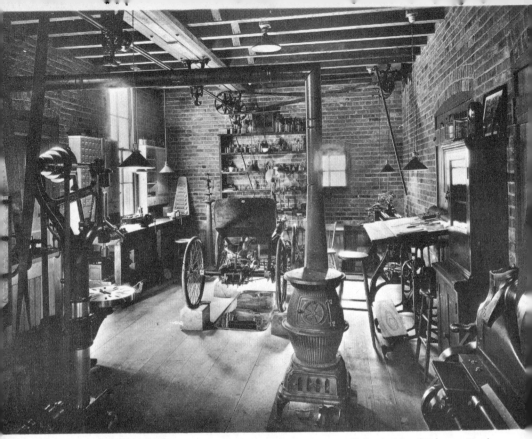

Fig. 1-27. Birthplace of the Ford car—in a little brick shed on Bagley Avenue, Detroit, Henry Ford began his first automobile in 1893. This replica of the shop stands at Greenfield Village, Dearborn. (*Courtesy: Ford Motor Company; from Brody and Stack, "Highway Safety and Driver Education," Prentice-Hall.*)

"Carriage folk," with their private rigs, were wealthy and socially important people. To them, owning and breeding fine horses was a matter of honor, the tradition of centuries. All the world regarded the horse as an indispensable factor in civilization. Even the poorest man treated himself to a holiday, when he could afford it, by hiring a horse and carriage from one of the many livery stables that flourished throughout the land. To everyone, however, a trip of 50 miles by private carriage meant many hours of jolting over dusty, undependable, and often treacherous roadways. It was an adventure not to be taken lightly or without proper preparation.

Throughout this period the automobile was only a vague idea —a dream in the minds of visionary and ambitious back-yard tinkers such as Duryea, Apperson, Dodge, Seldon, Olds, Ford,

Buick, and others. Generations of inventive pioneers had struggled to perfect a vehicle that would move efficiently under its own power, provide dependable, personalized, inexpensive transportation, and be available to the great masses of people. The invention of the locomotive in 1814 was the first successful step in the direction of fast, comfortable transportation. But the locomotive was not a complete solution; it was not something every man could own and operate at his convenience. With the railroad train, man had to adjust himself to the limitations imposed by timetables and fixed tracks. Passengers and freight had to be loaded and unloaded at one spot—the depot. Thus, the urge for a self-moving vehicle available to everyone—an "automobile"—kept spurring inventors on and on.

Fig. 1-28. Uriah Smith of Battle Creek, Michigan, designed this model so that it would not frighten horses it met on the road. (*Courtesy: General Motors Corporation.*)

FROM HORSELESS CARRIAGES TO STREAMLINED HORSEPOWER

Charles and Frank Duryea built the first successfully-operated, marketable automobile in America. It was completed at their Springfield, Massachusetts, workshop in 1892. On Thanksgiving Day, 1895, the Duryea car defeated four others in a contest from Jackson Park, in Chicago, to Evanston, Illinois, and back, to win the first automobile race ever held in the United States. The 52-mile route was traveled at an average speed of 5.05 miles per hour. The very next spring, Barnum and Bailey advertised the horseless carriage as the strangest attraction in their circus: "The famous Duryea motor wagon . . . the identical Horseless Carriage that won the great race at Chicago last November—to be seen every day in the new street parade." Even though the motor

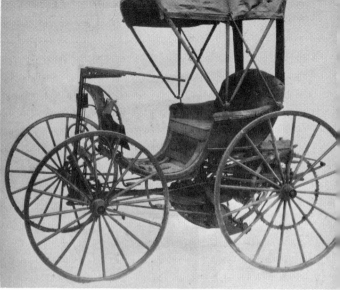

Fig. 1-29. (Left) A recent picture of J. Frank Duryea, builder in 1893 of America's first gas-propelled automobile. (Right) The original Duryea car, now on exhibit at the National Museum in Washington. Credited to the Duryea brothers, it was first operated on the streets of Springfield, Mass. in 1893. The second Duryea, designed and built by J. Frank Duryea, won America's first automobile race at Chicago on Thanksgiving Day, 1895, with Frank at the wheel. (*Courtesy: Dr. Arthur Pound.*)

car was only a curiosity at the time, many recognized that a new age in human mobility had arrived.

In the beginning, automobiles were little more than motorized buggies, and they thoroughly deserved the name "horseless carriage." Their bodies were built to order by carriage manufacturers and designed so that the engine could be placed either under the carriage or directly behind the driver's seat. The large, high wheels were connected to the source of power by a system of chains and belts. Not all of these mechanical contraptions were powered by the gasoline-burning, internal combustion type of engine generally used today. Many were driven by electric motors or steam engines. If there was any protection for passengers from the weather (and often there was none) it consisted of a flimsy wagon top. Clumsy and awkward in appearance, these "cars" were indeed makeshifts. They were so much a part of the horse-and-buggy age that one model was even equipped with a whip socket. Another, designed by Uriah Smith, of Battle Creek, Michigan, had an artificial horse head protruding from the front so as

Fig. 1-30. The merry Oldsmobile of 1901 was the first smash hit of the auto industry. (*Courtesy: General Motors Corporation.*)

not to frighten horses on the road! For more than 50 years now, the automotive industry has been trying to get away from its original hybrid design.

The "Merry Oldsmobile"

The first smash hit of the automotive industry was the 1901 Oldsmobile. The popularity of the "Olds," the first mass-produced car, spread like wildfire, and soon Gus Edwards' popular song, "In My Merry Oldsmobile," was tops on the "hit parade." This car had a curved dashboard to give it a high-speed look. "Mudguards" were draped over the wheels to keep off the splatter and then connected to a continuous platform, the running board, which replaced the buggy steps. Some early car bodies were so high they required two running boards.

The Model T Ford

Certainly one of the most outstanding cars in the history of automotive development was the Model T Ford, the "universal car" of the people, and introduced in 1907. It was strictly a utilitarian beast of burden, stripped of all nonsense. "They can have any color they want," Henry Ford used to say, "as long as it's black." Earlier experience with the production of high-priced cars had convinced Ford that he would be more successful by manufacturing smaller, cheaper cars in large quantity rather than expensive cars in small lots. The construction of only a few cars necessarily

Fig. 1-31. The 1912 Cadillac—the first self-starting sedan. (*Courtesy: General Motors Corporation.*)

Fig. 1-32. This 1916 Chevrolet gave the "Tin Lizzie" stiff competition. (*Courtesy: General Motors Corporation.*)

Fig. 1-33. An illustrious ancestor of our modern cars was the 1924 Chrysler. It offered four-wheel hydraulic brakes, leather upholstery, and a high-powered engine. Needless to say, it was a leader at that time. (*Courtesy: Chrysler Corporation.*)

Fig. 1-34. This Hudson sedan provided enclosed riding comfort and convenient self-starting at a relatively low cost. (Courtesy: Hudson Motor Car Company.)

Fig. 1-35. Plymouth entered the low-priced field with this flashy 1928 model. (Courtesy: Chrysler Corporation.)

Fig. 1-36. The 1930 Model "A" Ford. (Courtesy: "Scholastic Magazines.")

resulted in high cost; many parts had to be made by hand, because the limited production did not permit the purchase of expensive machinery. But when thousands of parts were made, each like the other, the cost of turning out each unit through the use of special machinery was comparatively low. Ford produced over 15 million Model T's during the next 20 years through the development of greatly improved methods in the assembly-line technique of mass production.

The Self-Starting Sedan

The low-priced, practical Model T dominated the industry until pride and convenience began to take precedence over practicability. The new trend started with the first enclosed body, developed by the Fisher brothers in 1908. Four years later Charles Kettering sold his electric self-starter to Cadillac, and motoring, until then a pastime strictly for the hardiest he-man, suddenly became ladylike. There was no more manful puffing with arm-breaking cranks on cold mornings; no more suffering from wind, rain, and dust. These improvements completely revolutionized the industry within a few years when Hudson made them available to the ordinary buyer by producing an inexpensive self-starting sedan.

The first to go as a result of the self- starter and enclosed body was the rival electric automobile, which had hung on because women could operate them. These now proved to be too slow. Next went the steamers, which took too long to start and could not be operated well in winter, as the new self-starting sedans could. Finally, the useful but ungainly Model T passed out of the picture. From that time on, the cheapest car in America had to appear to be an attractive, comfortable, dependable, mechanical "magic carpet" before people would buy it.

The Streamlined Look

The design of the motor car changed rapidly, owing to constant emphasis on appearance, comfort, speed, and power. The dashboard became higher and higher, until it was transformed into a virtual windshield with a glass window for the driver. A wheel replaced the lever used originally to steer the vehicle, and the

Fig. 1-37 (facing page). Motor Cars of the Future. (Courtesy: Ford Motor Company and General Motors Corporation.)

Fig. 1-38. Automotive engineers are constantly working to improve the design and construction of the car. Here an engineer tests the endurance of a new power brake unit. (*Courtesy: "Scholastic Magazines."*)

driver's seat was shifted from the right side to the left, closer to the center of the road. As roads improved, the floor was lowered closer and closer to the ground until standard clearance became one foot. More recently this has been reduced to eight or nine inches, and in some models as low as five inches. Losing its function, the running board was absorbed into the body. Meanwhile, the body swelled to accommodate more passengers and the fender-to-fender, straight-line design of today appeared.

EARLY FAITH IN THE MOTOR CAR

In spite of the early discomfort and inconvenience connected with the automobile, it gained popularity rapidly. What if it was undependable and expensive—it would soon be efficient and cheap! What did it matter that springs were weak and roads rough—the one could be made stronger, the other smooth and

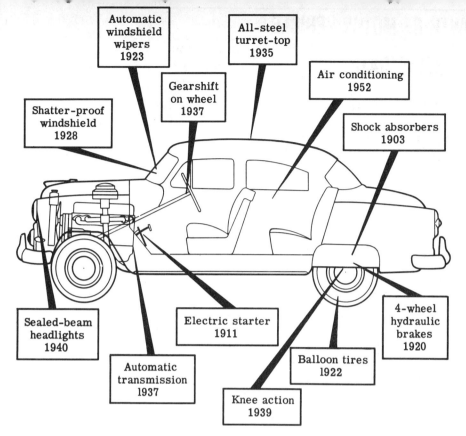

Fig. 1-39. Since the early days, every part of the engine, chassis, and body has undergone vast improvement. (*Courtesy: "Scholastic Magazines" and General Motors Corporation.*)

pleasant! Who could object to the frightful bang and clatter of the engine if he had the faith that, before long, it might be made to run as smoothly as a Swiss watch? Could progress be stopped because horses were frightened by a machine that might soon replace them altogether? A vision had appeared! Man was oblivious to everything but the fact that the motor car was the realization of his desire for free mobility.

Thousands of improvements have come to pass since the early days of the automobile. A list of the developments would include every part of the engine, body, and chassis. The modern car is virtually everything that its forerunner was not: it is beautiful, smooth-running, easy to operate, comfortable, and efficient. If handled with skill and care, today's car is dependable, long-lived, and safe. Breakdowns are so scarce that many a motorist has no reason other than mere curiosity to look under the hood. Only two

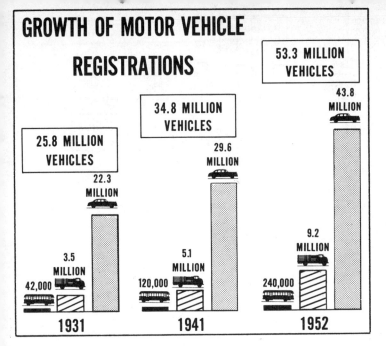

GROWTH OF MOTOR VEHICLE REGISTRATIONS

25.8 MILLION VEHICLES

22.3 MILLION

3.5 MILLION

42,000

1931

34.8 MILLION VEHICLES

29.6 MILLION

5.1 MILLION

120,000

1941

53.3 MILLION VEHICLES

43.8 MILLION

9.2 MILLION

240,000

1952

Fig. 1-40. (*Courtesy: "Scholastic Magazines."*)

generations ago the motor car was a circus freak; to us, however, it has become a prized possession and a faithful servant.

OBSTACLES TO ADEQUATE TRAFFIC CONTROL

By 1896 about 25 new cars were being made annually, but three years later production had been upped to almost 4,000. When the motor vehicle output soared to nearly 23 thousand in 1904, some of the nation's financial wizards warned automotive manufacturers that they were building more cars than they could sell and would soon be bankrupt! In 1930, there were 20 automobiles for every one existing in 1913, or a total of over 26 million. Today there are more than 60 million vehicles in use—over twice the number on the roads in 1930.

Although we Americans comprise only one-seventh of the world's population, we own over 80 per cent of all motor cars. We have one passenger car for every three persons, while the rest of the world averages only one for every 250 individuals. If every automobile owner would bundle his family and a guest or two into his car at the same time, it is literally true that the entire nation would be on wheels!

The amazing growth in the development, production, and use of the automobile has proven to be a tremendous asset to America and its people. However, it has also resulted in many new and

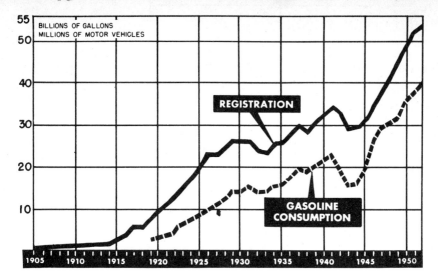

Fig. 1-41. Automobile registrations and gasoline consumption indicate that today more cars travel more miles than ever before. (*Courtesy: Automobile Manufacturers' Association.*)

perplexing problems. The entire traffic situation has grown all out of proportion to society's ability to cope with it.

Numbers and Speed

The rapid increase in numbers of vehicles, coupled with the constant trend toward increased power and speed, has resulted in a serious obstacle to adequate traffic control. Early automobiles rattled and jolted along rough, "washboard" roads. When they went faster than 40 miles an hour, it was like riding a bucking broncho, and the driver was glad to slow down in order to ride more comfortably. But the millions of modern automobiles do not rattle or jolt. It is difficult for a driver, seated on soft cushions in a sound-resistant car, to realize that speed and hazard are constant companions. A modern car, purring along at high speed, can lull its driver into a feeling of complacent security that can change to disaster and sudden death in a split second. Too many motorists think that because they cannot hear or feel the wind whistling past, the vibration of the speeding car, or the high-pitched hum and rumble of tires on the pavement, the danger has been taken out of the speed. Nothing could be more erroneous. Whether a new, streamlined convertible or an old Model T strikes a stationary object at 60 miles an hour, there is little difference in the result. Both hit with the same impact as if driven off the top of a nine-story building!

Fig. 1-42. The design and construction of roads has lagged badly behind the increase in motor vehicles. (*Courtesy: Allentown (Pa.) "Call-Chronicle."*)

The Lag in Road Construction and Design

Another major obstacle to adequate traffic control is the fact that *road design and construction have lagged badly behind improvements in the automobile.* Old streets and highways, built for horse-drawn vehicles, were suddenly "taken over" by "horseless carriages." Narrow city streets could not easily be converted into avenues suitable for hordes of the new vehicles. There are still many places where 200-horsepower cars are speeding over narrow, rough roads that were built over 30 years ago. In fact many highways, constructed less than a decade ago and designed to be adequate for long periods, are today already obsolete. The results: congestion and accidents.

The Need for Uniform Regulations

One of our great difficulties has been *the lack of uniformity in traffic regulations among the various cities and states.* It was natural that each locality should work out its own rules. The problem was a local one because the early cars did not travel far from home. But when the range of the automobile increased, the problem grew too big for local treatment. Today, with our modern high-speed cars and our national highway system, the motorist can easily drive through a half-dozen important cities between daylight and dark. Thus, he may encounter numerous variations in local traffic laws within a single day of travel.

The Problem of Effective Traffic Law Enforcement

Traffic law enforcement has been hampered by a widespread lack of understanding of traffic laws as well as of the services rendered by traffic patrolmen. Furthermore, some of the motoring public have always had a feeling of resentment toward traffic laws and enforcement officials. This unco-operative attitude still constitutes a serious obstacle to adequate traffic control. However, new educational programs for the motoring public are proving helpful in traffic law enforcement, and special programs for enforcement personnel are raising their proficiency.

Fig. 1-43. Driver education might improve this picture. (*Courtesy: Travelers Insurance Company.*)

Public Apathy and the Driver

We have spent millions of dollars to improve our automobiles and our highways, but in general the performance of our drivers has not progressed much beyond the days of high-crowned roads and two-wheel brakes. That is probably why *the driver remains the outstanding obstacle to adequate traffic control.* For example,

Fig. 1-44.

relatively few motorists understand the physical laws of motion and energy as they apply to an automobile on the highway. Altogether too many ignore our traffic laws. Some regard enforcement as a game between driver and policeman and take the attitude, "may the best man win." Many think of driving as an inherent right, despite the fact that legislatures and courts have repeatedly declared it to be a privilege that may be revoked. And, in general, such personal traits as showing off, transferring blame, abusing the use of power, and trusting that "everything will come out all right" blossom into full flower behind the wheel of a car. It would seem that we have not yet sufficiently matured to use the automobile properly.

THE TRAFFIC PROBLEM

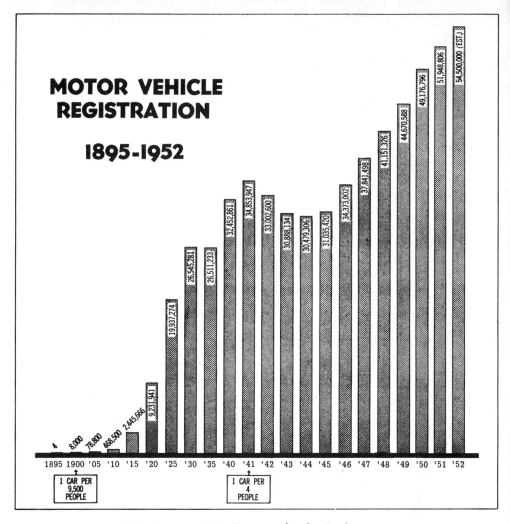

MOTOR VEHICLE REGISTRATION 1895-1952

Year	Registration
1895	4
1900	8,000
'05	78,800
'10	468,500
'15	2,445,666
'20	9,231,941
'25	19,937,274
'30	26,545,281
'35	26,511,233
'40	32,452,861
'41	34,853,947
'42	33,002,600
'43	30,888,134
'44	30,479,306
'45	31,035,420
'46	34,373,002
'47	37,841,498
'48	41,151,326
'49	44,670,588
'50	49,176,796
'51	51,948,806
'52	54,500,000 (EST.)

1 CAR PER 9,500 PEOPLE

1 CAR PER 4 PEOPLE

Fig. 1-45. (*Courtesy: F.B.I. Cartographic Section.*)

Certainly present-day driving is far more complicated than it was when most drivers first took the wheel. Memorizing a few traffic laws and learning how to start, steer, and stop a car are not sufficient preparation for safe and efficient driving in today's—or tomorrow's—traffic. Only a small number of our 70 million drivers have ever had any systematic instruction in how to drive. The majority "just took it up." They learned to drive in a haphazard fashion without any systematic plan. When instruction was provided, it was usually given by some other driver who did not actually know the essentials of good driving. These "instructors" generally passed on to their pupils many of their own bad habits,

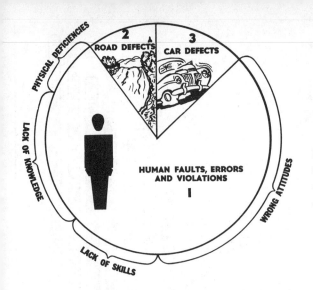

Fig. 1-46. The relative importance of the three basic elements in accidents. (*Courtesy: F.B.I. Cartographic Section.*)

poor attitudes, and faulty techniques. When we consider this inadequate preparation of the great majority of our drivers, we cannot be surprised at reports in *Accident Facts*, which indicate that *drivers themselves—not bad roads or faulty vehicles or acts of chance—are primarily responsible for over 85 per cent of all traffic accidents!*

DO YOU ACCEPT THE CHALLENGE?

The great changes wrought by the automobile have come so rapidly that we have not been able to adjust efficiently to them. The result has been a complex traffic problem. It is now up to the new generation to accept the challenge and take the leading role in the solution of this problem. It is unthinkable that we shall continue to kill almost 40 thousand people and maim about two million year after year. The nation's youth today have it in their power to set an example to be followed by older motorists and those of the future. If they determine to set a good example, the problem is sure to be solved. Are *you* ready to do your part?

DISCUSSION TOPICS

1. Do you agree with the statement, "No one man invented the automobile; it is a composite of many inventions"? Support your opinion with a general account of the development of the motor car as we know it.
2. "Today's automobiles are not as good as those made 20 years ago." Do you agree or disagree with this statement? Support your views with facts.
3. Explain the nature of some of the problems that the rapid increase in the number of automobiles has brought to the American people. How might these problems be solved?

THE TRAFFIC PROBLEM

4. What have been five basic obstacles to the development of adequate traffic control? Can you give practical examples of each from your own experience?

PROJECTS AND PROBLEMS

1. Prepare a chart showing the increase (by decades) in motor car registration, drivers, speed and power of cars, gasoline consumed, and traffic accidents. How would you interpret this chart? What predictions might you make about the future?
2. Interview five experienced drivers. Find out the methods by which they learned to drive. Outline the advantages and disadvantages of each.
3. Make a survey of your community to determine if any of the roads are inadequate. What specific recommendations would you offer to improve them?
4. Interview one of the officers in your local police department. Find out the history and problems of traffic law enforcement in your community.

SELECTED REFERENCES FOR UNIT I

1. *Accident Facts,* National Safety Council. Chicago: annual publication.
2. *Annual Traffic Accident Booklet,* Travelers Insurance Company. Hartford: annual publication.
3. *Automobile Facts and Figures,* Automobile Manufacturers Association. Detroit: annual publication.
4. *Fill 'er Up,* Bellamy Partridge. New York: McGraw-Hill, 1952.
5. *100 Million Motor Vehicles,* Automobile Manufacturers Association. Detroit: 1949.
6. *Motor Truck Facts,* Automobile Manufacturers Association. Detroit: annual publication.
7. *Sportsmanlike Driving,* American Automobile Association. Washington, D. C.: 1948.
8. *The Fundamental Principles of Driving,* H. James Tysor. Dallas: Banks Upshaw and Company, 1953.
9. *The Highway Transportation Story in Facts,* National Highway Users Conference, Washington, D. C.
10. *The Public's Attitude on Traffic Safety,* Opinion Research Corporation. Princeton: 1946.
11. *The Teenage Driver,* National Safety Council. Chicago.
12. *Those Wonderful Old Automobiles,* Floyd Clymer. New York: McGraw-Hill, 1953.
13. *Traffic Accidents and Congestion,* Maxwell Halsey. New York: John Wiley and Sons, Inc., 1941.
14. *Transportation Progress,* General Motors Corporation. Detroit.
15. *Who, Me? Forty Years of Automobile History,* Chris Sinsabaugh. Detroit: Arnold Powers, Inc., 1940.

LEARNING FUNDAMENTAL DRIVING SKILLS

In classrooms and on practice driving streets are sown the seeds that on later days in other places will bear the fruits of better living.

PROBLEM ONE

How can the instruments, switches, and controls help you?

PROBLEM TWO

How is good form in driving developed?

Fig. 2-1. The safety of you and your passengers will depend on your ability to use effectively the instruments, switches, and controls in the driver's compartment of your car, just as the safety of the crew of this plane depends on the pilot's ability to use these devices. (*Courtesy: Grumman Aircraft Engineering Corporation.*)

How Can the Instruments, Switches, and Controls Help You?

Planes fly safely and efficiently in various weather conditions thanks to instruments, switches, and controls that the pilots understand and use properly. Complete familiarity with these devices is essential. Skillful driving, also, demands adequate knowledge and proper use of the instruments, switches, and controls in the driver's compartment of the car.

If you ever have been in a car that has run out of gas or has been stopped for speeding, you know how much trouble and embarrassment can be saved by watching such instruments as the gasoline gauge and the speedometer. Although some seem to think that a few of the other instruments and devices in the driver's compartment have been added for decorative effect, each is designed to serve a very definite purpose. A thorough understanding of their functions will not only help you to drive more skillfully, but will also help you to prevent trouble and expensive repairs.

According to their functions, these devices may be organized into three classifications: information instruments, regulating switches, and driving controls.

INFORMATION INSTRUMENTS

The information instruments include the fuel gauge, the ammeter, the oil pressure gauge, the engine temperature gauge, the speedometer, and the odometer. The six gauges might be com-

Fig. 2-2. The instruments will help you to diagnose any "illness" your car may have. (*Courtesy: General Motors Corporation.*)

pared to a doctor's instruments for making a medical examination. The "symptoms" that they reveal will often point the way to the ounce of prevention, which, if administered promptly, may avoid the need for a pound of cure later on. These six information instruments, then, keep you posted on the functioning of vital units, forewarn you of impending trouble, and help you get the most out of your car with the least effort and expense. Cultivate the habit of glancing at the dials regularly!

Fuel Gauge

The fuel gauge indicates the amount of gasoline in the tank. Keeping the tank filled avoids the danger of running out of gas and also lessens the possibility of water vapor condensing in the tank and reducing the effectiveness of the fuel.

Ammeter

The ammeter indicates the flow of electricity to and from the battery. A positive (+) reading means that the generator is putting more electricity into the battery than is flowing from it—the battery is being charged. A negative (−) reading means that electricity is being used from the battery faster than it is being replaced—the battery is being discharged.

As soon as the ignition is turned on, the pointer should show discharge (−). After the engine has been started and brought to

Fig. 2-3. (Left) Battery is neither being charged nor discharged. (Center) Battery is being discharged. More electricity is flowing from it than is being supplied to it by the generator. (Right) Battery is being charged. More electricity is being supplied to the battery than is being taken from it. (*Courtesy: General Motors Corporaton.*)

a fair rate of speed, the pointer should move over to the charge (+) side. The speed at which the maximum charge is obtained differs with various makes of cars, but almost all of them should show best charging rate at about 35 miles per hour.

When the ignition is turned off and no electrical equipment is being used, the pointer should be directly in the center of the gauge at zero. If it is not, a short circuit in the wiring is indicated and should be investigated at once, although there is a possibility that the instrument itself may be at fault.

Most cars built today are equipped with a voltage regulator and a generator control device to prevent too much electricity from flowing to the battery. On cars equipped with these devices, if the battery is fully charged the ammeter will show a relatively low charging rate under ordinary driving conditions. As long as the needle stays on the "plus side" or in a neutral position and only shows discharging at short intervals (for example, when the engine is idling), you know that the charging circuit is in good order. Violent fluctuations or prolonged readings of discharge call for an investigation.

If the indicator should fail to move over from the minus or discharge side even after the car attains a good rate of speed, these are the most likely causes:

1. Too many electrical accessories in use at once.
2. Generator stopped due to a loose or broken belt.
3. Generator out of order.
4. Voltage regulator out of order.

Fig. 2-4. The Ammeter indicates whether more or less electricity is flowing to the battery than is taken from it. (*Courtesy: General Motors Corporation.*)

Oil Pressure Gauge

The oil pressure gauge indicates the pressure at which oil is flowing through the lubrication lines of the engine. It does not indicate the amount of oil in the crankcase; that is measured by the dip stick on the side of the engine block. Oil pressure, like blood pressure in the human body, is an important thing to watch. Normal oil pressure differs with various makes of cars, but with a little observation the driver can determine the average pressure for his particular car. Extra high pressure right after starting, particularly in cold weather, usually means that the oil is "stiff" from the cold. Avoid speeding the engine under these conditions. The cold oil must be given time to warm up and circulate properly; otherwise damage to the engine is likely to result.

OIL PRESSURE

Fig. 2-5. The Oil Pressure Gauge indicates whether or not oil is flowing properly in the lubrication lines of your engine. Investigate violent fluctuations or abnormally low readings immediately. (Courtesy: General Motors Corporation.)

A smart driver always operates at a slower rate of speed until the oil pressure is normal. If the instrument records unduly high pressure after the engine is warmed up, it usually means that the oil being used is too heavy or that there is an obstruction in the oil line. On the other hand, if the oil gauge shows little or no pressure at ordinary driving speeds, stop and investigate at once. Trouble may be due to any one of several causes:

1. The oil level may be too low.
2. The oil may be too thin.
3. The oil pump may be out of order.
4. An internal leak may be sidetracking the oil flow.

If the pressure is jumpy and irregular, have it checked at the earliest opportunity. If it drops to zero, it is wise to stop the car immediately. Running the engine without proper oil pressure is likely to cause expensive repairs.

Engine Temperature Gauge

The engine temperature gauge or heat indicator is simply a type of thermometer that indicates the temperature of the liquid in the cooling system of the engine. An undue rise in engine temperature indicates that something is wrong in somewhat the same sense as does a fever in the human body.

"Normal" operating temperatures vary between 160 and 180 degrees among different cars, and depend to some extent on the

Fig. 2-6. An overheated engine is just as sick as a person who is running a fever. (Courtesy: General Motors Corporation.)

TEMPERATURE

outside air temperature and on driving conditions. For example, driving very slowly in heavy traffic or on bad roads, or driving in the mountains or across a desert is likely to cause the engine to get hotter than usual.

Whenever the temperature gauge indicates that the engine is "running hot" it is a danger signal, and you should investigate as promptly as possible. If it is necessary to proceed to a service station, drive slowly.

Aside from operating conditions such as those mentioned above, overheating may be due to one of these causes:

1. Insufficient liquid in the cooling system, resulting from a leak or evaporation.

2. Loose or broken fan belt.

3. Water pump failure; a frozen radiator that prevents circulation of liquid.

4. An obstruction in water passages of radiator or cylinder block.

5. An obstruction in front of radiator, or an accumulation of insects on the radiator grillwork, cutting off the flow of air around the core.

6. Thermostat out of order.

7. Some internal trouble with the engine itself, such as inadequate lubrication.

Speedometer

The speedometer indicates how fast the car is traveling. Since most speedometers are not absolutely accurate, it may be well to have your speedometer checked occasionally. The size of tires used, the condition of the tires, and the condition of the instrument itself all affect speedometer readings.

Odometer

The odometer tells how far the car has traveled. The reading of the odometer cannot be tampered with easily by the driver.

"Six Honest Serving Men"

"I keep six honest serving-men;
(They taught me all I knew)
Their names are *What* and *Why* and *When*
And *How* and *Where* and *Who.*"

—KIPLING

Fig. 2-7. (Courtesy: General Motors Corporation.)

However, garagemen and mechanics using special tools can change odometer readings; therefore, the odometer readings on used cars may or may not be accurate.

Beam Indicator

Cars are usually equipped with a headlight beam indicator, which is located on the instrument panel. When the high beam is on, a red light warns you that your lights are "up" where they will dazzle the eyes of drivers coming toward you. When the headlight beam is depressed, the red light on the beam indicator goes out.

REGULATING SWITCHES

The regulating switches most commonly found in modern automobiles include the ignition switch, starter switch, choke, hand throttle, windshield wiper switch, light switch, dimmer switch, directional signal switch, horn button or ring, and accessory switches.

Ignition Switch

The ignition switch is usually key operated and located in a central position on the instrument panel. When in the "on" position, the ignition switch permits electricity to flow through the ignition system, providing the spark to ignite the fuel mixture and run the engine. When in the "off" position, the ignition switch breaks the circuit, making it impossible for electricity to flow through the ignition system. In some cars, removing the key when the ignition switch is in the "off" position locks the ignition; on other cars, however, "off" means only that the electricity in the ignition system has been turned off—the ignition is not locked and can be turned on without the key. These cars have a third position on the ignition switch, the "locked" position. When in the "locked" position, the ignition is "off" and cannot be turned on without a key. A car should never be left unattended without locking the ignition switch. Many cars have been stolen because of drivers' negligence in this matter.

The ignition switch should not be left in the "on" position when the engine is not running. There are two important reasons for this: first, if the battery is forced to supply electricity for the ignition system when the car is not going, it will be unnecessarily discharged; and second, since the engine is not running, electricity will be flowing constantly through the same spark plug circuit. This may result in undue burning and wear to spark plugs and to the delicate electrical contacts called *points*, and will cause difficult starting and poorer gas mileage.

Starter Switch

The starter switch is located in different places on various makes and models of cars. The most common locations for the starter switch is a button on the instrument panel, a separate pedal on the floor, or combined with another pedal or control such as the ignition switch, accelerator, or clutch pedal. The starter switch permits the flow of electricity from the battery to the starter motor, which in turn starts the engine. When starting the car, you should release the starter switch as soon as the engine starts running. Do not make the mistake of pressing on the starter switch when the engine is running—this may result in serious damage to the starter gears.

If the engine does not start within five to ten seconds, discontinue using the starter, then try again in a minute or two. If you smell gasoline it is probable that the carburetor is "flooded." In this case, hold the accelerator all the way down and turn on the starter again. If the engine still does not start, wait a short time and try again.

Choke

The choke controls the amount of air to be mixed with gasoline in the engine. Starting or running a cold engine requires a richer

Fig. 2-8. The driver's compartment of a dual control training car.

fuel mixture (more gas and less air). The choke regulates the amount of air that is mixed with the gasoline. When the choke is pulled out very little air is allowed to enter the engine; when the choke is pushed in, the normal air supply enters. Proper use of the choke makes starting easier, but choking an engine after it has warmed up interferes with smooth operation and wastes gasoline. On many cars the choke operates automatically.

Hand Throttle

The hand throttle is used to regulate the speed of the engine when the car is *not in motion*. A driver should not use the hand throttle to control the speed of a moving car. This is a practice that may result in loss of control, especially in an emergency situation.

Windshield Wiper

The two common types of windshield wipers are those powered by the vacuum from the engine and those run by electricity. The electric wiper has two major advantages: (1) it assures steady wiping performance under all driving conditions, whereas the vacuum powered wiper sometimes stops when the engine is laboring in climbing a hill, pulling a heavy load, or the like; and (2) the electric wiper may be operated even though the engine is not running. The electric wiper is driven by an electric motor; the vacuum wiper is driven by a motor that is operated by air pressure from the engine. The wiper switch located on the panel regulates the speed of these motors, thereby controlling the speed of the wiper blades.

Light Switches

The light switches permit the flow of electricity to the outside and inside lights. They operate on the same principle as the light switches in your home. The instrument panel lights and the outside lights are usually regulated by the same switch. Various positions on this switch control the headlights, parking lights, and panel lights.

Dimmer Switch

Most head lamps are now equipped with two filaments, so arranged that one throws the standard direct light and the other throws a beam down and to the right. This "depressed beam" is controlled by a switch located on the floor, to the left of the steering column. In most states the use of "depressed beam" when meeting or passing other vehicles at night is required by law.

Signal Switches

The directional signal switch is usually attached to the left side of the steering column just below the steering wheel. When the switch is on, it signals the driver's intention to turn by means of blinking lights at the front and rear of the vehicle. A right turn is signaled by pushing the switch in a clockwise direction, and a left turn is signaled by pulling it counterclockwise. Another signal switch operates with the brake pedal. When the pedal is pushed down the switch turns on red lights at the rear of the car.

Horn

The horn, another electrically-operated signalling device, is controlled by a button or ring type switch located on the steering wheel. This is similar to the electric doorbell assembly in your home. Some horns have an adjustment switch to lessen the intensity of the sound for city driving.

Accessory Switches

Accessory switches such as the heater switch, radio switch, spotlight switch, cigarette lighter, and others are simply electrical switches that permit electricity to flow from the battery to these various electrical devices.

Driving controls regulate the operation of the automobile. These controls include the accelerator, brake pedal, hand brake, clutch pedal, shifting lever, and steering wheel.

Accelerator

This is a pedal, operated by the right foot, that controls the amount of fuel reaching the engine and consequently the speed of the car. Depressing it causes the engine to run faster. When not actually depressed by the foot, it returns automatically to a position that permits the engine to run at a slow speed, called the idling speed.

Brakes—Hand and Foot

An automobile has two brake controls: a foot pedal, which operates a braking system connected to the four wheels, and a hand brake lever, which operates a set of brakes affecting the two rear wheels.

The foot brake pedal is located to the right of the steering-post. When depressed with the right foot, it sets the brake mechanism in operation, reducing the speed of the car. Its effect is somewhat proportionate to the amount of pressure you apply; a light pressure will slow the car only slightly, but a heavy pressure will cause the wheels to lock so that they will not turn at all.

The hand brake is used chiefly to keep the car stationary while parked, although it is also used in certain maneuvers such as starting on hills. It is usually controlled by a vertical lever located at the side of the shifting column, and is operated by pulling the lever toward you to apply and lock the brake. It is released by gripping the lever firmly, squeezing or turning, and moving it forward. However, the parking brake on some cars consists of an auxiliary pedal to the extreme left of the steering column.

Clutch Pedal

The clutch pedal, similar in appearance to the brake pedal, is located at the left side of the steering column. It engages and disengages the clutch mechanism. When the clutch pedal is pushed down, the engine is disconnected from the rear wheels; when the clutch pedal is up, the engine and the rear wheels are connected. Pressing the clutch pedal down makes it possible for a driver to shift gears without clashing or grinding them. It also makes possible stopping the car without stalling the engine. *The clutch pedal should always be pressed down before and during the shifting of gears and immediately before stopping.*

Shifting Lever

The shifting lever, located on the right side of the steering column, permits the selection of three forward speeds and one reverse speed by adjusting the gear arrangement in the transmission. A fifth gear arrangement, in which the gears are disconnected, can also be selected. This "no action at all" position is called neutral. You may locate neutral by moving the gearshift lever around experimentally. You will find that it slips easily into four fixed positions which correspond to the four corners of an "H" and into a fifth position which corresponds to the cross-bar of the "H." This central position is neutral.

Your hand position on the shift lever is extremely important in shifting effectively. Let us suppose that you have the gearshift lever in neutral. To shift to *first gear*, place the right hand (*palm up* and horizontal) under the shifting lever, and lift up through neutral. Then, with upward pressure, pull the lever back toward you until it feels firmly set in place in the top back corner of the H. The gears are now arranged in first or "low"—an arrangement

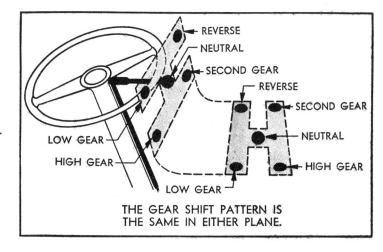

Fig. 2-9.

REVERSE
NEUTRAL
SECOND GEAR
REVERSE
SECOND GEAR
LOW GEAR
HIGH GEAR
NEUTRAL
HIGH GEAR
LOW GEAR

THE GEAR SHIFT PATTERN IS
THE SAME IN EITHER PLANE.

that is not designed to be used for speed, but rather to produce a great deal of power at slow speed. This is the gear arrangement used for starting the car in motion. It can be used efficiently at speeds under 10 miles per hour.

When the speed of the car reaches about 10 miles per hour the driver should shift to second gear. To shift to *second gear*, place the right hand (*palm down* and horizontal) on top of the shifting lever and push away from you. The lever should go down through neutral and forward until the shifting lever becomes snugly set in the bottom forward corner of the H. Second gear is designed to provide a considerable amount of power at moderate speeds. It is efficient at speeds under 15 miles per hour.

When the speed of the car exceeds 15 miles per hour, the driver should shift to third gear. To shift to *third gear*, place the right hand (*palm down* and horizontal) on top of the shifting lever and, with a downward pressure, move it toward you so that it settles into the bottom back corner of the H. Third gear is not designed to be used for power, but rather to provide smooth, quiet performance at regular driving speeds. It is mechanically efficient from 15 miles per hour up to the fastest speed of the engine. The engine will "labor" and may vibrate, buck, or even stall at speeds less than 10 miles per hour in third gear. Therefore, it sometimes becomes necessary to shift from third back to second.

The other gearshift position is reverse. To shift to *reverse,* place the right hand (*palm up* and horizontal) under the shifting lever, lift up through neutral, and with upward pressure push away from you until the lever fits snugly into the top front corner of the H. Reverse gear is designed to provide power at slow speed for backing.

Shifting Lever on Older Cars

These directions apply to conventional transmission cars, which have the gearshift lever mounted on the steering column. On older cars, where the gearshift is on the floor, the same general procedure for selecting gears is followed. In such cases, the letter H and the gear positions are identical. The only difference is that shifting motions are carried out in a horizontal plane, rather than in a vertical plane.

Selector Lever for Automatic Transmissions

Cars with automatic transmissions have no conventional gear-

Fig. 2-10. This is the driver's compartment of an automatic transmission vehicle. (*Courtesy: "Scholastic Magazines."*)

shift lever. Instead they have a corresponding *selector lever*. This lever has an indicator showing the position for various *speed ranges*. Since automatic transmission cars do the driver's shifting for him, all that has to be done is set the selector in the desired position and drive. The various speed range positions are selected by merely moving the lever and setting it at the proper position.

Depending on the make of car, there are either four or five positions on the selector. A driver should carefully examine each position on the selector of any automatic transmission car he may

Fig. 2-11. Selector Lever Indicator. (*Courtesy: General Motors Corporation.*)

INSTRUMENTS, SWITCHES, AND CONTROLS 65

be called upon to operate so that he is sure he understands where each position is and what it means.

These are the positions most commonly found on selectors:

N....This is the "Neutral" or out of gear position. It is provided for starting and as a safe means of allowing the engine to idle when the car is stopped.

D or Dr....Use this "Drive" position for all normal cruising in the city or country. It is the range to be selected for almost all forward driving.

L or Lo....For exceptionally heavy going the "Low" position should be used. In some makes this position also utilizes engine compression to help slow the car when descending steep hills.

S or Ds....Some cars have an intermediate range. It is used primarily for driving in hilly country or when increased acceleration is needed in traffic. For increased acceleration, a lower gear ratio can also be obtained by pushing the accelerator to the floor.

R....Whenever it is necessary to use "Reverse" position, the car should be brought to a full stop. Then raise the selector lever upward toward the steering wheel and move it into position. This position is used for backing, and on some makes of cars locks the car in gear to hold in stationary position when parked.

P....In this position the car is locked in gear and held from rolling forward or backward when parked. The position can be used whether or not the engine is running. It should be used when the car is parked or when it is standing still for a long period of time.

Steering Wheel

The steering wheel, together with the steering mechanism, controls the directional movement of the car to the right or left. On most standard makes of cars the steering wheel will make two complete turns to the right or to the left from a straight ahead position.

AT THE CONTROLS

Make sure first that your position is comfortable and that you can reach all the switches and controls easily, without straining. To do this you may have to adjust the seat by raising it, lowering it, or moving it backward or forward. Experiment until you have found the best position, and *always adjust the seat to that position before starting to drive.* You may have to use a cushion if you are shorter than average. You should sit high enough so that when you look straight ahead you will be looking over the top of the

FUNDAMENTAL DRIVING SKILLS

steering wheel and not between the spokes. Without changing your position in the seat, you should be able to extend both feet so that heels and toes can rest flat on the floor beside the clutch and brake pedals. You should also be able to reach the accelerator pedal easily with the ball of your right foot. Adjust the rear-view mirror, which is located near the top of the windshield just above your eyes, so that you can see the road behind you clearly for about 200 feet. If your car has a rear-view mirror attached to the side, adjust it carefully also. Make sure that your view through all windows is clear and unobstructed. Now you are ready to begin your practice driving activities.

But remember, your switches, instruments, and controls supply you with information, regulation, and control. It is only through a complete understanding of the functioning of these devices and the ability to use them properly that you can become a good driver.

DISCUSSION TOPICS

1. Discuss how the switches, instruments, and controls can help you.
2. What does a minus (−) reading on the ammeter mean? Under what conditions might this indicate trouble?
3. Does the oil pressure gauge indicate the amount of oil in the engine? Explain. What warnings can this gauge give you?
4. What are some of the factors that may influence the accuracy of a speedometer reading?
5. Compare the conventional gearshift lever with the selector lever found on automatic transmission cars. What similarities exist between them? How do they differ?
6. Explain the use of the dimmer switch. What is its relationship to the beam indicator?
7. Describe the proper adjustment of the seat and mirrors in the driver's compartment.

PROJECTS AND PROBLEMS

1. Draw a picture of the driver's compartment of a late model car. Clearly label the various instruments, switches, and controls.
2. Make a diagram of the shifting lever and its various positions; or draw a picture of a selector lever and its position options. Explain the proper hand position for shifting into the various positions and the purpose of each.
3. Draw a simple diagram showing how each of the instruments, switches, and controls functions.
4. Prepare a diagram illustrating the best adjustment of the seat and the mirror for driver comfort and safety.

Fig. 2-12. Good form is a characteristic of an accomplished performer, both on the athletic field and on the highway.

FUNDAMENTAL DRIVING SKILLS

How Is Good Form in Driving Developed?

Good form—the ability to perform skills in a smooth, well co-ordinated and efficient manner—is one of the basic characteristics of an expert. Outstanding craftsmen, champion athletes, and good drivers all exhibit good form. This means that if you would rather be recognized as a top-notch driver than as a second-rater you will need to develop the good form that characterizes the expert behind the wheel. Good form is developed through intensive and purposeful practice.

Developing good form in any skill necessitates forming new habits and refining many of your present ones. Good habits increase your efficiency. They free your attention from small details so that you can concentrate on more important matters. Habits are the foundations of good form and dependable performance.

FORMING HABITS

Habits are learned by practice and repetition. When you perform an act or a series of acts over and over again, you form habit patterns. Every time you perform an act, it becomes easier to do it again. Certain pathways in your nervous system gain in efficiency, and your new habit grows to be a part of you. Consider some simple process such as starting a car. The first time it is done it will have to be performed wholly under conscious direction.

GOOD FORM IN DRIVING   69

However, you will start a car many thousands of times, and you cannot afford to have your mind completely occupied with this relatively simple act when there are so many other things with which it must be concerned. Fundamental driving acts such as starting a car should therefore be made into habits. When a habit is formed, the effect is to set the mind free, or at least partially free, to attend to other things.

A large part of the information you learn in the classroom is of little use until it has been converted into habits. You can see, therefore, how important it is to have classroom work followed up with wisely-directed safe driving activities.

Simple acts, firmly established in an orderly sequence, are the foundation for performance in complex situations. Habits are built one upon the other. Your driving skill will be made up of the simple acts you practice from the first time you get behind the wheel. This means that unless you *practice exactly as you want to perform* and *never permit exceptions to occur,* you will never be a skillful driver. If, however, you always practice correct acts, the time will come when you will perform the fundamental skills almost automatically, with a minimum amount of effort and thought. You then will have developed a set of reliable driving habits—the first step toward becoming an efficient and accomplished driver.

FUNDAMENTAL DRILLS

Purpose of the Drills

Practice is the key factor in the development of any skill. You can learn to perform a skill only by actually doing it. Practice, however, must be purposeful and organized in an orderly fashion if it is to produce the desired results. Athletic coaches often conduct special practice drills, to help the players to develop the greatest amount of skill and "know-how" in the shortest amount of time. They allow each athlete to practice "on his own" while the coach is giving special help to an individual or a small group. Drills of this type are also valuable in learning to drive. The eight drills that follow are study and activity guides to help you and your teacher in organizing and operating your practice sessions. They are designed to help you to perfect the skills that you will use in everyday driving situations.

Fig. 2-13. On the highway as on the athletic field, high-quality performance demands attention to detail. (*Courtesy: Travelers Insurance Company.*)

Fig. 2-14. Practice drills are just as effective in learning to drive as in learning to play basketball. (*Courtesy: State Board of Education, Dover, Delaware and New York University.*)

GOOD FORM IN DRIVING 71

Using the Drills

Practice each drill carefully. Begin a new drill only after you have mastered the previous one. After you have had some practice under the direct supervision of your instructor, you may want to get additional practice under the supervision of a member of your family. A word of caution, however: do not practice too long at any one time.

A constant *repetition* of an act in the correct way, so that you can get a sense of successful progress and increasing control, is the way to learn quickly. Make a game out of driving drills just as you do of shooting baskets, practicing shots at a golf driving range, or pitching a baseball. *Read each drill through carefully and memorize the sequence of steps for each maneuver before beginning to practice it. Then repeat each maneuver, and be sure that you repeat it correctly, until you get perfect performance.*

NOTE: These drills can be used with conventional shift or automatic shift cars. Certain explanations relating to the drills will apply regardless of what make of car you are learning to drive. Where driving techniques differ between the two types of cars,

Fig. 2-15. This practice driving area at Pershing High School in Detroit makes it possible for one instructor to supervise as many as 12 student drivers simultaneously.

the explanation of the technique to be used for automatic transmission cars is given in italic type.

DRILL I: PREPARING TO DRIVE

This drill involves getting ready to drive, starting the engine, stopping the engine, and leaving the car. It is designed to help you to learn the proper techniques for performing these basic operations and to acquaint you with the general procedure to be used in the more complex drills which follow.

Location for Drill

The automobile should be *out of doors*. Use an off-street area or a street that has been closed to other traffic.

General Procedure

This is the procedure to follow in practicing this drill:

1. Get ready to drive.
2. Start the engine.
3. Change the engine speed by increasing and decreasing pressure on the accelerator. (Do not race the engine!)
4. Read the gauges.
5. Stop the engine and leave the car.

Explanation

In each of these drills you will find a detailed description of the sequence of steps that, as a result of experience and careful study, have been found to be an efficient method of performing the fundamental driving maneuvers. The following is a detailed description of the proper techniques to be used in performing the tasks involved in this drill.

Getting Ready to Drive. Some licensing examiners have remarked that they can rate a driver's ability fairly accurately just by the way in which he gets ready to drive. This is the sequence of steps that is recommended for carrying out this preliminary operation.

1. **Check to see that there are no obstructions near the car.**
2. **Enter car, key in hand, via curb side.**
3. **Put key in switch (do not turn "on").**

4. **Adjust seat** (assume an erect and alert driving position).
5. **Adjust mirror(s).**
6. **Check doors** (see that they are closed securely).

Fig. 2-16. An orderly, step-by-step procedure eliminates confusion in learning the fundamentals. (*Courtesy: National Association of Secondary School Principals.*)

At first consideration, this task of getting ready to drive may not seem very important to you. However, if the necessary preparations and adjustments are not made before the driver begins moving the car in traffic, serious difficulties may needlessly develop.

Starting the Engine. You are now ready to turn your attention to starting the engine. First press the clutch pedal down, and keep it depressed throughout this entire operation. This is important for two reasons: (1) since the clutch is a device which connects the power of the engine with the transmission and rear wheels, the clutch pedal must be pressed down to break this connection if the engine is to be started and gears are to be shifted without moving the car; and (2) depressing the clutch pedal makes starting easier, especially in cold weather, because it relieves the engine of the task of turning the gears in the transmission.

Even though the clutch pedal is depressed, it is recommended that the shifting lever be placed in neutral. Now, even if you

FUNDAMENTAL DRIVING SKILLS

mistakenly let the clutch pedal up, the car will not leap ahead and the engine will not stall.

Next, turn on the ignition switch and at the same time depress the accelerator. If the car has an automatic choke and throttle, these can be pre-set by pressing the accelerator to the floor and then releasing it. Now turn on the starter. The engine will begin turning by itself in two or three seconds. Release the starter switch as soon as the engine is running. Do not grind the starter gears by turning the starter on when the engine is running. If, after releasing the starter, you are in doubt about whether or not the engine is actually running, check by pressing the accelerator down slightly. If the engine is running you will hear it as its speed increases. After the engine has started, let the clutch pedal up and allow the engine to slowly "warm up" for at least 60 seconds, because oil cannot lubricate moving parts until it is pumped or splashed around them.

If you have difficulty in starting the engine when it is cold and your car has a hand-operated choke, pull the choke about half way to give the engine a richer fuel mixture. When the engine starts, push the choke in slightly. As soon as the engine will run properly without it, return the choke to the normal position.

Let us summarize now the sequence of steps to be used in starting the engine of a conventional shift car:

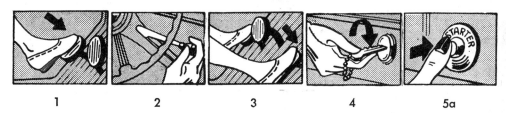

1   2   3   4   5a

1. Clutch down.
2. Place gear shift lever in neutral.
3. Press accelerator to the floor once, then release (this pre-sets automatic choke and throttle).
4. Ignition on.
5. Starter on and release as soon as engine begins running.
6. Clutch up (allow at least 60 seconds of "warm up" for oil to begin circulating in engine).

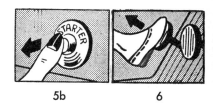

5b   6

Fig. 2-17.

The same general technique applies to starting cars with automatic transmissions but, of course, no clutch manipulation is involved. This is the recommended method for starting the engine of an automatic transmission vehicle:

1. *Place selector lever in neutral.*
2. *Press accelerator to floor once, then release (this pre-sets automatic choke and throttle.)*
3. *Ignition on.*
4. *Starter on and release as soon as engine begins running (allow engine to idle for at least a 60-second "warm up").*

Changing the Speed of the Engine. Now, experiment with the accelerator pedal. Notice how the engine speed increases as the pedal is depressed and how it slackens as you ease pressure. Do not run the engine above a moderate speed. Running the engine fast when the car is standing still is called "racing." It is a practice that greatly increases engine wear.

Fig. 2-18. Racing the engine results in excessive wear. (Credit: General Motors Corporation.)

Reading the Gauges. Now read the gauges. How much gasoline is in the tank? Is the battery being charged or discharged? How is the oil pressure? What do you notice about engine temperature? Do any of these readings change as engine speed varies? How do you explain these changes?

Stopping the Engine and Leaving the Car. To complete this drill it is necessary to turn off the engine and leave the car properly. Before you are ready to turn off the engine and leave the car in a typical driving situation you will have to stop your car. Therefore, you would be pressing down on both the brake and the clutch. In order to simulate the actual driving problem begin this part of the drill by pressing down on the brake and clutch.

Fig. 2-19. This driver is inviting an accident.

Fig. 2-20. The smart driver enters and leaves by the curb side.

A driver preparing to turn off the engine and leave his car is confronted with two basic problems: (1) How to make the car secure so that it cannot be stolen, and (2) how to hold the car stationary so that it will not roll away. The steps in this part of the drill are designed to solve these problems.

After the car has been stopped in the place the driver wishes to leave it, the next step is to set the hand brake; then he may remove his foot from the foot brake. Then shift to first gear. This will help to hold the car stationary. It has been argued that if a car while parked in gear were pushed by another vehicle damage would result to the transmission. Automotive engineers, however, state that there is very little danger of this. The greater danger is that even on apparently level ground the car may roll. Therefore, putting the shift lever in first gear as well as setting the hand brake provides a double safeguard.

Now turn off and lock the ignition, and let up the clutch pedal. Remove the key from the switch and close and lock windows. With the key in hand leave the car through the door on the curb side. Make a habit of locking the doors before leaving a car unattended.

And so, the operation of *stopping the engine and leaving the car* involves the following steps:

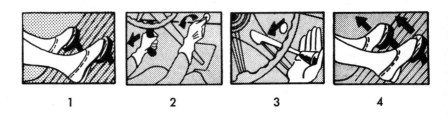

1. Stop car—brake and clutch down.
2. Set hand brake and lock ignition.
3. Place shift lever in first gear.
4. Brake and clutch up.
5. Remove key from switch.
6. Close and lock windows.
7. Leave car, key in hand, via curb side.
8. Lock doors.

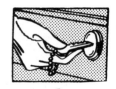

5

Fig. 2-21.

This procedure applies to automatic transmission cars except for the directions regarding the clutch pedal. Also, Step 3 for automatic transmission vehicles is PLACE SELECTOR LEVER IN PARK POSITION. If your make of car has no Park position, place the selector lever in Reverse.

Practice. Keep repeating this drill until you have mastered it. You will find that you will learn faster if you memorize the sequence of steps for each operation in the drill before actually getting into the car. Have your instructor or someone designated by him check your performance during each trial using the following score card. Study your score card after each performance and make a mental note of your strong and weak points.

FUNDAMENTAL DRIVING SKILLS

SCORE CARD FOR DRILL I

Operation	Point Value	Check errors and Record Point Deductions											
		1	2	3	4	5	6	7	8	9	10	11	12
1. Getting ready to drive.													
a. Entered car on wrong side.	3												
b. Failed to have key ready.	1												
c. Failed to put key in switch promptly.	1												
d. Failed to adjust seat properly.	3												
e. Failed to assume an erect, alert, driving position.	3												
f. Failed to adjust mirror(s).	3												
g. Failed to check doors.	2												
h. Failed to follow steps in proper order.	3												
2. Starting the engine.													
* a. Failed to depress clutch.	2												
b. Failed to check neutral.	2												
c. Failed to turn on ignition.	1												
d. Failed to depress accelerator properly.	2												
e. Failed to release starter promptly.	1												
f. Used starter after engine was running—clashed starter gears.	2												
g. Failed to allow engine to warm up.	2												
h. Failed to use choke when needed.	1												
i. Failed to read gauges correctly.	2												
j. Unable to control engine speed smoothly.	3												
k. Raced engine.	3												
l. Failed to follow steps in proper order.	3												
3. Turning off engine and leaving car.													
a. Failed to set hand brake.	3												
b. Removed foot from foot brake before setting hand brake.	3												
* c. Released clutch before turning off ignition while car was in gear.	3												
d. Failed to shift to proper position.	1												
e. Failed to lock ignition.	3												
f. Failed to close and lock windows.	1												
g. Left car via wrong side.	3												
h. Failed to take keys.	3												
i. Failed to lock doors.	1												
j. Failed to follow steps in proper order.	3												

* Does not apply to automatic transmission cars.

DRILL II: MOVING THE CAR

This drill involves driving forward and backward in a straight line at speeds less than one mile per hour. It also involves driving at these speeds forward and backward in an off-set alley layout. The drill is designed to develop skill in steering and controlling the car at low speeds while driving forward and backward.

Location for the Drill

A closed level street or suitable off-street area marked off as indicated below should be used:

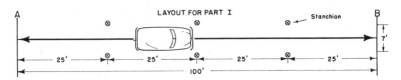

General Procedure

This is the procedure to be followed in practicing this drill:

Part I:

1. Get ready to drive.
2. Start the engine.
3. Starting with front bumper at Point A, drive at about the speed at which a child would crawl; keep within boundary lines.
4. Stop with front bumper directly over line B.
5. Drive backward at the same speed and stop with front bumper directly over line A.
6. Repeat this procedure until your performance is perfect.

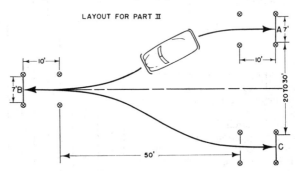

Part II:

1. Starting with rear bumper directly over line A, drive forward at a speed at which a child would crawl, stopping with front bumpers directly over line B.

2. Drive backward at the same speed and stop with rear bumper directly over line C.
3. Repeat driving forward and backward, driving forward into stall B each time and backing alternately into stall C and stall A.

Explanation

Moving the Car. In the previous drill you were required to start the engine, but you did not move the car. Now, you are ready to put the car in gear and move it forward and backward. This is the recommended sequence of steps for putting a car in motion:

  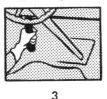 

1   2   3   4a

1. **Clutch down.**
2. **Place shift lever in first or reverse (palm up and horizontal).**
3. **Release hand brake.**
4. **Accelerator down slightly. (If turning into traffic from the right curb, take a look out of the left side window and give hand signal for left turn.)**
5. **Clutch up to friction point, hesitate and continue to let up smoothly; maintain steady pressure on accelerator.**

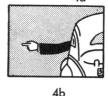

4b   5a

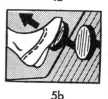

5b   5c

Fig. 2-22.

This is the recommended method for putting an automatic transmission car in motion:

1. *Brake down.*
2. *Place selector lever in "drive" or "reverse."*
3. *Release hand brake. (If turning into traffic from the right curb look out left side window and give hand signal for left turn.)*
4. *Accelerator down gradually.*

Moving the Car at Very Slow Speeds. One of the most important objectives of this drill is to develop skill in locating and using the "friction point" of the clutch. "Friction point" is the name given to that point at which the clutch begins to connect the power of the engine with the rear wheels. You can locate the "friction point" when the engine is running by shifting to first gear and letting the clutch pedal up about half way. At this point the engine can be heard to work a little harder, an increased vibration of the clutch pedal is noticeable, and the car will start to move. Skill in locating and using the "friction point" is essential for smooth operation, especially for starting and for close-quarters maneuvering.

Close-quarters maneuvering, such as angle and parallel parking, turning around in narrow streets, and the like, requires very slow speeds to insure precise control. This slow speed can be attained only by smoothly and efficiently controlling the speed of the car with the clutch. This is done by moving the clutch pedal up and down slightly in relation to the friction point, while steadily keeping the accelerator pressed down slightly. This process connects and disconnects the turning motion of the engine from the rear wheels, thus controlling the speed of the car. The proper procedure for controlling car speed, in first and reverse, with the clutch is as follows:

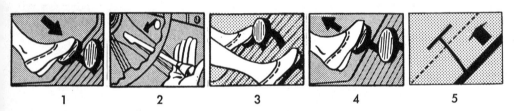

1.   2.   3.   4.   5.

1. **Clutch down.**
2. **Place shift lever in first or reverse.**
3. **Accelerator down—moderate and steady during entire maneuver until ready to stop.**
4. **Clutch up to friction point (car will begin to move slowly).**
5. **To go faster, clutch up about half an inch above friction point.**
6. **To go slower, clutch down about half an inch below friction point. (Speed is controlled by connecting and disconnecting the clutch.)**

6

Fig. 2-23.

In driving automatic transmission cars it is necessary to develop skill in locating the "motion point" of the accelerator—the point at which the engine develops just enough speed to move the car. This corresponds in function to the "friction point" of the clutch in conventional shift vehicles. Skill in manipulating the accelerator in relation to this point is essential for smooth control at very slow speeds. To operate at very slow speeds use regular "Drive Range" to go forward and "Reverse," of course, to go backward.

Slowing Down and Stopping. When in first, second, or reverse gear, in order to insure smooth operation the clutch should always be pressed down before easing pressure on the accelerator. The method recommended for slowing down and stopping when driving in any other gear than third is as follows:

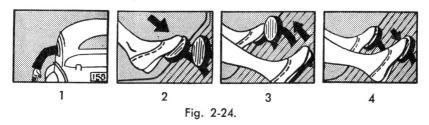

Fig. 2-24.

1. Check rear view mirror and give hand signal.
2. Clutch down.
3. Accelerator up.
4. Brake slowly and evenly as needed.

Slowing down and stopping automatic transmission cars is accomplished through these steps:

1. *Check rear view mirror and give hand signal.*
2. *Accelerator up.*
3. *Pump brake, applying gradual pressure as needed. (Just before forward motion stops ease up slightly on the brake, then resume pressure after the car has rolled to a stop.)*
4. *For brief stops keep foot on brake pedal until time to move. For longer stops set hand brake or move selector to park position.*

GOOD FORM IN DRIVING

Steering. Hands should be placed in a stable position on opposite sides of the steering wheel to facilitate control. The hand position for good control and driving comfort is right hand at about 4 o'clock and left hand at about 10 o'clock on the wheel. When driving for long periods of time, it is desirable to vary your hand position frequently to avoid muscular fatigue. For example, right hand at 2 o'clock and left hand at 8 o'clock is a good alternate position.

Turning should be executed by a co-ordinated hand-over-hand technique. Because some drivers turn in short jerky motions rather than in long, smooth sweeps, it often appears that the steering wheel will make five or six complete turns in either direction. However, any driver who has learned to turn the steering wheel properly realizes that it will make only two complete turns either clockwise or counter-clockwise from a straight ahead position of the front wheels.

Do not turn the wheels unless the car is moving. Turning while the car is stationary puts a strain on the delicate steering mechanism and may cause damage.

Backing. A difficult part of this drill is controlling the car while driving backward. An easy way to remember the principle of steering while backing the car is this: when driving backward, turn the wheel in the direction you want the rear of the car to go. For instance, if you want to back to your left, turn the steering wheel to the left. One of the greatest difficulties of beginners in steering backwards is that they "over steer." To overcome this difficulty when backing, drive very slowly and steer very carefully.

There are three recommended positions that the driver may take to look to the rear while backing. Each one has a definite purpose and should be used according to the visual range required by the operation. If you are planning to drive straight backward place your right elbow behind the top of the back seat, thus pulling your body around in a comfortable position. Get a firm grip on the top of the steering wheel with your left hand. This position permits you to look over your right shoulder and out the rear window and provides a wide range of vision. If you are planning to back to the right, turn your body part way around to the right so that you can get a wide range of vision out of the right rear window as well as the back window. Retain a grip on the wheel with both hands so that you can steer easily. If you

SCORE CARD FOR DRILL II

Operation	Point Value	Check Errors and Record Point Deductions											
		Trials											
		1	2	3	4	5	6	7	8	9	10	11	12
1. Failed to get ready to drive properly.	3												
2. Failed to start engine properly.	3												
3. Moving the car forward and backward.													
a. Selected wrong gear.	2												
b. Failed to handle shifting lever properly.	2												
c. Failed to release hand brake.	3												
d. Jerked or bucked car.	3												
e. Stalled or raced engine.	2												
* f. Failed to slip clutch properly.	3												
* g. Attempted to control speed by varying pressure on accelerator.	3												
h. Moved car too fast.	3												
i. Failed to steer properly.	3												
j. Failed to look around properly when backing.	3												
* k. Failed to depress clutch before releasing accelerator when preparing to stop.	2												
l. Failed to stop smoothly and accurately within one foot of designated point.	3												
4. Moving and turning.													
* a. Failed to slip clutch properly.	3												
b. Failed to select proper gear.	2												
c. Failed to handle shift lever properly.	2												
d. Failed to use hand-over-hand technique in steering.	3												
e. Moved car too fast.	3												
f. Failed to steer car into stall, or hit stanchions.	3												
g. Raced or stalled engine.	2												
h. Bucked or jerked car.	2												
* i. Failed to depress clutch before releasing accelerator when preparing to stop.	3												
j. Failed to stop smoothly and accurately within one foot of designated point.	3												
k. Attempted to turn wheels while car was stationary.	3												
5. Failed to turn off engine and leave car properly.	3												

* Does not apply to automatic transmission cars.

plan to back to the left, turn your head and body so that you can look backward out of the left side window. Keep both hands on the wheel to facilitate steering. If at any time when backing you have any doubt about whether or not your path is clear or about the exact position of your car with respect to its path of travel, stop at once and check carefully.

DRILL III: DRIVING IN LOWER GEARS *

This drill is designed to help those learning to drive conventional-shift cars to develop smooth, co-ordinated action in putting the car in motion, accelerating, shifting from first to second gear, driving in second gear, and stopping.

Location

Use a closed street or suitable off-street area.

General Procedure

This is the procedure to be followed in practicing this drill.

1. Get ready to drive.
2. Start the engine.
3. Move the car forward, accelerating in first gear.
4. Shift from first to second.
5. Drive in second gear; gradually increase car speed up to 15 mph, then gradually reduce speed to 5 mph. Repeat this several times.
6. Stop the car.

Explanation

Shifting Gears. During the last drill you learned how to put the car in motion and drive in first and reverse. Obviously, however, the very slow speeds attained in these gears are satisfactory only where heavy pulling or precise maneuvering is needed. Now you need to learn how to shift from first gear into a gear arrangement that provides more speed. This is how it is done.

Imagine that you have put the car in motion and have steadily increased the speed of the car so that you are now moving at about 10 mph. It takes about four car lengths to reach that speed. At this point press the clutch pedal down and as the clutch passes the friction point let the accelerator up. Handling the shift lever

---

° Student learning to drive automatic transmission vehicle should omit this drill.

as described earlier in the Unit, move it into the neutral position. Hesitate, then move it to second gear. The accelerator should be depressed slightly just before the clutch pedal reaches the friction point. After a momentary hesitation at the friction point, continue gradually letting up on the clutch and simultaneously increasing pressure on the accelerator.

The steps in shifting gears can be summarized in a compact, easily remembered formula, which will serve as a practice guide. (This formula assumes that you know the various gear shift positions, that you know how to handle the shifting lever, and that you will never attempt to shift to first or reverse while the car is in motion.) This is the formula:

1   2   3   4

1. **Clutch down.**
2. **Accelerator up.**
3. **Shift to desired position (hesitate an instant in neutral point).**
4. **Accelerator down slightly.**
5. **Clutch up (hesitate at friction point) and gradually increase pressure on the accelerator.**

5

Fig. 2-25.

Controlling Speed in Second Gear. You learned that when driving in first gear it was necessary to control car speed entirely with the clutch pedal. For example, if you tried to slow down by letting up on the accelerator the car bucked and jerked, so you depressed the clutch instead. In second gear, however, it is desirable to increase car speed with the accelerator. But the accelerator must be used very smoothly and evenly. Uneven pumping on the accelerator, for instance, would result in a very uncomfortable ride.

Carefully memorize the shifting formula, then practice this drill. Have your performance checked with the following score card:

SCORE CARD FOR DRILL III

Operation	Point Value	Check Errors and Record Point Deductions Trials											
		1	2	3	4	5	6	7	8	9	10	11	12
° 1. Failed to get ready to drive properly.	3												
° 2. Failed to start engine properly.	3												
° 3. Moving the car.													
a. Selected wrong gear.	2												
b. Failed to depress clutch.	3												
c. Failed to release hand brake.	2												
d. Failed to look out window and give hand signal when necessary.	3												
e. Failed to hesitate at friction point, causing car to buck.	3												
f. Stalled engine.	3												
g. Released pressure on accelerator before depressing clutch, causing car to jerk.	3												
h. Failed to handle shifting lever properly.	1												
i. Clashed gears.	2												
j. Failed to maintain smooth, forward movements.	3												
k. Drove too long in 1st gear.	3												
l. Shifted into 2nd gear too soon.	3												
m. Rested elbow on window sill.	3												
n. Failed to maintain a stable grip on the steering wheel.	3												
4. Stopping:													
a. Released pressure on accelerator before depressing clutch.	3												
b. Raced engine.	2												
c. Failed to make smooth stop.	3												
° 5. Failed to turn off engine and leave car in proper manner.	3												

° If pupil has difficulty in executing these maneuvers properly he should go back and work on previous drills.

Fig. 2-26. (Courtesy: National Association of Secondary School Principals.)

DRILL IV: ADJUSTING DRIVING SPEED

This drill is designed to help you to develop skill in adjusting speed to driving conditions. In driving conventional shift cars this involves shifting through the forward gears, driving in third gear, reducing gears and stopping.

Location

Use a closed street or a suitable off-street area.

General Procedure

This is the procedure to be followed in practicing this drill:

1. Get ready to drive.
2. Start the engine.
3. Move the car forward.
4. Shift through the forward gears (1st, 2nd, and 3rd). (This does not apply to driver of automatic transmission vehicles.)
5. Drive in third gear. (In automatic transmission cars use "Drive" range.)
6. Adjust driving speed to the following commands, which your instructor will give sometimes in sequence a, b, c^1, and sometimes in sequence a, b, c^2.

Explanation

Shifting Through the Forward Gears. Now that you are thoroughly familiar with the operation of most of the driving controls,

GOOD FORM IN DRIVING 89

the time has come to shift into third gear—and really drive! Remember that driving in high gear means increased attention to steering and smoother co-ordination in shifting. By the time you finish this drill you should be able to shift gears automatically, without taking your eyes off the road. You also should be able to keep your car in its proper lane and to stop smoothly and precisely at a given point. Hand signals should be given in advance of all stops. Your speed should not exceed 25 miles per hour during the drill.

As you recall, you shift from first gear to second at about ten miles per hour—after your car has traveled about four car lengths. You should shift from second to third gear at about fifteen miles per hour—after your car has traveled about eight car lengths. The same formula that was used in shifting from first to second applies in shifting from second to third. The complete process of *shifting through forward gears* can be summarized in the following steps:

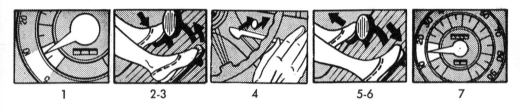

1   2-3   4   5-6   7

1. With shifting lever in first gear, accelerate to about 10 miles per hour.
2. Clutch down.
3. Accelerator up.
4. Shift to second gear (palm down and horizontal). Hesitate an instant in neutral.
5. Accelerator down slightly.
6. Clutch up to friction point, hesitate, and up smoothly.
7. Increase speed to about 15 miles per hour.
8. Clutch down.
9. Accelerator up.
10. Shift to third gear (palm down and horizontal). Hesitate an instant in neutral.

8-9

10

Fig. 2-27.

11. Accelerator down gently.
12. Clutch up to friction point, hesitate, and up smoothly.
13. Gradually increase pressure on accelerator until desired speed is attained.

11-12   13

Shifting will be very smooth if you start pressing the accelerator down just an instant before the clutch reaches the friction point on the way up. Be careful, however, not to apply too much pressure to the accelerator and thus race the engine.

After you have shifted into third gear and let the clutch up, keep your foot off the clutch pedal unless you are preparing to stop or shift gears. Resting the left foot on the clutch pedal while driving in third is called "riding the clutch." It is a practice that results in unnecessary wear and reduces the life of the clutch.

Elimination of the clutch pedal and the provision of fully automatic shifting through all forward speeds leaves little to do but select the proper operating range in automatic transmission cars. In driving these cars, concentrate on smoothness of operation. Press down on the accelerator evenly and gradually. Apply the brakes gently.

Stopping When Operating at Driving Speeds. Stopping a car, especially when driving in third gear, is not as simple an operation as it may at first appear. Of course, the emergency stop is fairly

Fig. 2-28. (Courtesy: National Association of Secondary School Principals.)

simple—just remove your right foot from the accelerator and press the brake pedal down as quickly and as hard as you can, after giving as much warning as possible to passengers and other highway users. However, this type of stop is very uncomfortable and quite dangerous. Therefore, it is used only in emergencies. The process of making a regular smooth stop in third gear involves three phases: preparing to stop, beginning to stop and stopping. These are the steps involved:

1   2   3

Preparing to stop.

1. Check traffic ahead and behind and give a hand signal.
2. Accelerator up.
3. Pump brake, applying pressure as needed. (Pumping the brake not only slows the car down smoothly and efficiently but also provides a flashing signal to warn cars behind you.)

Fig. 2-29.

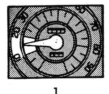 

1   2

Beginning to stop (about 50 yards).

1. Brake to slower than 15 miles per hour.
2. Clutch down.

Stopping.

1. Continue to pump brake, applying pressure as needed.
2. Coast up to stopping point.

FUNDAMENTAL DRIVING SKILLS

3. **Press brake down as needed.** (Just before forward motion stops ease up slightly on the brake, then resume pressure after the car has rolled to a stop.)

1-2-3

The Caution Habit. Caution in driving not only involves looking ahead to anticipate trouble, but it also involves making the proper responses well in advance to avoid emergency situations. The "caution habit," therefore, is an important one to develop. Whenever you see a situation down the road that may cause trouble, say to yourself, "Caution!" This means take your right foot off the accelerator and rest it on the brake pedal ready for use. This habit will keep you out of a good many tight spots. By taking your foot off the accelerator you reduce the speed of your car, thus reducing your braking distance. By placing your foot on the brake you cut down the time necessary for you to react if an emergency does develop, thus reducing your reaction distance. The caution habit, therefore, will shorten your stopping distance and save you trouble in traffic. Good drivers know that any time your right foot is not pressing on the accelerator it should be immediately rested on the brake pedal.

Reducing gears. If you have slowed to 5 mph and decide to speed up, letting the clutch up and pressing the accelerator down may cause the car to buck or stall. This is the recommended method of *reducing gears.*

| 1 | 2 | 3 | 4-5 |

Fig. 2-30.

1. Slow down to 15 mph or less.
2. Clutch down.
3. Shift from third to second gear.
4. Clutch up, hesitate at friction point, and up smoothly.
5. Accelerator down, as needed.

SCORE CARD FOR DRILL IV

Operation	Point Value	Check Errors and Record Point Deductions											
		Trials											
		1	2	3	4	5	6	7	8	9	10	11	12
1. Entered car improperly.	3												
2. Failed to get ready to drive properly.	3												
3. Failed to start engine properly.	3												
4. Moving the car.													
a. Failed to select proper gear.	3												
b. Handled shifting lever improperly.	2												
c. Failed to release hand brake.	3												
d. Failed to look out window and give hand signal.	3												
e. Bucked or jerked car.	2												
f. Stalled or raced engine.	2												
* g. Clashed gears.	2												
h. Failed to maintain smooth forward acceleration.	3												
* i. Drove too long in low gear.	2												
* j. Shifted into higher gear too soon.	2												
5. Stopping.													
a. Failed to respond properly to caution command.	3												
* b. Put clutch down too soon.	2												
* c. Let clutch up too long.	2												
d. Failed to stop gently and smoothly.	3												
e. Failed to give hand signal properly.	3												
f. Failed to stop at designated point.	3												
* 6. Reducing gears.													
a. Clashed gears.	2												
b. Handled shifting lever improperly.	2												
c. Failed to maintain forward motion of the car.	3												
d. Stalled or raced engine.	3												
e. Jerked or bucked car.	3												
f. Drove in 2nd too long.	2												
g. Shifted back to 3rd too soon.	2												
7. Failed to turn off engine and leave car in a proper manner.	3												

* Does not apply to automatic transmission cars.

As long as the car is rolling, second gear will keep it going. If, however, the car comes to a full stop, you must shift to first gear.

After you reduce gears (shift from third to second) you have three possible alternatives: (1) drive at a slow speed in second gear, (2) build up speed and shift back to third, or (3) bring the car to a full stop. As you work on this drill, practice all three.

This drill is the basis for the development of the skills needed for city and highway speed control. Practice it carefully until you can attain a perfect score on the accompanying score card.

DRILL V: RIGHT AND LEFT TURNS

This drill involves turning corners. It is designed to help you (a) to develop skill in estimating the proper speed at which any given turn should be made, and (b) to learn the proper procedures for turning various types of corners.

Location

Use a series of seldom-traveled or closed streets with left and right turns or an off-street area laid out as indicated:

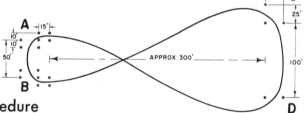

General Procedure

1. Drive over the route indicated in the diagram or a suitable substitute route that your instructor recommends.
2. Execute turns (a) and (b) as regular turns and turns (c) and (d) as fast turns.
3. When a perfect score is attained driving around the route in one direction, reverse the route and practice in the other direction.

Explanation

Turning Corners. This drill will serve a double purpose. It will help you to get additional practice in some of the skills you have already learned as well as prepare you for maneuvering in traffic. Much of your driving so far has been driving in a straight line —this drill introduces the problem of turning corners.

The speed at which a corner is turned depends upon several factors such as traffic conditions, sight distances and general visibility, the acuteness of the angle, and the condition of the pavement. A driver must take these factors into consideration as he approaches a corner in order to determine whether he will make a slow turn or a regular turn. A slow turn is one executed at speeds less than 10 mph. This is the recommended procedure for making such a turn:

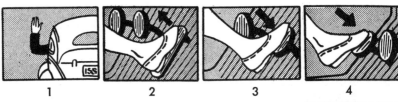

1. Check traffic conditions using rear vision mirror(s), and signal well in advance—by hand signal, mechanical signal, and position of the car.
2. Accelerator up.
3. Pump brake as needed to slow down to less than 10 mph. (Rest right foot on brake pedal so that it can be pressed down quickly if needed. Keep right foot in this position until it is again necessary to press down the accelerator.)
4. Clutch down.
5. Shift to second.
6. Turn corner slowly and accurately using proper hand-over-hand steering technique.
7. Halfway around the corner or when power is needed to keep the car moving (whichever comes first), clutch up to the friction point, hesitate, and up slowly; accelerator down slightly as clutch reaches the friction point. (Another acceptable method is to let clutch up before beginning to turn corner.)
8. Straighten wheels.

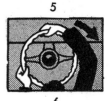

Fig. 2-31.

Whenever conditions require shifting in making a turn, the shifting should be done before entering the turn or after completing the turn; shifting should not be done while the turn is being made.

FUNDAMENTAL DRIVING SKILLS

There are many situations, however, where a turn can be made safely and efficiently without shifting. This type of turn, sometimes referred to as a *regular turn,* is made like this:

1. Check rear vision mirror(s).
2. Signal well in advance—by hand signal, mechanical signal, and position of the car.
3. Accelerator up.
4. Pump brake as needed and slow down to between 15 and 10 mph. (Rest right foot gently on brake pedal, ready for use if necessary, until car is halfway around the corner).
5. Turn corner smoothly and accurately, using proper hand-over-hand steering technique.
6. Halfway around the corner, right foot off the brake pedal and accelerator down slightly.
7. Straighten wheels.

The above steps are also used for making all turns in automatic transmission cars.

The general rule regarding speed control on corners and curves is slow down before entering the turn and then begin to accelerate slightly after half of the turn has been completed.

Steering Around Corners. Proper hand position on the steering wheel will make the turning operation smoother and more efficient. All turning should be done in long sweeps by a hand-over-hand technique. The recommended hand positions for turning to the right are as follows:

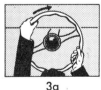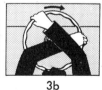

     1   2   3a   3b

1. Left hand moves from 10 to 3.
2. Right hand moves from 11 to 4.
3. Continue this "hand-over-hand" movement until wheel is turned sufficiently.

Fig. 2-32.

To turn to the left use these hand positions:

1. **Right hand moves from 4 to 10.**
2. **Left hand moves from 1 to 9.**
3. **Continue this "hand-over-hand" movement until wheel is turned sufficiently.**

When straightening the wheels, control the slipping of the steering wheel. If the wheel does not return to an exact straight-ahead position, make any adjustment that may be necessary.

In traffic situations, approach a corner for a left turn with the left wheels of your car about two feet from the center line; on a three-lane road approach from the center lane. This position will permit you to make your turn with a minimum of effort and interference. For a right turn, approach the corner with the right wheels about four feet from the right curb. If your wheels are much closer than this, the rear wheels may strike the curb while turning. On the other hand, if your car is much more than four

SCORE CARD FOR DRILL V

Operation	Point Value	1	2	3	4	5	6	7	8	9	10	11	12
		Check Errors and Record Point Deductions — Trials											
° 1. Clashed gears.	2												
° 2. Failed to reduce gears properly.	3												
3. Failed to slow down properly before making turn.	3												
° 4. Attempted to shift gears while turning.	3												
5. Bucked car or stalled engine.	3												
6. Hit stanchion or curb.	3												
7. Turned too wide.	3												
8. Operated too fast for conditions.	3												
9. Failed to signal properly.	3												
° 10. Failed to reduce gears when necessary.	3												
11. Failed to turn steering wheel properly.	3												
12. Failed to check mirror.	3												
13. Failed to position car properly for the turn.	3												

° Does not apply to automatic transmission cars.

feet from the right curb, another car may squeeze in between your car and the curb and interfere with your turn. Since the typical car is at least six feet wide, the margin of four feet will prevent such an interference.

Conclusion. Now use the score card below and practice until you can turn corners with good form and perfect control.

DRILL VI: THE Y TURN

This drill is designed to give you practice in turning around in limited areas, using the Y-turn method.

Location

Use two closed streets, one 40 feet wide, the other 25 feet wide, or an off-street area arranged as shown. Curbs can be made of cinder blocks or long boards.

General Procedure

This is the procedure to follow in practicing the drill:

1. Turn around in street A using Y-turn method until you achieve a perfect score.
2. Turn around in street B using Y-turn method until you achieve a perfect score.

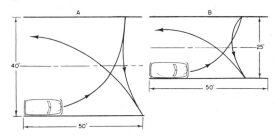

Explanation

Turning Around—Y-Turn Method. This is the sequence of steps for developing efficient habit patterns for executing a *Y turn:*

1. **Steer to right side of the road and stop with right wheels about six inches from the curb.**
2. **Shift to first gear.**
3. **Give hand signal for a left turn and take a look out the left side window for on-coming traffic.**
4. **Accelerator down slightly.**
*5. **Clutch up to the friction point and move ahead slowly, controlling speed with the clutch. (See Drill II.)**

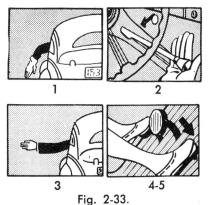

Fig. 2-33.

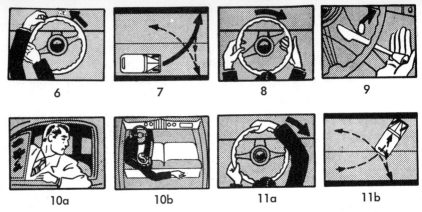

6   7   8   9

10a   10b   11a   11b

6. Turn the steering wheel as far as possible (two complete turns) to the left before the car has moved four feet. (See Drill II.)

12a

7. Move car across the street slowly.

8. When front wheels are within two feet of the curb or when the car is facing at right angles to the curb, straighten the wheels (two complete turns to the right) before the car is stopped. (Wheels may touch curb lightly, but *do not bump the curb.*)

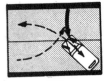

12b

9. Shift to reverse.

*10. Check traffic conditions, then back smoothly.

11. Before the car has moved backward two feet, turn the steering wheel as far as possible (two complete turns to the right.

13a

12. When front wheels are at the middle of the road or when the rear wheels are two feet from the curb (whichever happens first), straighten wheels by turning two complete turns to the left before stopping. (Again, wheels may touch curb lightly but *do not bump curb.*)

13b

Fig. 2-33 (cont.).

13. Shift to first, check traffic, and proceed into the right lane.

---

* Does not apply to automatic transmission cars.

Close-Quarters Maneuvering. Remember, the secret of success in close-quarters maneuvering is to be able to control the motion of the car efficiently at extremely slow speeds and to be able·to turn the wheels quickly and accurately. Keep these points in mind, and practice this drill until your score is perfect on this score card.

SCORE CARD FOR DRILL VI

Operation	Point Value	Check errors and Record Point Deductions											
		1	2	3	4	5	6	7	8	9	10	11	12
1. Failed to signal and stop at curb before turning.	3												
2. Failed to look for oncoming traffic and signal.	3												
3. Moved too fast.	3												
4. Failed to turn wheel properly.	3												
5. Bumped curb.	3												
6. Failed to look to the rear properly before and during backing.	3												
7. Failed to complete turning maneuvers in three movements.	3												
8. Stalled or raced engine.	2												
* 9. Failed to use clutch properly.	3												
10. Turned wheels while car was not moving.	2												

° Does not apply to automatic shift cars.

DRILL VII: MANEUVERING ON GRADES

This drill involves stopping and starting on upgrades and parking on grades.

Location

A hill on a closed street or on an off-street area.

General Procedure

This is the procedure to be followed in practicing the drill:

1. Drive uphill in third gear and stop. (Use "Drive" position on automatic transmission cars.)
2. Start in first gear, shift to second, and stop.

3. Repeat steps 1 and 2 until a perfect score is attained.
4. Drive uphill and park at the right-hand curb.
5. Drive downhill and park at the right-hand curb.
6. Repeat steps 4 and 5 until a perfect score is attained.

Explanation

In many parts of the country there are few hills or mountains. However, even if there are no hills in your locality, you will undoubtedly drive in hilly and mountainous areas before many vacations have passed. Therefore, if at all possible, this drill should be practiced on an incline—even a man-made one such as an inclined driveway, if necessary.

Starting on Upgrade. The procedure for starting on an upgrade is somewhat similar to the general procedure for starting that you have already learned. The use of the clutch, brake, and accelerator, however, is quite different. This is the best way to stop, hold steady, and start on an upgrade:

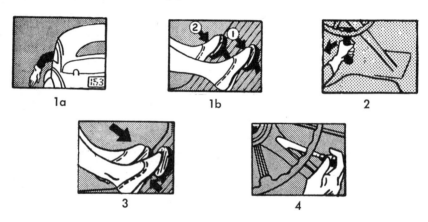

Fig. 2-34.

Stopping and holding steady:

1. Stop as you would on level ground.
2. Set hand brake.
3. Brake pedal up slowly to see if hand brake is holding the car perfectly still. If it is not, press the brake pedal down quickly and pull hand brake a little tighter.
4. If the stop will be of 60 seconds or longer, shift to neutral, let clutch up and relax.

1a   1b   2   3

Starting:

1. Clutch down and place shift lever in first gear.
2. Accelerator down moderately. Maintain a steady engine speed—faster than idling, but not racing.
3. Clutch up to friction point. (At this point, you will hear the engine slow down a little.)
4. Hold both feet steady, just where they are, and release hand brake. Car should now hold perfectly still. If, however, the car moves forward this indicates that your clutch is up too far; if the car rolls backward your clutch is not up far enough. If the engine stalls, it indicates that the engine is not getting enough fuel—the accelerator is up too far; or if the car does not move but the engine is racing, it indicates that the accelerator is down too far.
5. Take a look to check traffic condition— if clear, go.
6. Accelerator down a bit more.
7. Clutch up slowly and smoothly.

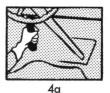

4a

4b

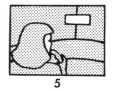

5

6-7

Fig. 2-35.

The technique of starting automatic shift cars on upgrades is somewhat different. These are the steps:

1. *Set selector lever in "low" position.*
2. *Accelerator down gently.*
3. *Release hand brake and adjust pressure on accelerator so that car holds still.*
4. *Check traffic conditions—if clear, go.*

GOOD FORM IN DRIVING

5. *Increase pressure on accelerator moving the car forward.*
6. *Move selector lever to "drive" position.*

Remember, whenever starting on an upgrade, the car must never roll backward even the slightest distance.

Parking on a Hill. Very few driving situations are more ridiculous or dangerous than a motorist chasing downhill after a car that he has just parked at the curb. This need never happen to you if you take the *proper precautions when parking on hills:*

1. **Pull hand brake on tight.**
2. **If the street has curbs or high shoulders, turn the front wheels so that as the car begins to roll downhill, the wheels will be blocked against the curb. On an upgrade, wheels should be turned as far as possible to the left, and on downgrades wheels should be turned as far as possible to the right. If the street does not have a curb or a high shoulder to block the wheels, turn the wheels as far as possible to the right in parking on both upgrades and downgrades.**
3. **Set shifting lever in first gear for parking on an upgrade and in reverse gear on a downgrade or, on automatic shift cars, place selector in "park" position.**

HOW TO PARK ON HILLS

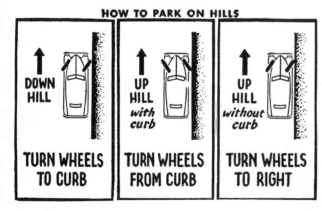

Fig. 2-36. A. *Downhill—* "Headed downhill with or without curb, turn wheels to the right."

B. *Uphill with Curb—* "Headed uphill with curb, turn wheels to left against curb."

C. *Uphill without Curb—* "Headed uphill without curb, turn wheels to right."

(*Courtesy: American Association Motor Vehicle Administrators an National Safety Council.)*

FUNDAMENTAL DRIVING SKILLS

Smart drivers treat even apparently level ground as if it were a slope. After all, they argue, rain water flows down nearly every street, so most streets have slopes steep enough to make a car roll away. Therefore, *always* park as if you were on a hill.

SCORE CARD FOR DRILL VII

Operation	Point Value	Check Errors and Record Point Deductions											
		Trials											
		1	2	3	4	5	6	7	8	9	10	11	12
1. Stopping and starting on grades.													
a. Failed to stop smoothly.	3												
b. Failed to set hand brake or use foot brake properly.	3												
c. Rolled back.	3												
d. Raced or stalled engine.	3												
e. Failed to hold car steady for a moment after releasing brake.	3												
f. Failed to release brake at proper time.	3												
° 2. Stopping and starting in first gear.													
a. Failed to use clutch properly.	3												
b. Rolled back.	3												
c. Raced or stalled engine.	3												
d. Failed to stop smoothly.	3												
e. Failed to hold car steady while stopped.	3												
3. Parking.													
a. Failed to set hand brake properly.	3												
b. Failed to turn wheels properly.	3												
c. Failed to put shift lever in proper gear.	3												

° Does not apply to automatic shift cars.

DRILL VIII: PARKING—ANGLE AND PARALLEL

This involves parking in angle and parallel parking spaces.

Location

A closed street or an off-street area arranged as follows:

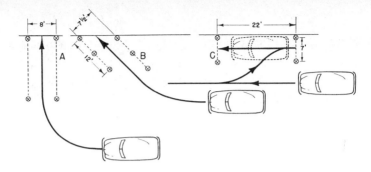

General Procedure

This is the procedure to be followed in this drill:

1. Park car in stall A; approach stall from the right side, parallel to the curb. Give proper signal and observe precautions which would be necessary in a traffic situation.
2. Drive out of the stall, observing proper traffic precautions.
3. Repeat this maneuver until you attain a perfect score.
4. Repeat the same procedure using stall B and stall C.

Explanation

The parking operation is one which requires considerable skill. In learning to park, it is best to practice angle parking first. This is the easiest and will help you to develop an awareness of the position of your car in close quarters.

Angle Parking. This is the procedure recommended for *angle parking:*

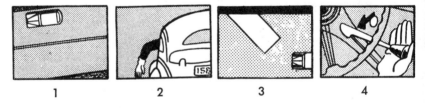

| 1 | 2 | 3 | 4 |

1. Approach the parking space with your car in the right lane.
2. Observe traffic behind and ahead; at least fifty feet before reaching the space, give hand signal to stop.
3. Stop just before reaching the space, about five feet from the entrance.
*4. Shift to first gear.

Fig. 2-37.

---

* Does not apply to automatic transmission cars.

FUNDAMENTAL DRIVING SKILLS

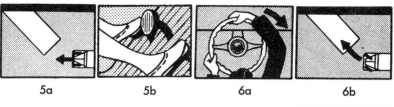

5a 5b 6a 6b

5. Move forward very slowly and control speed with the clutch.
6. When the front bumper is opposite the right edge of the parking space, begin turning to the right (clockwise).

7

7. Steer carefully so that the left edge of your front bumper does not strike the car on the left and the right rear fender does not hit the car on the right.

8

8. Touch the curb gently, but do not bump the curb; then back off a few inches.
9. Set hand brake, shift to first gear (or "park"), and lock the ignition.

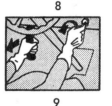

Fig. 2-37 (cont.)

9

Leaving an angle parking space is sometimes a greater problem than getting into it. This is the method to be used in leaving an *angle parking space:*

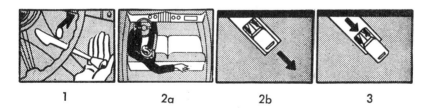

1 2a 2b 3

1. Shift into reverse.

Fig. 2-38.

2. Check traffic to the rear; back straight out slowly for two or three feet (to get a wider range of vision over your right shoulder); stop and check traffic carefully.
3. Proceed straight back when traffic permits.

4a

4b

5a

5b

4. As the front bumper passes the rear of the car on the left, turn wheels sharply to the right (clockwise).

5. When your car is lined up in the right traffic lane, stop, shift to first, and straighten wheels as you proceed forward.

5c

Fig. 2-38. (cont.).

Parallel Parking. Parallel parking is an operation that requires even more skill and control than angle parking. The steps to be followed for *parallel parking* at the right-hand curb are these:

1

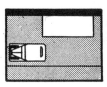
2

3

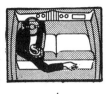
4

1. Locate the car behind which you wish to park; observe traffic behind and ahead. At least 50 feet before reaching the parking space, give a hand signal to stop.

2. Stop beside the car, about two feet to its left, and line up rear bumpers. (If cars are about the same length, line up steering wheels.)

3. Shift to reverse.

4. Back very slowly. (Do not race the engine.)

5. Before your car has moved backward two feet, turn steering wheel as far as possible (two complete turns) to the right. (Clockwise.)

Fig. 2-39.

FUNDAMENTAL DRIVING SKILLS

5	6a	6b	7a

6. As soon as the car is on a 45° angle with the curb, straighten wheels (two complete turns to the left) and continue to back up slowly.

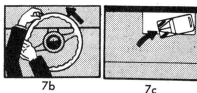

7b   7c

7. Just as your front bumper passes the rear bumper of the car ahead, turn the steering wheel two complete turns to the left (counter-clockwise). Continue backing slowly.

8   9a

8. Stop before touching the bumper of the car in the rear.

9. Move forward, turn wheels toward curb on level ground, and center the car in the space.

10. Set parking brake, shift to first (or "park") position, and lock ignition.

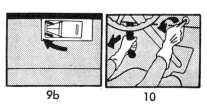

9b   10

The steps for parallel parking on the left side of a one way street are similar but opposite.

Leaving a parallel parking space is accomplished by using these steps:

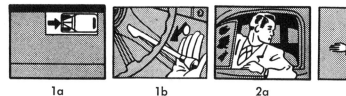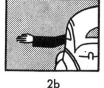

1a	1b	2a	2b

1. Back until bumper almost touches car to the rear; stop, and shift to first (or "drive") position.

2. Look out left side window to check oncoming traffic and give hand signal for left turn.

Fig. 2-40.

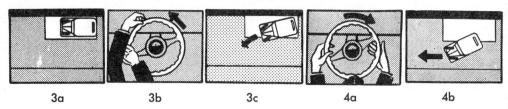

3a   3b   3c   4a   4b

3. When clear, move forward slowly, turning wheels as far as possible to the left (counter-clockwise).

4. When the front half of the car is in the right-hand traffic lane, straighten wheels (two turns to the right); then continue to move forward and steer into proper lane.

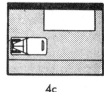

4c

Fig. 2-40 (cont.).

With some concentrated practice you will soon be able to park your car skillfully in angle and parallel parking spaces. Although this skill is essential if you are to park your car efficiently, the ability to locate parking spaces and park in them without creating a hazard for other drivers and pedestrians is of equal importance. The scramble for an empty parking space on a street where parking facilities are at a premium tends to bring out a driver's most aggressive characteristics. You should be aware of this factor, not only from the standpoint of avoiding such behavior in yourself, but also for the sake of becoming alert for other drivers engaged in this practice.

Fig. 2-41. Parallel parking is easy when you know how.

SCORE CARD FOR DRILL VIII

Operation	Point Value	Check Errors and Record Point Deductions Trials
		1 2 3 4 5 6 7 8 9 10 11 12
1. Angle parking.		
a. Failed to signal or observe proper traffic precautions.	3	
b. Failed to stop before attempting to enter stall.	3	
c. Failed to enter stall from correct lane.	3	
d. Entered stall too fast.	3	
e. Hit stanchion.	3	
f. Bumped curb.	3	
g. Front wheel more than six inches from curb.	2	
h. Failed to set hand brake.	3	
i. Failed to shift lever in proper position.	3	
j. Failed to lock ignition.	3	
k. Left stall too fast.	3	
l. Failed to observe traffic precautions when leaving.	3	
m. Raced or stalled engine.	3	
n. Turned wheels while car was not moving.	3	
2. Parallel parking.		
a. Failed to signal intention to stop, or failed to observe proper traffic precautions.	3	
b. Failed to stop in proper position to begin parking maneuver.	3	
c. Raced or stalled engine.	2	
d. Failed to turn wheels properly.	2	
e. Failed to move slowly and smoothly.	3	
f. Hit stanchion.	3	
g. Bumped or scraped curb.	3	
h. Failed to center car in stall.	2	
i. Wheels more than six inches from curb.	3	
j. Failed to shift lever in proper position.	3	
k. Failed to set hand brake.	3	
l. Failed to lock ignition.	3	
m. Failed to signal and look before leaving stall.	3	
n. Turned out unnecessarily wide when leaving stall.	3	
o. Turned wheels while car was not moving.	3	

SUMMARY

Learning to drive is a challenging personal adventure, but it is important to remember that it involves the welfare of the general public. For that reason, the right way to drive should be learned from the beginning, so that only good driving habits will be formed.

The game of driving requires a high degree of good sportsmanship, sound instruction, knowledge, foresight, and good attitudes. The difference between a poor driver and a good one depends to a large extent on his attitude toward learning to drive, and on the way he learns. *Good habits form the basis of good driving.* Each basic maneuver should be practiced, *in the right way,* until your overall skill as a beginner warrants your being classified as a driver. The next step is to apply these basic maneuvers to actual traffic situations!

DISCUSSION TOPICS

1. Make a comparison between learning an athletic sport and learning to drive. What similarities exist between these learning activities? Are there any differences?
2. What is a habit? How are habits formed? Is it easier to learn a new habit or unlearn an old one? Explain.
3. What are the advantages and disadvantages of learning to drive an automatic transmission car before learning a conventional shift.
4. What fundamental operational skills are essential to good driving?
5. What are the various steps to be followed in getting ready to drive, starting the engine, turning off the engine, and leaving the car? Explain the reason for each. What errors are sometimes made in these operations by inexperienced drivers?
6. Describe the process of "slipping the clutch." Why is this method employed for controlling car speed in first and reverse gear? How does it differ from "riding the clutch"?
7. Explain the proper technique for shifting the gears. What shifting errors do beginners most frequently make?
8. How does stopping when driving in third gear differ from the method used when driving in other gears?
9. Why is reduction of gears sometimes necessary? Can you give examples of everyday driving situations when this operation would be used? Describe the proper technique for shifting from third to first gear.
10. Describe the proper technique to be used in turning corners. What cautions should be observed?
11. From a standing position how does starting on an upgrade differ from starting on level ground? Downgrade?

12. Describe the techniques used in parking a car under various conditions, and explain the purpose of the various steps.
13. What can be learned from the observation of other drivers?

PROJECTS AND PROBLEMS

1. Observe several drivers, and make a list of their activities that are apparently habitual. Include not only the manipulations of the car but also habits of courtesy toward others.
2. Prepare a list of those driving acts that should become automatic and those which should not. Give reasons.
3. Prepare a poster or chart that illustrates the relationship of the front wheels to the direction in which the car will move, forward and backward.
4. Observe drivers in the act of parking parallel to the curb. List the errors they make. Prepare a diagram and list the steps which should be used for correct parking.
5. Prepare a diagram of proper hand positions on the steering wheel in each of these operations:
   a. Driving straight ahead.
   b. Hand-over-hand turning.
6. Prepare diagrams of the proper method of turning a corner to the right and to the left, indicating the point at which each step in the operation would be performed.
7. Debate the following question. Resolved: that hand signals are a more adequate means of informing others of your intentions than are mechanical or electrical directional signals. What general agreements and conclusions resulted from the debate?

SELECTED REFERENCES FOR UNIT II

1. *Automobiling*, Burton Marsh. New York: Boy Scouts of America, 1941.
2. *Behind-the-Wheel Driving Guides*, American Automobile Association. Washington, D. C.: 1948.
3. *Learning to Drive Safely*, Alvah R. Laurer. Minneapolis: Burgess Publishing Company, 1949.
4. *Safe Driving Can Be Learned*. Minneapolis: Burgess Publishing Company, 1952.
5. *Sportsmanlike Driving*, American Automobile Association. Washington, D. C.: 1948.
6. *The Fundamental Principles of Driving*, H. James Tysor. Dallas: Banks Upshaw and Company, 1953.
7. *Youth at the Wheel*, John J. Floherty. Philadelphia: J. B. Lippincott and Company, 1937.

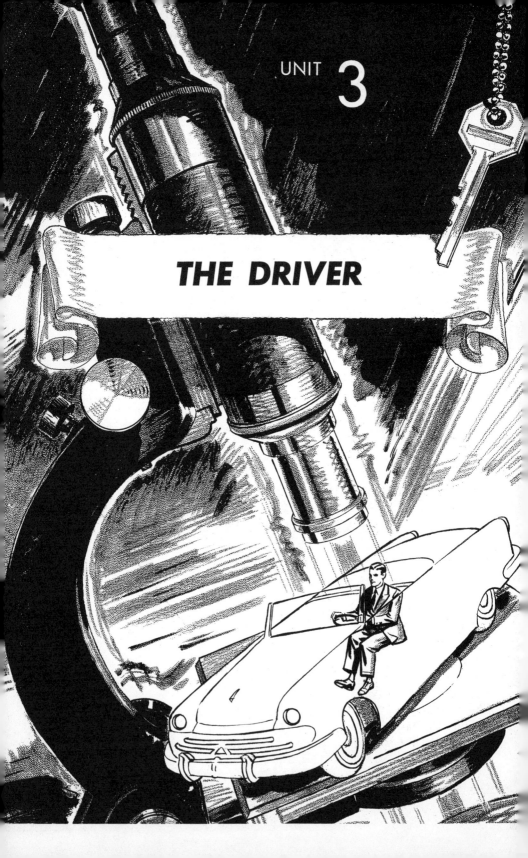

UNIT 3

THE DRIVER

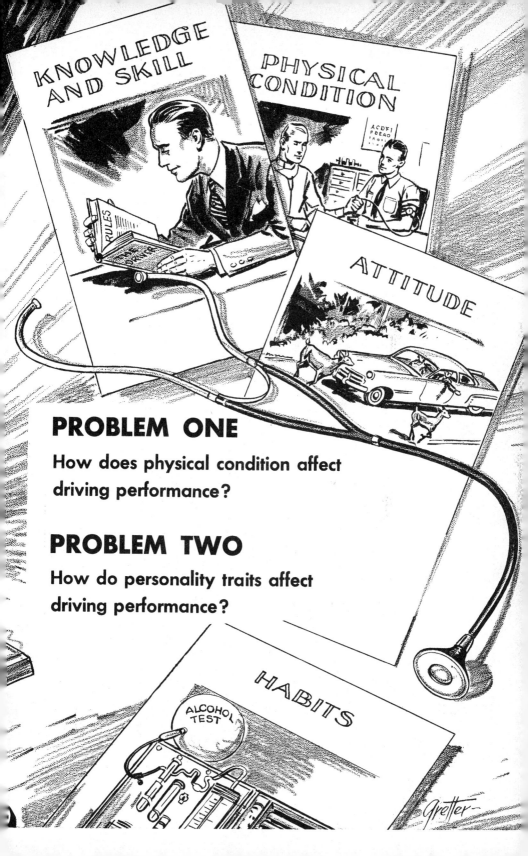

PROBLEM ONE

How does physical condition affect driving performance?

PROBLEM TWO

How do personality traits affect driving performance?

Fig. 3-1. This test determines the driver's field of vision. (*Courtesy: Porto-Clinic Instruments, Inc.*)

How Does Physical Condition Affect Driving Performance?

American engineers have produced the safest and most efficient cars in the world, but in traffic a car is no more safe or efficient than the person who is driving it. To operate effectively, an automobile must be guided with steady hands and feet, clear eyes, and an alert brain—all responsive to the influence of good attitudes, trained habits, and sound judgment.

If drivers performed as well as the vehicles they operate, there would be few accidents. It is relatively easy to pick a good car and keep it in order, but selecting a good driver and keeping him in order is a much harder job! However, just as there are specifications for cars, so there are specifications that are either necessary or desirable in connection with the physical, mental, and emotional make-up of drivers.

Every prospective driver should ascertain whether he is physically fit, or can be made fit, to perform the acts that will be required of him in driving. Such a physical examination, fortunately, is one that most persons can pass.

GENERAL PHYSICAL CONDITION

Not a great deal of physical strength is needed to drive well. Our present day automobiles, if they are in good operating condi-

Fig. 3-2. Visual acuity is measured by a Snellen Chart.

tion, are so efficient mechanically that very little strength is required to manipulate them. However, even though a ninety-pound girl may be strong enough to handle a car capably, there are other physical requirements that she must meet.

First and foremost is good health—the proper working together of sound body organs. No person suffering from a disease that is likely to result in sudden collapse should drive a motor vehicle—certainly not a person who, for example, has serious heart trouble. Other diseases or conditions entail special caution; for example, very high or low blood pressure. The primary consideration should be this: anyone whose health is such that he may lose control of his muscles or senses, without sufficient warning to allow him to bring his car to a safe stop, should not drive. In addition, anyone who is physically unable to respond quickly (and properly) to situations that call for fast action should refrain from driving. Individuals who have any doubt about themselves in this connection should consult a physician. That applies to present as well as prospective drivers.

Compensable or Correctable Disabilities

Many people have deficiencies that may limit their ability to drive. Fortunately, however, most of these disabilities are either correctable or compensable. It should be remembered, however, that a person who has a disability can drive with safety only as long as he is constantly on guard. An individual who has some kind of disability that may effect his driving should get professional advice, usually from his teacher and his physician, regarding the significance of the condition and the means of correcting or compensating for it. Naturally, it is important to learn to drive under a competent instructor who has a thorough understanding of common disabilities in relation to driving.

Fig. 3-3. A rough estimate of visual acuity can be obtained by reading the license plate of a parked car and calculating the distance.

Visual Acuity

By far the most necessary sense for driving is *good* vision. Visual acuity is one of several important qualities of vision. It has to do with sharpness of vision and is often measured in terms of ability to read the letters on a Snellen Chart. A person is considered to have normal visual acuity if, at a distance of 20 feet, he can read a line of letters on the chart that are approximately ⅜ of an inch high. He is then said to have 20/20 vision—which means literally that he can see at 20 feet what should generally be visible at that distance. If, however, at 20 feet he can see no better than the line of larger letters that are generally distinguishable at 50 feet, he is said to have 20/50 vision.

Fig. 3-4. Special controls to help orthopedically disabled drivers compensate for their limitations.

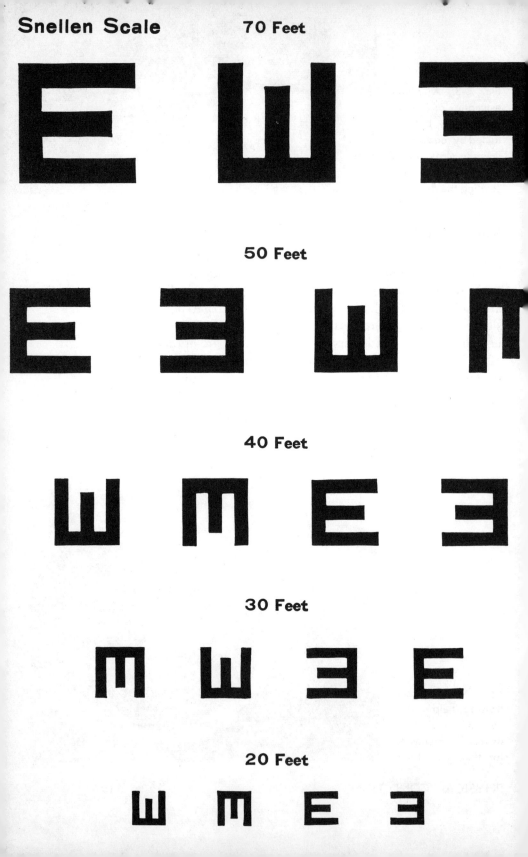

Use the Snellen Chart in this book to test your visual acuity, and then try the following test:

Most state license plates have four-inch numbers. If your visual acuity is 20/20, you should be able to read them at 200 feet. Pace off 200 feet from a car, and see if you can read the plate numbers. If not, walk toward the car until you can read them. If you can do this at 100 feet, your visual acuity is approximately 20/40. If you have to walk in to about 60 feet, it is only about 20/70.

Obviously, anyone who has defective visual acuity should have it corrected *before* attempting to drive. Perception of objects in the path of his car, as well as the ability to read warning signs in time, depends on this function. Fortunately, correction of common deficiencies in visual acuity can readily be made by eye specialists. But good visual acuity alone is not enough for good driving.

Fig. 3-6. Testing a student's field of vision in a traffic situation.

Field of Vision

A person's "field of vision" is the extent to which he can see to the sides while looking straight ahead. An adequate field of vision is important in safe driving; the driver must reckon with movements to the right and left of his car. When a person cannot see well to either side, he is said to have "tunnel" or "barrel" vision. Obviously, this is hazardous in traffic.

In some schools a side-vision testing device is used to measure students' field of vision. This device is essentially a large protractor, as shown in Figure 3-1. The student places the bridge of his nose in the small notch on the open side of the instrument and looks straight ahead, focusing his eyes on a white spot directly in

Fig. 3-5 (facing page). (Courtesy: National Society for the Prevention of Blindness.)

Fig. 3-7. This student is being tested for depth perception. (*Courtesy: Socony-Vacuum Oil Company, Inc.*)

front. The teacher then moves a white dot from the side of the device toward the center and asks the student to let him know as soon as he notices it. (The teacher must watch the student's eyes closely, for if they shift to either side, the test must be begun again.) This process is repeated three times for each eye, and the three scores are averaged. A field of 70 degrees or better to each side is desirable for drivers. Another method of testing one's field of vision more or less realistically is this:

> The person to be tested is seated behind the wheel of a car and is told to look ahead with both eyes open. Two spotters are stationed behind the car, one 20 feet of the left, and the other 20 feet to the right. At a horn signal, the first walks slowly ahead. He stops when the driver signals that he sees him. The second spotter performs similarly. If the field of vision is normal—about 180 degrees—the driver's head will be in direct line between the spotters. Smaller fields of vision may be measured with fair accuracy.

To compensate for "tunnel" vision, the person affected should develop the habit of looking frequently from side to side by turning his head. In addition, he should drive slowly and take special care at intersections.

Depth Perception

The ability to judge the relative distance of objects is known as depth perception. A deficiency in this characteristic, unless compensated for, can obviously have serious consequences in traffic.

One of the devices that can be constructed for measuring depth perception is based on the "rod test" given to pilots in the Air Force. The device consists of a small platform, with two toy cars and a stop sign. One of the cars and the stop sign are stationary. The other car is attached to a cord, so that it may be moved backward or forward by the person taking the test. The subject stands 20 feet away from the instrument and manipulates the control string until the cars appear to him to be side by side. A ruler is mounted alongside the stationary car and the stop sign for use in scoring test performance (the distance in inches separating the stationary and movable objects). See Figure 3-7.

The process is repeated until three trials have been recorded, and a total of three inches or more of deviation in each of the tests, or a sum total of six or more inches, is often taken to indicate a deficiency in distance judgment.

The following is an application of this test in an outdoor situation:

> Station two cars, facing in opposite directions and about 20 feet apart, so that they are 200 feet from the person being tested. With one car remaining stationary, the second is moved forward and back, as directed by an arm signal given by this person. When he is satisfied that the two bumpers are in line, marks are made on the pavement and their distance out of alignment is measured. Differences of over five feet should be investigated.

If depth perception is faulty, one can partly compensate by developing the ability to judge the distance of objects by their size. Obviously, it is important not to approach other cars too closely from the rear. A good rule is not to pass other cars unless the road ahead is clear—both of cars approaching from the opposite direction, and of cars ahead of the one that is to be passed. Parking and turning maneuvers must be executed at a slow rate of speed.

Night Vision

Night traffic accidents are three times as numerous per mile traveled as daytime accidents. This is partly due to drivers being temporarily blinded by oncoming headlights. Individuals vary in their ability to see clearly against strong light, and also in the rapidity with which the pupils of their eyes expand back to normal after the glare which caused them to contract has subsided. Sometimes defective night vision and slow glare recovery are due

USE HIGH AND LOW HEADLIGHT BEAMS PROPERLY

Use upper beam only when driving in the open country without other cars near. Even with the upper beam, speed must be lower than by day.

Always use lower beam when approaching other cars so as not to blind the driver. Also use lower beam when driving where there are street lights, in fog and when following another car closely.

Fig. 3-8. (Courtesy: American Association of Motor Vehicle Administrators and National Safety Council.)

to poor diet or a vitamin deficiency. Sometimes an improved diet high in Vitamin A, or Vitamin A capsules, may aid in correcting this deficiency.

The pupil of a normal eye will contract almost to a pinpoint size if exposed to a bright light for about a second. After the light is removed, it requires almost a minute for the pupil to expand again fully. This means that the night driver who looks directly into a glaring headlight may experience a few seconds of total blindness and close to a minute of reduced vision. At 50 miles per hour, for example, the average driver travels about 146 feet partially blind and nearly a mile with reduced vision if he has looked directly into glaring headlights! Persons whose eyes are abnormally sensitive to light undergo a correspondingly longer period of decreased vision.

DRIVE SLOWER AT NIGHT

Fig. 3-9. Drive more slowly at night so that you can stop within the distance your lights let you see things ahead on the road.

THE DRIVER

Fig. 3-10. The Glareometer measures a person's ability to see after being exposed to a bright light and to see under conditions of reduced illumination. (*Courtesy: Educational Device Company.*)

Of course, a good driver will always depress his headlight beam when meeting other cars. He will also reduce speed when he is faced with the glare from approaching vehicles or from the sun and will resume speed only when his eyes have recovered from the glare. Incidentally, if colored glasses are worn during the day to reduce the effects of sun glare, they should be removed before driving through dark tunnels. Dark glasses should not be worn at night.

It is obvious that in actual practice drivers should not look directly at glaring lights, but rather at the right side of the road. And, of course, added caution and alertness must be exercised in night driving.

Overdriving one's headlights is the practice of driving at speeds for which the stopping distance is greater than the illuminated distance in front of the car. This means that by the time the headlights illuminate a danger so that it can be seen, the driver is too close to be able to avoid it. In most states the law requires that the high beams of headlights illuminate an object 350 feet ahead. Many drivers, however, cannot see much more than 100 feet with their headlights, and it is hard to say what the average is when we consider the findings of a recent national survey of over three million cars: Seven out of every ten had defective lights.

Under favorable night conditions, "Safe headlight speed" is about 40 miles an hour. To drive faster invites an accident if unexpected conditions arise.

Color Blindness

Traffic signal lights throughout the country are not yet arranged with the same sequence of colored lenses. The recommended American standard calls for red at the top, meaning

Fig. 3-11. A driver's ability to distinguish colors is measured by means of various lights on the front of this machine.

"stop," amber next, meaning "caution," and green at the bottom, meaning "go" if the way is clear. If all signals were standardized (the trend is definitely in that direction), it might be helpful to drivers who cannot differentiate between red and green, but who can detect variations of the intensity of light.

Research findings, however, rather clearly indicate that color-blind individuals, even those who are not aware of this deficiency, generally have little difficulty distinguishing between red and green lights. As a matter of fact, they are able to distinguish certain qualities of these colored lights rather than depend on their position on the standards. This was demonstrated in one clinic, where the colors were distinguished despite the fact that the order of the lenses was varied. However, rare exceptions may be possible.

Color perception is tested by the use of colored balls or marbles, colored yarn, or the color-plate Ishihara test. If you are color blind, you are probably aware of the fact. Since color blindness cannot be corrected by glasses, it is wise insurance for the color-blind driver to depend on the movements of traffic as a guide in the event of possible error in interpreting traffic lights in unfamiliar localities. Fortunately, motor vehicle department records show but few instances where color blindness was a factor in accident occurrence.

Reaction Time

Slowness in reacting to situations where quick action is imperative can be dangerous. As a matter of fact, *no human being can*

THE DRIVER

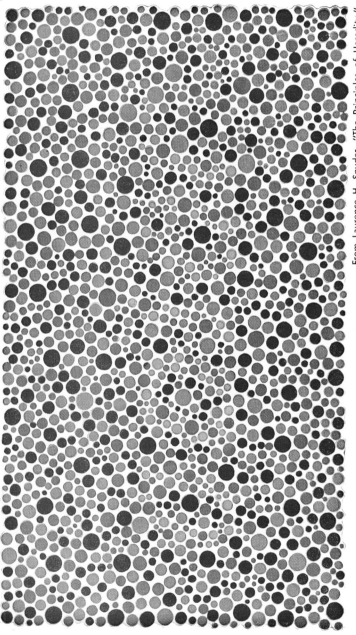

From Laurence H. Snyder, "The Principles of Heredity."
By permission of the author and D. C. Heath and Company

● Use this chart to test yourself for color blindness. If you have normal vision, you will see the word ONION. If you have red-green color blindness, you will see the word COLOR. Some color-blind persons will not be able to make out any word. Red-green color blindness is controlled by a gene inherited in accordance with the sex of the individual.

Fig. 3-12. Just as the fencer must react quickly and accurately to avoid the thrusts of the opponent, a driver must react quickly and accurately to avoid conflicting with other highway travelers.

act instantaneously. It takes a certain amount of time for the eyes to telegraph a warning to the brain, for the brain to decide what to do and to transmit its instructions to the muscles, and then for the muscles to get into action and complete the movement.

The time that elapses between the instant the eye perceives a situation that calls for a single, simple action and the instant the muscles perform that action is known as "simple reaction time." In the normal person it is about one-half of a second. If a choice of actions is offered, the reaction time is likely to be about three-fourths of a second, because the brain requires additional time to make the choice. This is known as "complex reaction time."

Fig. 3-13. Chemical tests show that the amount of drinking done before driving makes a tremendous difference in a driver's chances of having an accident. Licenses are revoked from those driving under the influence of alcohol. (*Courtesy: American Associations of Motor Vehicle Administrators and National Safety Council.*)

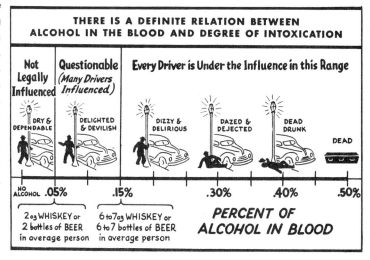

THERE IS A DEFINITE RELATION BETWEEN ALCOHOL IN THE BLOOD AND DEGREE OF INTOXICATION

Not Legally Influenced	Questionable (*Many Drivers Influenced*)	Every Driver is Under the Influence in this Range
DRY & DEPENDABLE	DELIGHTED & DEVILISH	DIZZY & DELIRIOUS — DAZED & DEJECTED — DEAD DRUNK — DEAD

NO ALCOHOL .05%   .15%   .30%   .40%   .50%

2 oz WHISKEY or 2 bottles of BEER in average person

6 to 7 oz WHISKEY or 6 to 7 bottles of BEER in average person

PERCENT OF ALCOHOL IN BLOOD

Fig. 3-14. Two students working together on psychophysical equipment of the Educational Device Company. (*Courtesy: J. Duke Elkow.*)

Suppose your reaction time is normal—about three-quarters of a second. You are driving along a residential street, lined with parked cars, at 30 miles an hour. 80 feet ahead, a child darts out in front of your car and stops, paralyzed with fright. You slam on the brakes, and your car comes to a halt—two feet from the child!

But suppose now that your reaction time is slower than normal —about a quarter-second slower. In that quarter-second your car would travel eleven additional feet before you began to apply your brakes. All other things being equal, your car would strike the child and travel nine feet beyond before coming to a halt! In both cases the braking distance was obviously the same, for the car was traveling at 30 miles per hour. But in one instance the distance traveled before the brakes were applied was only 33 feet, while in the other it was 44 feet. This is an illustration of the possible significance of reaction time. Figure 3-15 shows how far a car will travel during various reaction times.

There are various devices for measuring the length of time it takes to move the foot from the accelerator to the brake in response to a signal, usually the flash of a red light. The devices are constructed so that timing begins with the flash of the light and

Speed in m. p. h.	1/4	3/8	1/2	5/8	3/4	7/8	1 second
20	7	11	14	18	22	25	29	Feet
30	11	16	22	27	33	38	44	"
40	14	22	29	36	44	51	58	"
50	18	27	36	45	55	64	73	"
60	22	33	44	55	66	77	88	"
70	25	38	51	64	77	89	102	"
80	29	44	58	73	88	102	117	"

Fig. 3-15. Reaction Distances. Reaction time varies with individuals, ranging from ¼ of a second to one second or more. This chart indicates how far a car will travel in the interval between the time individuals of various reaction times perceive an emergency and the time that they apply the brakes.

stops with the depression of the brake pedal. The measurement is usually in hundredths of a second.

Of course, reactometers measure relatively simple reactions: The person responding knows what the stimulus will be, he knows what response is called for, and he is in a state of readiness to react. Driving reactions are usually much more complex. Driving is a psychological process involving numerous factors. These may be said to include, among others: *attention*—you are concentrating on driving; *perception*—you notice an object roll into the street; *interpretation*—you make it out to be a rubber ball; *decision*—you decide to stop because a child may be chasing it; *action*—right foot off the accelerator and down on the brake. In situations of this type the driver does not know in advance what the stimulus will be, and the correct response will vary according to many possibilities. Thus, when we talk of reaction time in relation to driving, the important question is how far is a car likely to travel before the driver clearly sees a danger, interprets all of the significant elements in the situation, and decides on the *correct* response. Obviously, fast reaction time alone is not enough. In fact, too quick a response may mean failure to select the right thing to do; the result could be an accident. The truly expert driver, then, is one who, regardless of how fast his reaction time is (as long as it is normal), will constantly try to avoid emergencies that call for desperately quick maneuvering. He *anticipates* possible trouble and drives accordingly. You will read more about this later.

Fig. 3-16. This timer is a piece of cardboard 11½ by 3 inches. The dimensions for calibrating it are shown in the diagram. The timer is held at the top, with its lower portion slightly above the hand of the person to be tested. He holds his thumb and forefinger apart. When the timer is dropped, he grasps it as quickly as he can. The point at which he grasps the timer is an appropriate indication of his very simple reaction time in thousandths of a second. (Courtesy: Transit Casualty Company.)

Hearing

Good hearing is an asset to the driver because it helps to make him aware of the distance, speed, and direction of cars in his immediate vicinity. In many instances poor hearing can be corrected by the use of amplifying devices. In other cases, the person who is hard of hearing or even totally deaf can to some degree compensate for this deficiency. He places more dependence on his vision, perhaps using an additional rear-view mirror. And he executes all maneuvers, such as shifting from one lane to the other, only after making doubly sure that the way is clear and after giving proper and obvious signals of his intention to shift.

Fatigue

Even if your health is good, there are times when your condition is so far below par that you should not attempt to drive. It is better at such times to *pull off the road* until you are fit to go on. Extreme fatigue, for example, may lead to drowsiness and, despite your best efforts, may cause you to fall asleep at the wheel. Almost as dangerous, your fatigue may deceive you into believing that you are driving safely when you are actually misjudging distances, speed, and driving conditions.

Several years ago Dr. Alexander H. Ryan of Chicago conducted a series of studies on driver fatigue. He found that the average drivers efficiency improves during the first three or four hours at the wheel; after five to six hours efficiency is reduced; and after six hours efficiency declines rapidly, regardless of how the driver feels. Many of those tested after five or six hours at the wheel made extremely poor scores on fatigue measurement tests, even though they insisted that they did not feel tired!

It is questionable whether much dependence can be placed on stimulants, such as strong coffee or tea, as a means of overcoming fatigue. There are certain times, however, when fatigue arises less from actual bodily weariness than from boredom and monotony. In such cases stopping at a roadside stand for a hot drink is beneficial. The exercise you get in standing up and walking helps too. However, if you are "dog-tired," nothing you may do to force yourself to keep awake is likely to be effective for long. When you are in that condition, the best thing to do is to drive your car to some area, preferably near lighted service station, and go to sleep for a while. There are too many instances where a car has gone off the road *after* the driver has fallen asleep.

Fig. 3-17. Measuring the degree of driver intoxication. (Courtesy: New York University.)

Fatigue sometimes comes very quickly. This is particularly true when one has gone through a siege of sickness and has not yet fully regained his strength. At such times one may feel "fit as a fiddle" for an hour or two, and then experience a reaction that blocks almost any physical or mental effort. If you are convalescing from an illness, do not drive until you have fully recovered. If you must drive, drive slowly and stop for frequent rests.

Effect of Alcohol

Records compiled by various states reveal the fact that drinking has a profound effect upon the accident situation; in fact, *in one out of every nine fatal accidents a driver has been drinking*. There is no doubt that drinking and driving do not mix. Even the manufacturers, distributors, and retail sellers of alcohol are all agreed on the verdict, *"If you drink, don't drive—if you drive, don't drink."*

Alcohol, when taken into the system *even in relatively small quantities,* definitely impairs vision, judgment, muscular co-ordination, and efficiency, and reduces accuracy and speed of reaction. Dr. Herman A. Heise, of Columbia Hospital, Milwaukee, tested two groups of drivers, giving one group a moderate amount of alcohol and the other group none. The alcoholic group made 60 per cent more driving errors. Its vision and muscular co-ordination were much poorer, and its reaction distance was 37 per cent greater! In addition to these effects, alcohol produces another that is perhaps the greatest accident hazard of all: it gives the drinker a *false* confidence that lures him into taking chances with his own and other people's lives—chances that would appall him when sober.

The drinking driver is likely to forget rules of safe driving, traffic laws, and regulations. If he remembers them, he is likely to observe them erratically. There is nothing that the man who has been drinking can do to compensate for the lowering of his driving skill and his impaired judgment. That is why the legislatures, the police, and the courts regard him as one of the most serious menaces in today's traffic and deal with him accordingly.

Recently developed chemical tests make it practically impossible for a person to conceal the fact that he has been drinking. These tests give scientific evidence, accepted in the courts of many states, as to whether or not alcohol is in the system—and, if it is, how much is present. Such chemical tests are playing an increasingly important part in keeping drinking drivers off the streets and highways.

One type of test commonly used is the "breath" test, which samples a person's breath by having him blow up a toy balloon. The air in the balloon is then passed through a chemical solution. The volume of breath required to change the color of the solution from purple to a light brown indicates the approximate *concentration* of alcohol in the blood stream and the brain tissue. Other tests check the individual's saliva, urine, or blood. They all yield similar results.

Since alcohol requires no digestion and is absorbed *directly* into the blood, it will reveal its presence within two minutes after consumption. The seriousness of the effects depends upon the amount and kind of alcoholic beverage, the physical stature and condition of the drinker, the amount of food and other fluids in the stomach, and the speed of the drinking. A concentration of more than 0.15 of one per cent of alcohol in the blood is generally accepted by legal and medical authorities as evidence that a man is intoxicated.

One of the most important rules that a prospective driver can adopt and follow is this: never drive an automobile after drinking —rather leave the car in the garage, or, if necessary, have someone else drive. If this rule were faithfully followed, one of the greatest killers on the road would be eliminated.

Carbon Monoxide Poisoning

Carbon monoxide gas, which is found in the exhaust of all cars, is the cause of many automobile accidents every year. It may be fatal if found in the air in concentrations greater than four-hundredths of one per cent. In the average car's exhaust, the concentration can be from five to ten per cent! It is colorless, odorless, and tasteless, and brings on drowsiness, followed by unconsciousness and death in an amazingly brief time. Several hundred persons are asphyxiated each year by this gas while sitting in their cars in closed garages warming the motors preparatory to starting out. It is possible that many accidents with obscure causes have been due to the drugging influence of this poisonous gas.

Keep your car in such mechanical condition that the gas from leaky exhaust manifolds and mufflers cannot seep in through broken floor boards and other openings. Keep a reasonable distance behind other cars, particularly large trucks or busses. It is wise to keep car ventilators partly open at *all* times and, at the first hint of drowsiness, to stop, get out of the car, and walk around, breathing deeply. When sitting for long periods of time in a parked car, such as at a drive-in movie, be sure to turn off the engine. Also, make sure not to park behind a car that has its engine running. In the event that some one is overcome by carbon monoxide, get the victim into fresh air and apply artificial respiration while awaiting the arrival of a doctor.

Age

With increasing age all persons suffer in varying degrees from gradual diminution of the senses, bodily strength, and endurance. Young drivers, however, are at an age when their physical powers are just approaching their peak. Eyesight is keener, reflexes are faster, and the body possesses more endurance and recuperative power than may be expected at, and beyond, middle age. To young drivers, then, the problem of age means only that they must exercise greater caution and courtesy when they are in the neighborhood of elderly drivers and pedestrians whose reaction time may be slow, who may not see clearly, and who may become confused in traffic and do the wrong thing in an emergency.

Because of his fine physical condition, the young driver many times fails to realize that *all* human beings have certain psychophysical limitations. Even the finest physical specimen has limits to his reaction time, co-ordination, vision, hearing, and endurance. As a person grows older he becomes more and more aware of his limitations. Perhaps this is one reason why older drivers, in spite of more handicaps, have far fewer accidents than young drivers!

SUMMARY

Every new driver should be aware of the importance of personal limitations and how they can affect his abilitiy to drive skillfully and safely. Factors such as vision, hearing, general health, physical strength, and mental well-being will naturally determine to a great degree the kind of driving he does. Often limitations in some of these respects, notably vision, may assume even more serious proportions as a result of external factors such as rain, snow, fog, and darkness.

The good driver, therefore, will learn his limitations and make needed corrections and compensations. He will be alert, too, to the fact that other drivers possess weaknesses, and he will drive "on the defensive" to protect himself against mistakes that they may make. Finally, despite what others may do, the good driver will always adhere to the principles of good sportsmanship.

DISCUSSION TOPICS

1. How and why does a driver's physical condition affect his driving?
2. Explain what is meant by each of the following, and indicate their relationship to safe driving: visual acuity, tunnel vision, depth perception, peripheral vision, double vision, glare resistance, color blindness.
3. What have scientists found the effects of alcohol to be on vision, reaction time, co-ordination, judgment, and attitudes?
4. What have many states done to help eliminate drunken driving? Explain in detail.
5. What is the effect of reaction time on driving performance? Define reaction distance. What physical conditions affect reaction time?
6. What is the effect of fatigue and monotony on driving? What can be done to overcome these difficulties?

PROJECTS AND PROBLEMS

1. Prepare a "driver's physical fitness chart," indicating the physical requirements needed for good driving. Indicate the disabilities or limitations that may be associated with each. Show which disabilities are temporary and which are permanent, and note any corrections or compensations that may be applicable.
2. Use two of the testing procedures described in the text and summarize your findings. What is the significance of your findings?
3. Prepare a series of recommendations for efficient driving that take into account the physical limitations of drivers.
4. What factors in a driver's physical makeup should be examined by the state before a driver's license is issued? Determine whether your present state examination tests these characteristics?

Fig. 3-18. Baseball star and Marine jet ace Ted Williams has said: "Whether you are in the batter's box on the baseball diamond, inside the cockpit of a jet plane, or behind the wheel of your car, alert attention, sound judgment, and smooth skill are vital for stellar performance." (*Courtesy: Boston Red Sox Baseball Club.*)

THE DRIVER

How Do Personality Traits Affect Driving Performance?

The physical limitations described in the preceding chapter are serious only for a small percentage of people. Where such conditions exist, the very carefulness that results from the effort to compensate may even have the effect of making the driver less likely to have accidents. Neither physical disabilities nor lack of manipulative skill produce the majority of traffic accidents today. The trouble with most dangerous drivers lies in the fact that their mental, moral, and emotional equipment is defective. If traffic experts could solve the problem of faulty attitudes and emotional maladjustments, they would need to be far less concerned with questions of vision, reaction time, or even driving skills.

When Dr. Lowell S. Selling was director of one of the world's foremost traffic court clinics, he had occasion to examine many hundreds of problem drivers. The following observations by Dr. Selling[*] are particularily appropriate to the present subject:

> The important thing which psychologists are beginning to discover is that there are habit patterns and consistent attitudes also which, incorporated within some of our bad drivers, are of extreme significance in the causation of automobile accidents. . . .

---

[*] Series T, No. 23, Psychopathic Clinic, Recorder's Court, Detroit, Michigan.

. . . there are some [drivers] who are sane, who are not feeble-minded, and who are not physically ill, yet who get into accidents, and the serious violators fall into this category. This is the group that has faulty attitudes. . . .

We classify attitudes primarily as temporary and permanent. A temporary attitude is the type which is found in an individual when he drives to work after having insufficient sleep, an argument with his wife, a poor breakfast, the promise of an unfriendly interview with the boss when he arrives at work, and similar occurrences which could make him apprehensive, fearful, or perhaps preoccupied. If the immediate problem which caused the difficulty is erased, that is, when the interview with the boss is over, when the wife has apologized, or when the problem driver has had a supplementary cup of coffee, the attitude may change. . . .

Permanent attitudes arise occasionally from an inherited mental weakness or more frequently from a faulty upbringing so that the person is antagonistic towards any discipline, as a result of trouble at home or in school, as a result of inferiority feelings from rivalry between older and younger children, or from other situations which would cause a change in the outlook of a person toward his life as a whole.

It must be remembered also that there is no such thing as an individual whose behavior is characteried entirely by a single attitude. . . . When we discuss the types of attitudes which we find in our drivers, therefore, particularly those of a permanent nature, we are dealing with the dominant trait only.

PROBLEM DRIVERS

The Self-Centered Driver

An egoist thinks or acts as though he were the only important person in the world. He looks at his car simply as another means of expressing himself and his importance, or as a means of imposing his will upon others. His disregard for the lives and feelings of others is limited only by his fear of punishment or injury.

This type of driver speeds whenever he is sure that no traffic officer is watching, even though he may have more time on his hands than he knows what to do with. He ignores traffic lights and stop signs; he forces other drivers out of his way. When parking, he stops in the center of a clear space, preventing another car from parking either ahead or behind, or he crowds in so closely that it is impossible for other parked cars to get out. He does not believe in signalling his intentions to other drivers; his motto is

"Let them look out." He will use his horn as a threat that he is coming through. If his disregard for the rights of others causes an accident, he is loud in his protestations of innocence. He always blames the other fellow; he will never admit making a mistake himself.

Fig. 3-19. Some drivers retain a Dr. Jekyll and Mr. Hyde personality when they get behind the wheel. (Courtesy: Travelers Insurance Company.)

Fig. 3-20. The really smart driver always keeps his attention on driving. (Courtesy: National Association of Secondary School Principals.)

We all probably have a certain degree of egoism. But as normal people we learn through experience that we are no more and no less important than the great majority of our fellow citizens. We learn that successful living in our modern democratic society is a process of give and take. We take pride in our ability to get along with people, on the road and off.

The Show-Off

First cousin to the self-centered driver—and just as dangerous —is the show-off. The show-off likes to draw attention to himself. He is often a frustrated individual who uses his car to get recognition and a feeling of power that he cannot get in some other way. For example, a young man who is not the athlete, artist, or scholar he would like to be may become a *frustrated* individual. How can he get people to notice him? Well, he can "take it out" on the accelerator and brake of his old car! So he roars down the street in a cloud of dust and comes to a halt with screeching brakes and squealing tires in an effort to satisfy that desire for attention and recognition. Needless to say, he does not know why he acts this way.

Obviously, the show-off is easy to recognize. He drives as wildly as he dares, particularly if he has passengers to impress. Only luck can save him, his passengers, and innocent bystanders from a horrible fate.

The Irresponsible Driver

Irresponsible people do not make good drivers either. They are usually just too indifferent to handle their cars efficiently and safely. Not willing to attempt to drive well, they are satisfied just to get by—and sometimes they don't!

Here are some common faults of the irresponsible driver: driving too fast for existing conditions; failing to signal; failing to grant the right of way; driving too closely behind the car ahead; passing whenever the fancy strikes him; disregarding signs, signals, markings, and other traffic regulations.

Thus, the irresponsible person drifts along in his driving just as he drifts along in life—avoiding things that require effort, *particularly where obligations to others are concerned.*

The Temperamental Driver

Most of us have the urge at times to express our dissatisfaction, sulkiness, temper, or ill-humor with people and events, but since childhood we have learned to control such impulses more or less successfully. Lack of such control in an otherwise normal, healthy, unfatigued adult usually means that he has not grown up emotionally. It means that he attaches exaggerated importance to the petty little annoyances of the moment. The person who cannot control his emotions under the stress of driving in traffic is definitely an accident hazard. This is true even if he manages to remain outwardly calm while inwardly he is seething, for his judgment is impaired and he is likely to take chances that, in calmer moments, he would not even consider.

The emotionally unstable driver shows his temperament in many ways: he honks his horn incessantly; he weaves in and out from one lane to another; he abuses other drivers, whether or not they are responsible for a delay; and he tries to make up for lost time whenever traffic starts moving. These, and many other dangerous and foolhardy acts, spring from his unwillingness or inability to accept even a minor or momentary annoyance. This pattern of immature behavior is easier to prevent by cultivating desirable attitudes in earlier years, than it is to correct after it becomes deep-seated.

The Inattentive Driver

The driver of an automobile can turn over to his "robot intelligence"—habit—some of the actual work of driving, but he must nevertheless be constantly on the alert to meet situations as they develop. Of course, one can and should perform certain driving operations more or less automatically, but there are many things that need conscious thought and attention. Driving is a full-time job that requires constant concentration on all the highly variable factors in traffic: the warning signs and signals, the pedestrians and bicyclists, road and weather conditions, and the actual and possible maneuvers of other cars.

Some authorities say that inattention is a factor in at least half of all accidents. We have all known drivers who carry on animated conversations with their companions, even gesturing and taking their hands off the wheel during an exciting topic; there are others who seem to become absorbed in interesting scenes alongside the street or highway. But the most common setting for inattention, no doubt, is preoccupation with personal problems. Even veteran drivers have found, to their sorrow, that expert skill and thorough familiarity with the road fail to make up for inattention.

The Accident-Repeater Driver

A large percentage of our accidents is caused by a small percentage of drivers. A study of the records of 30,000 drivers in Connecticut some years ago found that 4 per cent of these drivers had been involved in 36 per cent of the accidents recorded over a period of six years. This undoubtedly included many of the individuals we have described in the preceding pages—the drivers who lack good judgment and good attitudes or are emotionally maladjusted or disturbed. Also interesting in this connection is a research study of accident repeaters in Michigan and Connecticut conducted by the New York University Center for Safety Education. Among other things, the Safety Center's investigators found that:

1. There is a close relationship between accidents and violations. A cumulative record of both provides the best picture of the driving practices of the licensed operator.
2. Repeaters tend to have more personality maladjustments than accident-free drivers. These tend to increase among the more serious repeaters.
3. Repeaters also have poorer co-ordination, under normal conditions as well as under conditions of frustration and annoyance.

4. Serious repeaters tend to be more upset by frustrations and annoyances than comparable accident-free drivers.
5. The attitudes toward certain aspects of driving are significantly poorer among repeaters.
6. More repeaters than accident-free drivers have been arrested on charges other than traffic violations. They tend to drive as they live.

The investigators recommended that, in re-educating accident repeaters, major attention should be given to the improvement of attitudes and the development of mature judgment.

WHAT DO THESE DRIVERS MEAN TO YOU?

We have described various types of drivers who personify certain undesirable attitudes or maladjustments in driving. Still others could have been described, and no doubt some of those considered might have been labeled differently. But the implications are clear. You will find on the road every day drivers who have not matured sufficiently or who lack the mental, social, or emotional qualities to be entrusted with the control of a high-powered, two-ton projectile on public highways. It is particularly unfortunate that they endanger not only themselves but other drivers and pedestrians as well.

For the most part these drivers can be corrected—through educational programs, personal counselling, or psychiatric treatment. But to do these things on the proper scale will be expensive and time-consuming. In the meantime, it is most important that each new crop of drivers "gets off on the right foot." And that is where you come in.

First of all, by knowing about these maladjusted people and their traits, you will be better prepared to protect yourself through defensive driving. But even more important, by understanding these traits and recognizing desirable attributes, you are insuring yourself against becoming one of these types.

What Makes a Good Driver?

In the preceding pages we have emphasized the disturbed, anti-social nature of bad drivers; the characteristics of good drivers have been suggested only by implication. It would be well, therefore, at this point to state in positive terms the qualities that make for good driving, so that they may be recognized and cultivated

Fig. 3-21. You cannot consider yourself a well-educated or well-adjusted person in this mechanical age if you have not learned to live safely and efficiently with motor vehicles. (*Courtesy: Travelers Insurance Company.*)

by new and prospective drivers. The emphasis here, of course, is placed on personality traits, since without certain knowledges and skills, one cannot properly operate a motor vehicle.

Obviously, the desirable attributes include such factors as social responsibility, emotional maturity, and sound judgment. However, we need more specific standards for driving behavior. The following represent attitudes and other personal characteristics that have been established through research and experience as of primary importance:

A Sense of Social Responsibility

The good driver realizes that his license to drive is a privilege, not a right.

He fully understands that this is a privilege extended to all competent persons, not just to himself. Therefore, he is aware of the fact that he must share the road with countless other drivers.

With the many possible variations in drivers' abilities, in types of vehicles, in road capacities, and in weather conditions, the good driver realizes that smooth flow of traffic depends upon teamwork to which he must contribute for his own sake as well as for the sake of others. He will not hog the road; he will not "chisel" space; he will not act as if it were every man for himself.

He also strives to be a good citizen of the road; whenever possible he helps other motorists in distress.

Naturally, he maintains a friendly attitude toward police officers, recognizing that their function in traffic situations is for the common good.

Finally, he recognizes that by setting an example of really good driving for his family and his friends and by helping them to improve their performance he is making a contribution to the solution of our traffic problem and discharging an important responsibility as a citizen.

A Sound Concept of Himself in Relation to Other Drivers

He recognizes that drivers differ in abilities and personality traits (within the limits, of course, set by licensing requirements).

He has a realistic concept of his own abilities and personality. Thus, he recognizes that other drivers may be his equals or his superiors in driving performance; he does not envy their ability but instead strives to perform as well or better.

He recognizes, too, that some drivers are not as good as he, and, while he takes pride in the quality of his performance, he does not demonstrate his superiority and look down upon or take advantage of inferior performances.

Emotional and Physical Fitness

In order to discharge properly his social responsibility as a driver, he realizes that he must be attentive and constantly on the alert, ready to anticipate hazardous movements of other drivers, of bicyclists, and of pedestrians.

In the event of such hazardous movements or in the face of traffic delays, he recognizes the danger of "flying off the handle"; he is mature enough to be able to control his emotions.

Of course, like a champion athlete, he is aware that he cannot do his best job as a driver unless he is in good physical condition. So he tries to keep himself fit, and, when he is not up to par, he avoids driving.

He realizes, too, that his abilities mean nothing unless his car is in good condition, and he sees to it that it is, through proper inspection, maintenance, and repair.

An Active Interest in Self-Improvement

He recognizes that in these days of rapid change and spectacular progress, there are always new things to be learned about cars, roads, and drivers. So he continually seeks to improve himself as a driver.

In this connection he is open-minded and welcomes the suggestions and advice of traffic experts, such as motor vehicle and police officials.

Needless to add, *consistency* in recommended behavior, such as observing traffic rules and regulations, is an essential quality of the superior driver. It is tantamount to insurance against the one occasion when an accident could happen to him.

The Art of Driving and the Art of Living

From the desirable attributes that have been itemized above, one can readily see that the art of driving and the art of living have much in common. It is indeed true that a person drives as he lives! *How will you rate?*

This question is even more important than you may think at the moment. More and more business concerns and industries are giving personality tests to applicants for jobs of all kinds, from clerks and typists to skilled mechanics and store personnel. Even junior executives are being selected partly on the basis of test scores that reflect satisfactory personal adjustments. For management is vitally interested in human relations; it wants to know that its employees can get along with customers, with supervisors, and with each other. Some day you will discover that *how you share the road* with other drivers and pedestrians may also be a pretty good indication of how successful you are in getting along with people generally—at work, at home, and in your social life.

DISCUSSION TOPICS

1. What is personality? What is its relationship to good driving?
2. How are attitudes involved in operating an automobile? What types of drivers reflect undesirable attitudes?
3. Describe several instances where good judgment and fair play may influence driving action.

4. Compare the two concepts "right to drive" and "privilege to drive," and discuss their influence on driving attitudes.
5. What incentives are there for being a skillful and safe driver?
6. What qualities essential for good driving are lacking in a so-called irresponsible driver?
7. What are some of the factors that may affect the attentiveness of a driver?
8. How should the good driver react toward the reckless, discourteous driver?

PROJECTS AND PROBLEMS

1. Prepare a list of mental and emotional qualities that an outstanding athlete must possess. Which ones are also necessary for a good driver?
2. Find out what is being done in your state and community to prohibit physically and mentally deficient persons from driving. Are records kept of accident-prone or accident-repeater drivers? Are there any special regulations for such drivers?
3. Draw a series of posters illustrating various personality traits and their effects on driving.

SELECTIVE REFERENCES FOR UNIT III

1. *How to Drive Better and Avoid Accidents,* Paul W. Kearney. New York: Thomas Y. Crowell Company, 1953.
2. *Psychology and the Motorist,* Herbert A. Toops and S. Edson Haver. Columbus, Ohio: R. G. Adams and Company, 1938.
3. *Sportsmanlike Driving,* American Automobile Association. Washington, D. C.: 1948.
4. *The Fundamental Principles of Driving,* H. James Tysor. Dallas: Banks Upshaw and Company, 1948.
5. *The Motor Vehicle Driver—His Nature and Improvement,* Eno Foundation for Highway Traffic Control. Saugatuck, Connecticut: 1949.
6. *Uniform Vehicle Code, Act V,* U. S. Public Roads Administration. Washington, D. C.: Government Printing Office, 1945.
7. *Why We Have Automobile Accidents,* Harry R. De Silva. New York: John Wiley and Sons, Inc., 1942.

UNIT
4

UNDERSTANDING YOUR CAR
ITS CONSTRUCTION, OPERATION, AND MAINTENANCE

SPARKPLUG

ENGINE

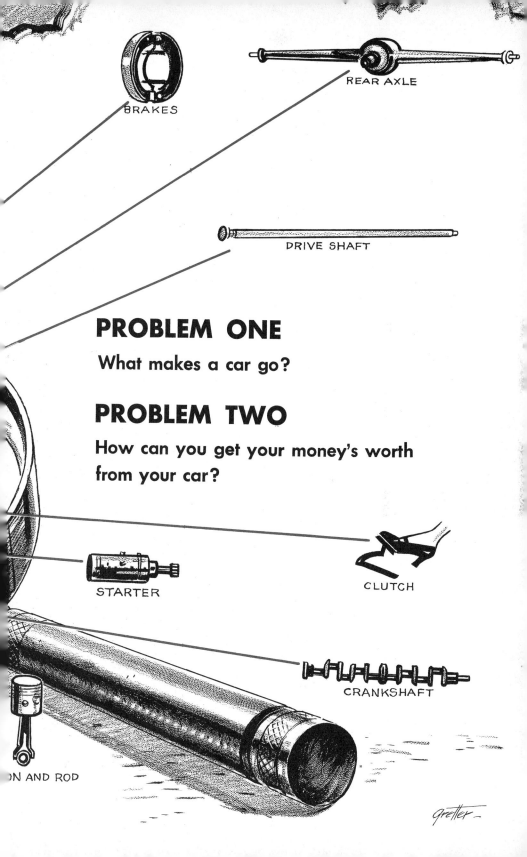

BRAKES

REAR AXLE

DRIVE SHAFT

PROBLEM ONE

What makes a car go?

PROBLEM TWO

How can you get your money's worth
from your car?

STARTER

CLUTCH

CRANKSHAFT

ON AND ROD

Gretter

Fig. 4-1. A schematic diagram of a car. (Courtesy: *Chrysler Corporation*.) After your car rolls off the assembly line, its life span depends upon the care you give it. (Courtesy: *Ford Motor Company*.)

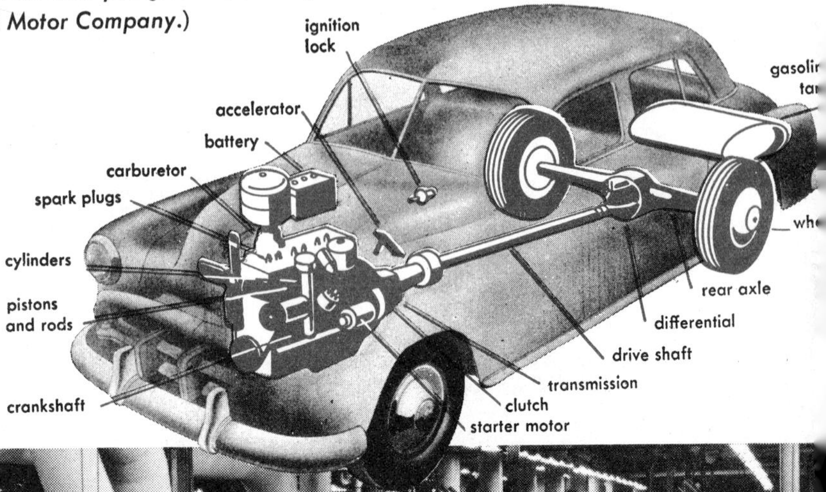

ignition lock

accelerator

battery

carburetor

spark plugs

cylinders

pistons and rods

crankshaft

gasoline tank

wheel

rear axle

differential

drive shaft

transmission

clutch

starter motor

UNDERSTANDING YOUR CAR

What Makes a Car Go?

Power is developed in the engine when a spark ignites a compressed gasoline-air mixture. Rapid burning of this mixture exerts a terrific pressure, which forces the pistons downward so that they rotate the crankshaft. When the clutch is engaged, this rotating motion goes to the gear box or transmission, where the speed or direction of the rotation can be changed as desired. A drive shaft then carries the rotating power back to the differential, which turns the two axle shafts that are connected to the rear wheels. And that is what makes the wheels go around in your car.

The modern car is so well made that a driver no longer needs to be an expert mechanic in order to operate it effectively. Most drivers feel little need to know what is going on under the hood or down among the wheels. However, the motorist who understands his car will be able to handle it more efficiently in any driving situation; he feels a sense of "kinship" with the machine and understands why he performs the various driving operations.

A motor car consists of four basic parts: the engine, the power train, the framework or chassis, and the body. Each part performs its own function. The engine produces the power to move the car. It is often called the "heart" of the car. The power train consists of a network of gears and shafts that transmit power from the engine to the rear wheels. The chassis is the framework or skeleton on which the engine and other parts are mounted. The body is the coach-like structure that provides a convenient enclosure for persons or goods. Let us consider each one of these parts in detail and find out "what makes our car tick."

THE ENGINE

The engine is simply a container in which fuel is burned to produce and harness power. Most of the engine's parts are designed to perform one of its four basic functions: (1) preparing the fuel to be burned; (2) providing a place for the burning to take place; (3) supplying a spark to ignite the fuel at the right time; and (4) harnessing the force created by the explosion.

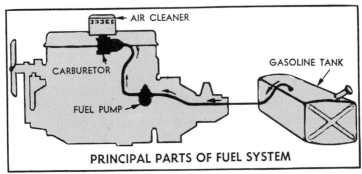

AIR CLEANER

CARBURETOR

GASOLINE TANK

FUEL PUMP

PRINCIPAL PARTS OF FUEL SYSTEM

Fig. 4-2.

Preparing Fuel to Be Burned

Gasoline and air are brought together and mixed in the *carburetor*. Gasoline is drawn by a *fuel pump* through a metal tube that runs from the gasoline tank to the float chamber of the carburetor. Air is drawn into the mixing chamber through a cleaner and silencer on top of the carburetor. This filter removes most of the dust and grit that might damage vital engine parts; it also helps to eliminate the hissing sound of air as it is "sucked" into the engine.

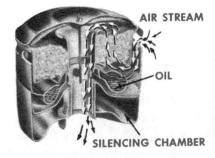

AIR STREAM

OIL

SILENCING CHAMBER

Fig. 4-3. The air filter on top of the carburetor removes impurities from incoming air and provides for quiet air intake. (*Courtesy: Chrysler Corporation.*)

UNDERSTANDING YOUR CAR

Fig. 4-4. Valves act as doorways to let fuel into and gases out of the combustion chamber. (*Courtesy:* General Motors Corporation.)

Similar to an atomizer or spray gun, the carburetor creates a fine spray or mist consisting of one part gasoline to about fifteen parts of air. This mixing process is essential, because liquid gasoline will not burn. The richness of the fuel mixture (proportion of gasoline to air) and the amount of fuel entering the engine are controlled by valves in the carburetor. These valves function quite similar to dampers in a stove pipe. The *choke valve* adjusts the richness of the fuel mixture for various driving conditions. The *throttle valve* regulates engine speed by controlling the amount of fuel entering the engine.

Providing a Place to Burn the Fuel

When the gasoline is properly mixed with air, it goes from the carburetor through a pipe called the *intake manifold* into one of the many combustion chambers where it is to be burned. The combustion chambers are cylindrical tubes bored in the cast-iron engine block. A typical automobile engine has four, six, or eight of these so-called *cylinders*. The cylinders are closed at the top by the *cylinder head*—a flat metal casting bolted to the engine block. Closing the bottom end of each cylinder, but free to move up and down, is a movable plug called a *piston*. Two doorways or *valves* are located at the top of each cylinder. Fuel enters the combustion chamber through the intake valve, and burned gases pass out through the *exhaust valve*.

Burning the Fuel

Just as a spark is used to ignite the fuel in a cigarette lighter, a spark is also used to ignite the gasoline-air mixture in the combustion chambers of the engine. Therefore, a spark plug is attached at the top of each cylinder. At the end of each plug are two wires or electrodes separated by an air gap about the thickness of a dime. Each time electricity jumps this gap a hot spark results. This is the fire that ignites the fuel mixture.

WHAT MAKES YOUR CAR GO

Fig. 4-5. The spark plug ignites fuel in the combustion chamber in much the same way that the fluid is ignited by the flint in a cigarette lighter. (*Courtesy: Chrysler Corporation.*)

To produce the spark a source of electricity is needed, and a means is needed to replace the electricity used. The source of electrical energy for the engine's ignition system is the battery. It consists of three cells that can be charged and discharged repeatedly. As the battery is charged, it stores chemical energy. When the battery is discharged, this chemical energy is transformed and released in the form of electric current.

Electrical energy taken from the battery is replaced by an engine-driven *generator*. This generator not only charges the battery but also operates the ignition system when the engine is running. It is composed of a coil of wire rotated between two magnets. The *field* between these magnets causes electricity to flow in the wire coil. Thus the generator converts mechanical energy into electrical energy. The generator-battery circuit is controlled by a unit called a *voltage-regulator*. This increases the flow of electricity to the battery when the battery is in a discharged condition and decreases the flow when the battery approaches a full charge.

Because a pressure of six volts produced by the battery is not powerful enough to jump across an air gap and ignite the fuel mixture, a *spark coil* is needed. Just as the nozzle on your garden hose operates so that when a considerable amount of water enters the hose at low pressure, a thin stream can be projected from the hose at high pressure, the spark coil in a similar way increases electrical pressure or voltage in the ignition system. Like the nozzle of the hose, the spark coil increases pressure and reduces volume. A moderate amount of electricity enters the coil at a pressure of six volts, but a very small amount of electricity is sent out from the coil at a pressure of about 18,000 volts—a pressure strong enough to easily jump the gap of the spark plug.

UNDERSTANDING YOUR CAR

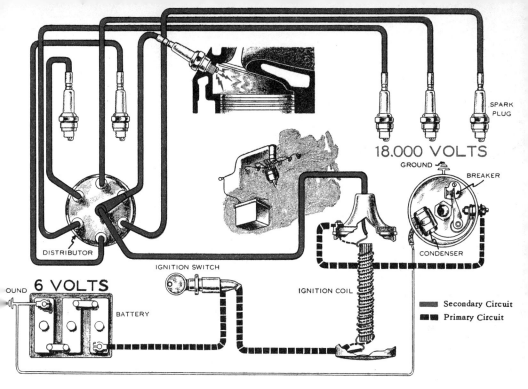

Fig. 4-6. Automobile ignition system. (*Courtesy: General Motors Corporation.*)

The other basic part of the ignition system is the *distributor.*
This is a revolving switch that sends an electrical impulse to each
spark plug at just the right time. It might be compared to a clock
—a clock with only one hand and with the hours marked in raised
numerals, which the hand rubs on as it moves around. Instead of
the hand going around once an hour, it may go around more than
2000 times a minute. A wire from the coil is attached to the center
of the distributor at the point where the hand or rotor is attached.
There is also a wire from each contact point (clock numeral) to a
spark plug. Thus as the rotor goes around electricity flows first to
one contact point then to another, and thus to one spark plug
after another, causing the fuel to explode in each combustion
chamber at just the right time.

In addition to supplying ignition for the engine, the electrical
system also performs many other functions. It provides power
for starting, lights, radio, instruments, and other accessories. Demands upon it are constantly increasing, so that larger batteries
and generators are required. For technical reasons some modern
cars are changing to 12-volt electrical systems to meet these needs
better.

WHAT MAKES YOUR CAR GO   155

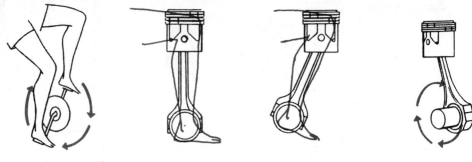

Fig. 4-7. The piston, connecting rod, and crankshaft assembly operate in much the same way your legs do in pedaling a bicycle. (*Courtesy: Chrysler Corporation.*)

Harnessing the Power

The pistons put power to work. They transmit power the way your legs do when you pedal a bicycle. The piston in a cylinder moves in much the same way your knees do when pedalling. The piston is forced straight downward with each explosion in the combustion chamber. The connecting rod below each piston corresponds to the lower part of your leg. The end of the piston rod that connects to the *crankshaft* is much like your foot on the pedal. When pedalling, your knees move straight up and down, but rotary motion is produced as you push down on the pedal. The piston-crankshaft assembly works in just the same way. (See Figure 4-7.) On a bicycle, one pedal is carried up through the last half of the circle by the downward push of your foot on the other pedal. In the engine, some of the pistons are moved upward by the crankshaft as the explosion in one cylinder pushes a piston down. The crankshaft receives power from all pistons in rapid succession. Each time a piston is forced downward, the crankshaft converts this straight-line, up-and-down motion into rotary power. The greater the number of cylinders in an engine, the more frequently power impulses are applied to the crankshaft, and hence the smoother the engine operates.

A heavy wheel called a *flywheel* is mounted on the back end of the crankshaft. This flywheel keeps the crankshaft turning smoothly between strokes of the pistons. Perhaps you have turned a grinding wheel very rapidly and then let go of the handle. You recall that the wheel continued to spin rapidly long after you released it because of the momentum that had been built up. This is the principle on which the flywheel operates 'to keep the engine running smoothly.

The Four-Stroke Cycle

Now let us consider how all of these engine parts work together to produce and harness power. The automobile engine is a four-cycle engine. That is, each power cycle consists of four piston strokes. A four-cycle engine and a muzzle-loading cannon have a great deal in common because they both go through the same basic operations each time they fire. (See Figure 4-8.)

The Intake Stroke. In the power cycle of the automobile engine, the first downstroke of the piston is the *intake stroke.* During this stroke the intake valve is open, and the descending piston sucks the gasoline-air mixture into the combustion chamber. At the bottom of this stroke, when the cylinder has been filled with the mixture, the intake valve closes. This intake stroke corresponds to the loading operation of the cannon.

The Compression Stroke. During the second stroke the piston is moved upward by the revolving crankshaft. Both valves are closed. This stroke squeezes or compresses the fuel mixture into a small space at the top of the cylinder, just as the charge in a cannon is rammed or tamped into the firing chamber. At one time or other you may have experimented with a coil spring and found that the more you compress it before releasing it, the greater rebound you get. Similarly, the more the fuel is compressed before igniting it, the more power it produces. The stroke that accomplishes this squeezing or compressing is called the *compression stroke.*

Fig. 4-8. The power cycle of the internal combustion engine. (*Courtesy:* General Motors Corporation.)

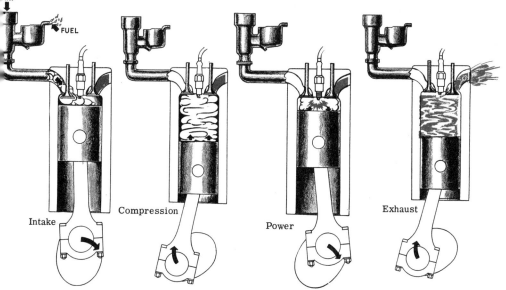

Intake Compression Power Exhaust

Smooth combustion can be obtained only if the fuel is squeezed just the right amount. Under the proper conditions the flame spreads evenly across the combustion chamber to produce steady pressure—quiet, efficient power. Squeezing fuel excessively creates terrific heat and may ignite the fuel prematurely. This causes engine "knocks." Knocking results if compression is higher than fuel can withstand or if the fuel burns unevenly.

Between the second and third strokes the firing occurs. In the cannon the initial fire may be caused by a match. The firing in the engine is accomplished by the electric spark, which occurs when the fuel mixture is fully compressed. The pressure in the cylinder is raised to about 400 pounds per square inch in a fraction of a second by the force of the explosion. The force pushing down on the piston is over two tons!

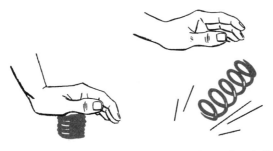

Fig. 4-9. Just as squeezing a spring increases the power of its recoil, squeezing a gasoline-air mixture increases the power of the explosion. (Courtesy: Chrysler Corporation.)

Sealing in the Power. To utilize the full force of the burning fuel, the expanding gases must be sealed above the piston. This can be compared with the precision fit needed in a cannon so that the force of the powder explosion cannot escape around the projectile and be wasted. An efficient seal is obtained in the engine by attaching expanding rings in grooves around the side of the piston. These rings press outward tightly against the cylinder walls.

Each piston is equipped with several of these rings. The upper *compression rings* seal combustion pressure above the piston, thus preventing power loss. The lower *oil-control rings* keep lubricating oil in the engine from splashing or seeping up above the top of the piston into the combustion chamber and burning away.

The Power Stroke. The exploding gases pushing down on the piston produce the *power stroke.* The valves remain closed as the spark ignites the fuel mixture. When the gun powder explodes in the firing chamber of the cannon, the cannon ball, the only movable part of the chamber, is forced out of the barrel by the force

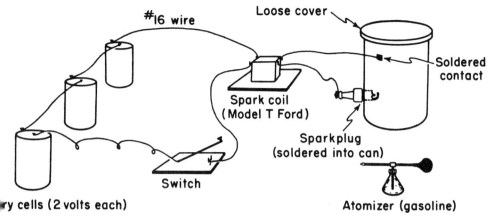

Fig. 4-10. The apparatus above can be used to demonstrate the basic principles of internal combustion. (*From Brody and Stack, "Highway Safety and Driver Education," Prentice-Hall.*)

of the explosion. In like manner, the rapid expansion of hot burning gases pressing against the walls of the combustion chamber in the engine forces the piston, the only movable part of the chamber, downward, turning the crankshaft.

The Exhaust Stroke. The fourth stroke of the cycle is the *exhaust stroke.* The gases have now spent their energy, and it is necessary to clear the cylinder to make way for a new charge. Just as the ramrod is used to clean out the cannon barrel before the next loading, the piston moves up in the cylinder forcing the burned gases, carbon dioxide and carbon monoxide, out past the open exhaust valve, into the exhaust manifold, through the exhaust pipe, and into the muffler.

This chamber smooths the flow of exhaust gases and absorbs most of the engine noise. From the muffler, the gases pass to the outside through the *tail pipe.* The cylinder is then ready to begin another four-stroke cycle.

Regulating Engine Speed

The power developed on the power stroke in each cylinder can be increased by burning more of the gasoline-air mixture, and a more powerful power stroke drives the engine faster. The speed of a car can, therefore, be regulated by controlling the amount of gasoline-air mixture reaching the cylinders. This is accomplished by means of the throttle valve in the carburetor, which is operated with the accelerator pedal.

When the engine is running at low speed this valve is almost closed, checking the flow of gasoline-air changes. In consequence, when the piston completes an intake stroke, only a small amount of gas has been sucked into the cylinder. On the other hand, when the accelerator pedal is pressed down to the limit, the valve opens wide and permits a full-size charge to enter the cylinder. This results in a higher compression and more violent explosion. The engine then moves at top speed.

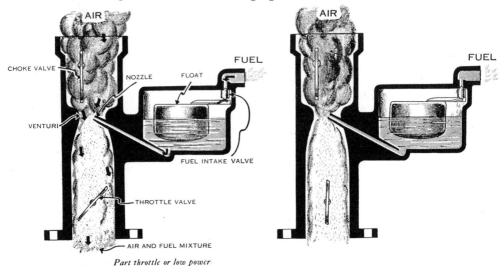

Part throttle or low power

Fig. 4-11. Both the choke and the throttle valves operate like dampers in a stove pipe. The choke valve controls the amount of air that is mixed with the fuel. The throttle valve controls the amount of air-fuel mixture that enters the combustion chamber. (*Courtesy: General Motors Corporation.*)

Timing

In hitting a baseball or golf ball you get more power and better performance if your timing is accurate. Perfect timing is just as important in getting full power from an automobile engine. The valves, pistons, and spark must all function in perfect synchronization.

The camshaft controls the movement of the valves. It is a straight shaft with egg-shaped sections called "cams" located underneath push rods attached by *rocker arms* to each valve. The camshaft is connected to the crankshaft by a chain or gears. Since the crankshaft regulates piston movement, the camshaft regulates valve operation, and the distributor regulates the spark, it is apparent that perfect timing is needed between the three.

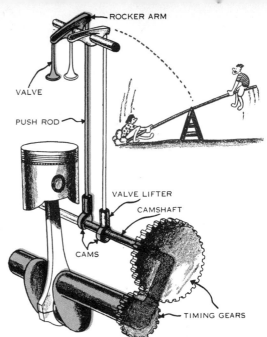

Fig. 4-12. The timing gears, camshaft, and rocker arm assembly control the opening and closing of the valves. (*Courtesy: General Motors Corporation.*)

Cooling the Engine

At the moment of the explosion of the fuel mixture in the combustion chamber, the temperature within the cylinder is raised to about 4500 degrees Fahrenheit. Water boils at 212 degrees, and iron melts at about 2500 degrees. This comparison illustrates what a high degree of heat 4500 degrees really is. If cooling were not provided, the pistons, valves, cylinders, and other vital engine parts would be molten, misshapen scraps of metal in just a short time. This tremendous heat must be carried away from the engine, not only to protect engine parts from melting, but also to help keep moving parts in proper adjustment. Since heat causes metal to expand, engine temperatures must be carefully controlled to maintain just the right spacing and fit between various precision parts.

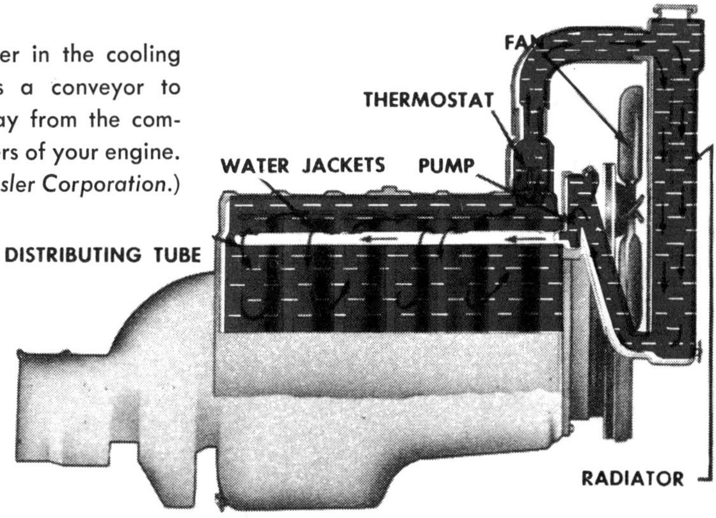

Fig. 4-13. Water in the cooling system acts as a conveyor to carry heat away from the combustion chambers of your engine. (*Courtesy: Chrysler Corporation.*)

The cooling system is a conveyor that carries away heat. Circulating water, as it flows through the hollow jacket that surrounds the cylinders, picks up heat from the engine. The hot water then flows to the radiator and down through the many small tubes in the radiator grillwork. The forward motion of the car, together with the fan that is mounted directly behind the radiator, forces the air to pass through the grillwork and around the tubes, thereby cooling the water.

A *thermostat* is used on many cars to regulate the flow of water. To warm up a cold engine, the thermostat stops the flow of water to the radiator. As the engine reaches its best operating temperature, the thermostat gradually opens the outlet to the radiator. It automatically adjusts itself to maintain the most efficient temperature, regardless of weather.

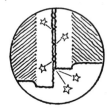 

Fig. 4-14. Lubricants provide a smooth cushion to prevent metallic surfaces from rubbing together, thereby reducing heat, friction, and wear. (*Courtesy: General Motors Corporation.*)

Lubricating the Engine

Without proper lubrication an automobile engine would quickly wear out. No matter how highly polished, metal surfaces are covered with unseen minute "teeth." Two such surfaces rubbing together produce friction, which results in heat, excessive wear, and eventual ruin of moving parts. Lubrication puts a cushion of oil, grease, or graphite between metal surfaces, eliminating metal-to-metal contact, reducing friction, and aiding in the cooling of parts that may spin thousands of revolutions per minute. The film of oil between the closely-fitted engine parts is many times thinner than this sheet of paper, yet it keeps precision surfaces gliding smoothly instead of rubbing and grinding each other down.

The main supply of oil for engine lubrication is contained in the oil pan attached to the bottom of the cylinder block. The oil pump sends oil under pressure from this reservoir to all moving parts of the engine. Oil is also sprayed and splashed against cylinder walls and connecting rod bearings. By means of these two engine lubrication systems—pressure system and spray system—oil in the various parts of the engine reduces wear and saves power.

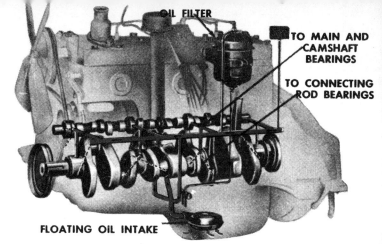

OIL FILTER

TO MAIN AND CAMSHAFT BEARINGS

TO CONNECTING ROD BEARINGS

FLOATING OIL INTAKE

Fig. 4-15. The pressure lubrication lines of the engine. (Courtesy: Chrysler Corporation.)

Oil needs to be kept clean. Some dirt always gets into the engine and, if carried by the oil, causes extra wear. To keep the oil clean, the oil entering the pump passes through a strainer. Some manufacturers provide an additional oil filter, which can be obtained for other cars not so equipped. These filters are more efficient, and contain a unit that can be replaced as it becomes clogged with dirt. Although an oil filter will remove many impurities it will not remove impurities such as small amounts of gasoline and water, which dilute the engine oil. Therefore, it is apparent that while oil filters may postpone the necessity for changing oil they cannot eliminate it.

Starting the Engine

Unlike an electric motor, an automobile engine will not start by itself. The automobile engine must be "turned over" a few times before it can run under its own power. To start the engine, a gasoline-air charge must be ignited in one of the cylinders to force the piston in that cylinder through its power stroke. When this happens the piston causes the crankshaft to rotate, sending another piston through its compression stroke and into its power stroke. As soon as each piston, one after another, produces its power stroke, the engine begins to run under its own power.

The power for starting the early automobile was furnished by hand cranking, but in the modern car it is furnished by the "self-starter." This is an electric motor, which, when put into operation, spins the flywheel. This causes the crankshaft to rotate and forces the pistons up and down until at least one of them completes a power stroke. As soon as this happens, the starter motor is disengaged, and the engine runs under its own power.

WHAT MAKES YOUR CAR GO   163

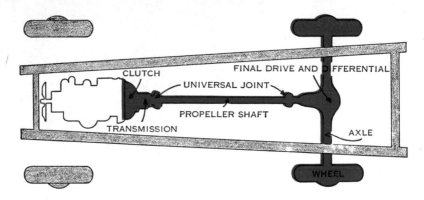

Fig. 4-16. The power train delivers the force of the engine to the rear wheels. (Courtesy: General Motors Corporation.)

THE POWER TRAIN

After the power has been produced and harnessed by the engine, it is necessary to transmit it to the rear wheels. This is accomplished by the power train, which consists of the clutch, transmission, universal and slip joints, propeller shaft, differential, and rear axles.

The Clutch

The clutch enables the driver to connect or disconnect the power of the engine from the rear wheels. Disconnecting the power makes it possible to run the engine while the car is standing still and permits shifting from one gear to another without clashing.

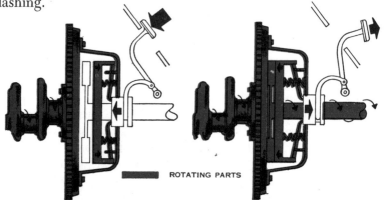

Pedal down, clutch disengaged. *Pedal up, clutch engaged.*

Fig. 4-17. By means of friction between the clutch disc and the flywheel, the clutch assembly connects and disconnects the engine from the power train. (Courtesy: General Motors Corporation.)

UNDERSTANDING YOUR CAR

The clutch engages somewhat like a phonograph record on a turntable. The flywheel of the engine can be compared to the turntable of a record player. Just as the turntable is in motion all the time the power is on, so the flywheel turns constantly when the engine is running. The disc of a clutch compares to the phonograph record. The record turns as soon as it is forced (by gravity) to make frictional contact with the turntable. Similarly, the clutch disc turns when it is pushed tightly against the flywheel by a pressure plate backed by powerful springs. Since the disc is connected to the transmission shaft, this shaft turns with the engine when the clutch is engaged. When the clutch pedal is pushed down, the pressure of the spring is relieved and the clutch disc stands free; hence no power is delivered to the rest of the power train.

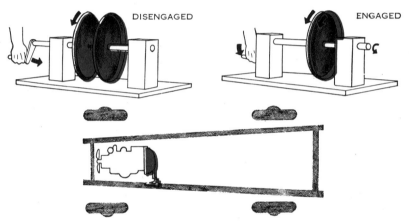

Fig. 4-18. Two pie tins attached to separate shafts provide a working model to demonstrate the friction clutch. (*Courtesy: General Motors Corporation.*)

The Transmission

The transmission, or gear box, is an arrangement of gears that enables the driver to utilize the power of the engine in the form of increased turning force or increased speed. By means of gear arrangements in the transmission a given amount of engine power can be used to produce great turning force at low speed for heavy pulling, or low turning force at high speed for fast traveling under a light load. Gears are simply spinning levers. For example, with a lever you can double your ability to move a stone: if the stone is 5 feet and you are 10 feet from the fulcrum, your end of the lever will move twice as far as the stone, but you

Fig. 4-19. A given amount of power can be geared to produce a high speed and low turning force, or a high turning force and low speed. (*Courtesy: General Motors Corporation.*)

can lift a stone twice your weight! You have sacrificed distance for increased force, and, since your end of the lever had to move farther in the same amount of time, it moved faster.

Added power is provided by gears in much the same way. These spinning levers or gears may be described as wheels with teeth on the edge. If two gears with an equal number of teeth are meshed so that the teeth on one gear fit into the notches on the other, they would both complete one revolution simultaneously. However, if one gear has 60 teeth and another only 20, the 20-tooth gear will turn around three times while the sixty-tooth gear turns once. But, *to the same degree to which a gear loses turning speed, it gains turning force.* Therefore, a gear with 60 teeth driven by a gear with 20 teeth will have ⅓ the speed but three times the turning force. When a small gear drives a large gear, speed is sacrificed for increased turning force; when a large gear drives a small gear, turning force is sacrificed for increased speed.

The conventional transmission offers five gear-arrangement options: (1) low or first gear, (2) intermediate or second gear, (3) high or third gear, (4) reverse, and (5) neutral. First gear pro-

Fig. 4-20. This cartoon shows the gear operation of the principle described in Fig. 4-19. (*Courtesy: General Motors Corporation.*)

ÚNDERSTANDING YOUR CAR

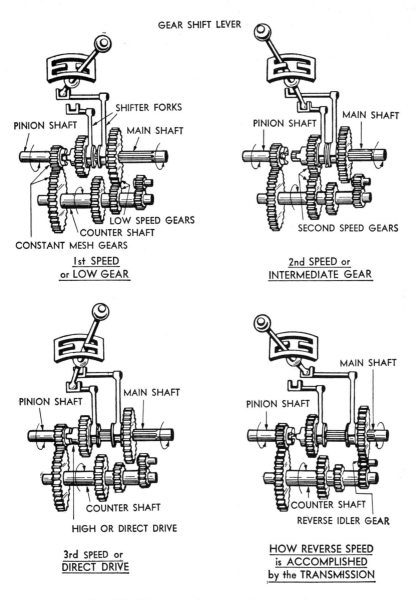

GEAR SHIFT LEVER

SHIFTER FORKS
PINION SHAFT
MAIN SHAFT

LOW SPEED GEARS
COUNTER SHAFT
CONSTANT MESH GEARS

1st SPEED
or LOW GEAR

MAIN SHAFT
PINION SHAFT

SECOND SPEED GEARS

2nd SPEED or
INTERMEDIATE GEAR

PINION SHAFT
MAIN SHAFT

COUNTER SHAFT

HIGH OR DIRECT DRIVE

3rd SPEED or
DIRECT DRIVE

MAIN SHAFT
PINION SHAFT

COUNTER SHAFT
REVERSE IDLER GEAR

HOW REVERSE SPEED
is ACCOMPLISHED
by the TRANSMISSION

Fig. 4-21. Schematic diagram of a transmission.

vides maximum power for starting, hill climbing, or heavy going. It permits the engine to run fast, thus developing power, but delivers a slow, powerful turning force to the rear wheels. After the car has been given an initial push in low, shifting to second gear allows the car to roll along faster, even though the engine speed is about the same. Third gear is usually a direct drive; that

Fig. 4-22. A supervised inspection of the mechanism of the car is helpful in understanding its operation.

is, it simply connects the clutch and the drive shafts so they turn as a unit. Thus in third gear the car can travel as fast as the engine will allow. Since an automobile engine rotates the crankshaft in the same direction all the time, a special gear arrangement called reverse gear is used to change the direction of rotation of the drive shaft. A neutral gear arrangement is also provided, to disconnect the engine from the drive shaft. In this arrangement the gears do not mesh; therefore, shifting to neutral gives the same general result as disengaging the clutch. (See Figure 4-21.)

Automatic Drive

Many cars now have some form of automatic drive in which the friction clutch and clutch pedal are eliminated and the transmission is much different. There are various types, but nearly all automatic drives are based upon the *fluid coupling* principle. The fluid coupling is really a form of clutch. It is shaped like a doughnut sliced through the middle, with blades on the inside of each

168   UNDERSTANDING YOUR CAR

half. One half is connected to the engine and the other half to the transmission. These two discs are sealed in a tight casing filled with oil. When the half connected to the engine is rotated it throws oil against the blades of the other. At slow engine speeds the disc connected to the engine does not throw the oil with enough force to turn the other disc. As the disc connected to the engine turns faster, however, it creates more force and the other disc begins to turn. The second disc begins to pick up speed until, under ordinary driving conditions, both halves are turning at about the same speed. It is something like arranging two electric fans face to face and plugging in only one of them. The force of the air from one will cause the other fan to rotate.

A complex gear arrangement responds more or less automatically to the needs of the car in terms of the amount of turning force delivered to the rear wheels. This gear arrangement in most cases is combined with the fluid clutch to form an *automatic transmission* unit.

Under ordinary circumstances, the driver of a car with an automatic transmission will find that there is no clutch pedal and no shifting to do except when he wants to back up. For forward driving, all he has to do is step on the accelerator or the brake pedal.

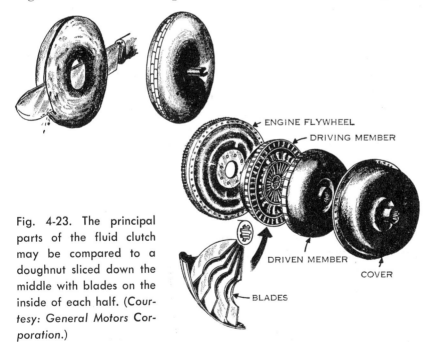

Fig. 4-23. The principal parts of the fluid clutch may be compared to a doughnut sliced down the middle with blades on the inside of each half. (*Courtesy: General Motors Corporation.*)

ENGINE FLYWHEEL

DRIVING MEMBER

DRIVEN MEMBER

COVER

BLADES

Propeller Shaft and Universal Joint

Power is transmitted back from the crankshaft as a twisting force. The *propeller shaft* provides the power connection between the transmission and the rear axle. This shaft is tubular to provide great strength at minimum weight. It is carefully balanced to eliminate vibration and noise. The propeller shaft is connected to the transmission shaft by a *universal joint,* a flexible connection that allows the shaft to move with any of the up-and-down motion of the rear wheels without damage or undue wear to other parts of the power train.

Another result of the flexing of the rear springs is that the distance between the transmission and rear axle changes slightly. To meet this problem a *slip-joint* is included at the universal which allows the propeller shaft to slide in and out according to spring position.

The Differential and Rear Axle

The rotary power from the propeller shaft is transferred on a right angle to the rear axle shafts by a complex gear arrangement in the rear axle housing. These gears not only perform this function but also permit the rear wheels to turn at different speeds when the car goes around a corner. In turning a corner, the wheels on the outside of the turn must rotate faster to cover a greater distance than the wheels on the inside. This is similar to a column of marching men turning a corner: the man on the outside must march much faster than the man on the inside, who in some cases merely pivots.

THE CHASSIS AND RUNNING GEAR

The Frame

The *frame,* which supports the body, the engine, and the transmission, as well as providing mounting for the running gear, is the "foundation" of the automobile. Most frames are made of two hollow "box" section beams, running the length of the car. However, in some automobiles the frame and body are combined to form one structure. Use of cross-braces and/or body panels makes a very rigid structure able to resist bending or twisting as the automobile strikes holes or bumps.

UNDERSTANDING YOUR CAR

The Springs and Shock Absorbers

A comfortable ride for the passengers is provided by the *springs* and *shock absorbers* between the frame and the axles. These units absorb most of the jolt as a car strikes irregularities in the road.

Coil springs and leaf springs are most commonly used. A coil spring is generally used for each front wheel and a leaf spring for each rear wheel, but some cars have a coil spring for all four wheels. Coil springs enable each wheel to move up or down independently of the others. This aids steering and improves the ride.

Unless checked, the springs would continue to compress and extend for some time after each jolt, so that the body and frame would be constantly moving up and down. To prevent this, shock absorbers, which slow up the spring action and stop the vibration, are connected to the spring and the frame. Shock absorbers are quite similar in construction and operation to the devices attached to doors to close them without slamming.

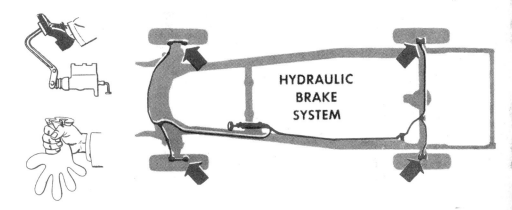

Fig. 4-24. The hydraulic braking system is designed to provide equal brake pressure on all four wheels. It consists of a master cylinder connected by four fluid-filled lines to wheel cylinders. (*Courtesy: Chrysler Corporation.*)

Brakes

Brakes are simply devices for converting energy of motion into heat, thereby stopping the moving car. The energy of motion of the car is converted into heat by the friction of the brake lining rubbing against a section of the inside rim of the wheel called the *brake drum,* and by the friction between the tires and the road surface.

Fig. 4-25. Brake shoes and the brake drum, essential parts of the braking system, attached to each wheel. (Courtesy: Chrysler Corporation.)

This is what happens when the driver steps on the brake pedal. Pushing on the brake pedal moves a piston in the *master cylinder*. This piston pushes on fluid in the cylinder. Since liquid cannot be compressed, it is forced out of the end of the cylinder through small tubes to the brakes on each wheel, and exerts equal pressure on each brake. Each wheel is equipped with another hydraulic cylinder that works just the opposite of the master cylinder. Fluid is pushed into them, and forces the pistons in these brake cylinders outward. This outward motion pushes two shoes in each brake outward against the drum, which is mounted rigidly on each wheel. It is the frictional drag of the brake shoes against the drums that slows up the revolving wheel.

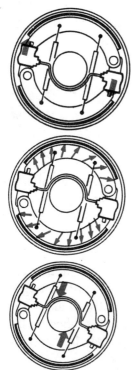

Fig. 4-26. A. Pressure in the hydraulic lines causes brake shoes to move out and press out and press against the brake drum.

B. The friction caused by the pressure of the shoes on the drum stops the drum from turning.

C. When the driver's foot is removed from the pedal, springs cause the brake shoes to return to their original position and the brake drum is again free to turn.

UNDERSTANDING YOUR CAR

When the driver lifts his foot off the brake pedal, pressure and movement in the system are reversed. Return springs on the brake shoes pull them back, moving wheel cylinder pistons with them. This action forces fluid back through the lines and into the master cylinder.

Some cars are equipped with power brakes. These utilize air pressure from the exhaust system of the engine to apply pressure to the hydraulic system. This allows full braking force with tip-toe pressure on the pedal.

Parking Brake

In order to prevent a car from rolling when parked, it is provided with a hand-operated auxiliary brake known as the hand brake or "parking" brake, which not only applies the brakes, but holds them in place until the hand-brake lever is released. This brake holds the rear wheels only. In some cars, the parking brake is a separate unit attached to the drive shaft, and when applied, prevents the shaft from turning. If the shaft cannot turn, the rear wheels cannot turn.

The parking brake is not as effective as foot brakes and is not designed to be used in stopping a moving car. It is intended merely to hold the car stationary after the driver has brought it to a stop. In case the foot brakes fail, however, the parking brake can be of some help in slowing the car down.

Steering Mechanism

The steering mechanism enables the driver to direct the car in motion. It multiplies the effort applied by the driver and absorbs most of the road shocks which tend to twist the steering wheel. This is how it works. When the driver turns the steering wheel (A), a shaft (B) on which it is mounted turns inside the steering column. A worm gear (C) on the end of the shaft meshes with a sector gear, which causes the Pitman arm (D) to swing to one side or the other, depending on which way the wheel is turned. Swinging of the Pitman arm moves the two tie rods (E), which connect to the steering arms (F) that turn the wheels, which are mounted on steering knuckles. These steering knuckles and their supporting assemblies are very similar to hinges on which a door is mounted. Precise alignment of the wheels is necessary if the steering mechanism is to operate efficiently and stay in good condition.

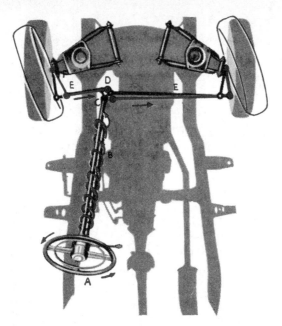

Fig. 4-27. The steering mechanism. (*Courtesy: Chrysler Corporation.*)

Some cars are equipped with power steering. One such device utilizes two small hydraulic pumps, which start operating when the driver begins turning the wheel and stop when he stops turning. This makes steering possible with finger-tip control.

THE BODY

The modern automobile's body is constructed of steel. A rigid unit is obtained by welding the floor, pillars, panel, and top of the body into one strong piece. This one-piece steel body provides greater riding comfort as well as greater safety.

Hundreds of rubber parts in the chassis and body contribute to quiet car operation and long life. Nearly all of the major suspension parts are separated from the frame by rubber cushions. This absorbs vibration, cushions rock shock, and prevents wear. Many other kinds of insulation materials are used in modern motor cars to cut down road noises and eliminate metal-to-metal contact, thus preventing squeaks and rattles.

CONCLUSION

Obviously the modern automobile is a great achievement of inventive genius, precision engineering, and manufacturing skill. Our problem is to use it with a skill and intelligence comparable to that used in its development and manufacture.

UNDERSTANDING YOUR CAR

DISCUSSION TOPICS

1. What are the four basic parts of the car?
2. What are the four main jobs to be done by the various parts of the engine? Describe the main parts that accomplish each of these jobs.
3. In terms of the construction of the car, explain the effects of the following:
   a. Riding the clutch
   b. Prolonged application of the brakes
   c. "Jack-rabbit" starts and short stops
   d. Racing a cold engine
   e. Leaving the ignition on when the engine is not running
   f. Driving with the parking brake partially set
   g. Attempting to shift gears without depressing the clutch pedal
   h. Turning the wheels when the car is stationary
   i. Striking curbs or holes with the front wheels
   j. Using the clutch to "hold" a car when stopped on a hill.

PROJECTS AND PROBLEMS

1. Make working, but schematic, models of a combustion chamber, clutch, and brake.
2. Visit a garage and examine various parts of a car. Talk with a mechanic, and try to learn what driving practices most frequently result in a need for repairs.
3. Write to an automobile manufacturer, and try to learn what efforts are being made to construct safer cars.
4. Draw simple diagrams showing the assembly and indicating the operation of each of the following:
   a. The four strokes of the internal combustion engine
   b. Conventional clutch; fluid clutch
   c. Conventional transmission
   d. Power train (show general flow of power)
   e. Hydraulic brake system
   f. Steering mechanism
   g. Ignition system
   h. Cooling system
   i. Lubricating system.

Fig. 4-28. Compulsory periodic motor vehicle inspections in many states provide an added incentive for drivers to keep their cars in safe operating condition. (*Courtesy: New Jersey Motor Vehicle Department.*)

UNDERSTANDING YOUR CAR

How Can You Get Your Money's Worth from Your Car?

Next to the cost of owning and operating a house, the expenses involved in owning and operating a car are ordinarily the greatest undertaken by the average family. These costs vary widely, however, depending upon the owner. Whether your automobile expenditures will reflect economic savings or wanton waste depends on the manner in which you maintain, operate, and protect your car.

An expert takes pride in keeping his equipment in good condition. In driving, your life depends on it. Some of the marks of unskilled, unsafe driving are battered fenders, unaligned wheels, faulty headlights, loose brakes, and a squeaky, noisy car body. The way to keep your car in safe, economical condition and avoid these difficulties is by regular lubrication, inspection, and adjustment.

LUBRICATION

Lubrication is the protector of every moving part of a car. A lubricant, such as oil, grease, or graphite, forms a protective coating, eliminates metal-to-metal contact, and reduces friction and wear, adding to comfort, pleasure, and safety in your driving.

Engine Lubrication

Motor oil should be kept clean, free from dirt, dust, water, and sludge. Under normal driving conditions, motor oil should be

Fig. 4-29. The dip stick on the side of the engine block provides a measure of the oil level in the crank case. (Courtesy: Standard Oil Co. of New Jersey.)

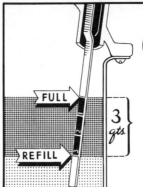

OIL LEVEL GAUGE

SAFETY MARGIN

Maintain oil level between "FULL" and "REFILL" marks on oil level gauge. Do not let oil level go below "refill" or above "full".

changed every 2000-3000 miles. Experience has shown, however, that driving conditions must be considered: a car that is driven in dusty areas, operated at high temperatures, or taken on short runs in cold weather usually requires more frequent oil changes. Check oil level and texture each time you buy gasoline.

High-speed driving increases the amount of oil that is used, and even at normal driving speeds it is perfectly natural for a car to consume a small amount of oil between changes. However, if your car uses an excessive amount of oil—say, one quart every two hundred miles—the time has come to have the piston rings checked. They probably need to be replaced.

Chassis Lubrication

The chassis should be lubricated at regular intervals. Chassis parts are exposed to dust, dirt, rain, and the like. A general rule is: lubricate every 1000 miles or once a month, whichever comes first. Some newer cars, however, only require lubrication at 2000-mile intervals or every two months. The oil level in the transmission and rear axle housing should be checked each time the chassis is lubricated. This oil should be changed about once a year, either in the spring or fall. About once a year or every 15,000 miles, the front wheel bearings should also be inspected to make sure they are properly greased. Some cars, however, are equipped with bearings that do not need to be lubricated periodically.

The Right Type and Amount of Lubricant

The lubricant is really a structural part of the mechanism of your car. To use the wrong type or amount of lubricant is almost as bad as putting in a replacement part that does not fit! Therefore, follow the advice of the engineers who designed your car. Read your instruction book and consult with your dealer. The safest and simplest way to handle the entire lubrication problem, without going into all the detailed instructions for various parts of the car, is to have this work done by the dealer whose mechanics have been trained to service your particular make and model. Oil is cheaper than metal, and repairs are expensive. It is not very much of an exaggeration to say that "a well-lubricated part never wears out."

INSPECTION, ADJUSTMENT, AND REPAIRS

The typical driver has neither the time, the tools, nor the technical training to master all of the details of automotive mechanics. The mechanism of the modern automobile has become so complicated that even expert mechanics tend to specialize on one make or group of cars. The day has passed when a driver can afford to tinker with his car to any great extent, or attempt to make complicated repairs. If you confine yourself to keeping a careful check on the condition of your car and tending to simple adjustments as the need arises, you will find that you can prevent costly wear and damage that would otherwise take place.

Fig. 4-30. Visibility is improved when windshield wiper blades are properly fitted.

BATTERY — RADIATOR

WINDSHIELD AND WIPERS

STEERING GEAR — BRAKES — TIRES   LIGHTS

Fig. 4-31. Good cars deserve good maintenance. Regular inspection and servicing assure smooth performance.

Cooling System Maintenance

Since the explosions going on in the cylinders of the engine produce heat enough to fuse steel, it is important, at all times, that this heat be carried away by the water that surrounds the cylinders. This water must be clean and must circulate freely. It must not be allowed to run low. Whenever you drive into a service station, have the water checked.

When winter is just around the corner, have the entire cooling system, including radiator, hose, couplings, and gaskets, thoroughly flushed and checked for leaks. Make sure everything is watertight, and then put in antifreeze. Use a sufficient amount, as specified by the car manufacturer, to keep the water in the cooling system from freezing at the lowest temperature you expect the car to meet. It is a good plan to test the strength of the antifreeze in the cooling system at regular intervals throughout the winter, for it is possible that through leakage or evaporation it has become so diluted that it will no longer afford adequate protection at low temperatures. In the spring, drain off the antifreeze, flush the cooling system thoroughly (using a rust-removing preparation if necessary), and refill with fresh, clean water.

Maintaining the Ignition System

It is necessary to keep the ignition system in good condition if you are to get first-class performance and prevent gasoline waste.

Battery Care. The battery should be thoroughly checked each time the chassis is lubricated. It should never be allowed to become excessively charged or discharged. This causes the plates to buckle and ruins the battery. The ammeter will warn you against this. Water level in the battery must be kept above the battery plates. Distilled water, free from impurities, is best for this purpose. The specific gravity of the solution should be checked at least once a month.

Check the Points. To keep the ignition system in good condition, the distributor points should be adjusted and the timing reset about twice a year—preferably in the spring and in the fall.

Spark Plugs. It is surprising how little things like spark plugs can so greatly affect the performance of your engine. Tests by the Engineering Research Department of the University of Michigan have indicated that faulty spark plugs may often waste as much as one gallon of gasoline in ten. In addition, bad plugs cause hard starting and reduce engine power. Smart drivers have their spark plugs cleaned and adjusted about every 8000 miles.

Check Connections. Be sure that all electrical connections are tight and that there is no worn or frayed insulation. This is far more than a matter of losing current due to leakage; it is vitally important from the safety point of view. The cable from the battery to the starter, for instance, carries such a powerful current that if it is allowed to get out of order a fire may result.

Exhaust Leaks

If the car develops a rumbling sound, check the muffler. Muffler and exhaust leaks are not only noisy but dangerous. Carbon monoxide gas in exhaust fumes is a deadly killer!

Fig. 4-32. The pressure of one finger should be enough to push the clutch pedal down an inch before the resistance of the clutch springs is felt. If there is little or no "play" the clutch may be slipping; if there is too much, it may not be disengaging completely. (Courtesy: General Motors Corp.)

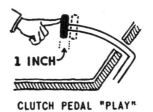

1 INCH

CLUTCH PEDAL "PLAY"

Maintaining the Power Train

Clutch Adjustment. You should be able to depress the clutch pedal about one inch with the pressure of one finger. If there is too little play, excessive wear to the clutch mechanism results. If there is too much play, you may have trouble shifting, because the clutch is probably not disengaging completely.

The Transmission and Differential. Excessive wear in either transmission or differential results in a "growl," "hum," or "rumble," which first becomes evident at higher speeds in each gear range. It is possible to make adjustments in the differential to correct this, but wear in the transmission can only be corrected by replacement of worn parts. However, automatic transmissions can be adjusted to correct for faulty gear selection. Extreme wear in conventional transmissions result in a tendency of the gear shift lever to continually "jump out of gear." A mechanic should be consulted when any of these difficulties arise.

The Universal Joint. If you hear a metallic "clash" when you are putting your car in motion or when you release pressure on the accelerator, it is a signal that the universal joint needs repair or replacement.

The Rear Axle. A common difficulty is wear of the bearings in the rear axle, which often causes noises similar to those of a worn transmission or differential, and may cause a wobble in a rear wheel. However, a wobble may also be indicative of a loose or bent wheel, or a bent axle. Lines of grease radiating from the hub cap is a sign that the grease seal at the outer end of the axle needs to be replaced.

The Springs and Shock Absorbers

"Tired" springs are readily noticeable because they cause the car to sag down close to the wheels. Springs in this condition have little resiliency and pass on most of the jolts to the rest of the car and to the passengers.

Worn "shocks" can be detected by forcing the bumper up and down vigorously. When released it should stop its motion almost instantly. If the bumper continues to bob up and down, the shock absorbers are faulty. Both "tired" springs and worn "shocks" should be replaced.

Steering System Maintenance

The steering system should always be kept "tight." There should be no more than two inches of free "play" at the steering wheel. Too much "play" causes a lag in steering, which can be very dangerous, especially in emergency situations such as skids. "Play" may be caused by wear in the tie-rod ends or by wear in the steering column. Wear in the steering column usually can be corrected by adjustment, but worn tie-rod ends demand replacement. Neglected tie-rod ends eventually may come completely apart, allowing the front wheels to turn freely in any direction.

Fig. 4-33. Your brakes need attention when the brake pedal can be pushed to within two inches of the floorboards or when the brakes "take the steering out of your hands." (Courtesy: General Motors Corporation.)

Care of the Brakes

To insure that your car can be stopped quickly, and that it will keep to its course and not thrust or swerve to one side or the other, the brakes should always be kept in proper adjustment. If the brake pedal can be pushed to within two inches of the floorboards, or if the brakes "take the steering wheel out of your hands," it is high time to have them checked and adjusted. It is a good rule to have your garage man examine the brake linings after the third adjustment. Also watch for evidence of leaks in the hydraulic system. Check fluid every time brakes are adjusted. Only brake fluids recommended by your dealer or a reputable service station should be used. Improper fluids are very dangerous because they may deteriorate or damage vital parts of the braking system.

The parking brake should not be overlooked when you are caring for the brakes. Make sure that it will hold the car stationary even on steep slopes, and that it will supply braking force for an emergency.

Fig. 4-34. From the speed of 20 miles per hour your car must be able to stop within 25 feet with the foot brake and 55 feet with the hand brake, but your car *should* be able to stop much more quickly. (Courtesy: American Association of Motor Vehicle Administrators and National Safety Council.)

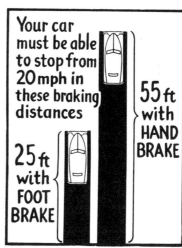

Fig. 4-35. Proper inflation is vital to the life of your tires. (*Courtesy: General Motors Corporation.*)

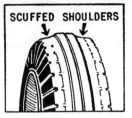

SCUFFED SHOULDERS

A RESULT OF
UNDERINFLATION

CHECK TIRE PRESSURE REGULARLY

CORRECT★ PRESSURE	5 LBS. UNDER	6 LBS. UNDER	9 LBS. UNDER
	Reduces Tire Life 32%	Reduces Tire Life 38%	Reduces Tire Life 52%

Tire Care

Studies show that improper air pressure will greatly reduce tire life as well as decrease comfort and safety. Check tire pressure at least once a week, and give special attention to any tire that shows a significantly great loss of air. This may indicate a slow leak. Air pressure should be checked while the tires are cool—before the car has been running very far. Most automotive stores sell pocket gauges, which, when properly calibrated and used regularly, provide a much more accurate reading than the pressure gauges on the air pumps at service stations. Remove stones, bits of glass, or metal that may have stuck in tire treads. Uneven or "feather-edged" treads may be due to one of the greatest enemies of long tire life—improper alignment. It is wise economy to check front wheel alignment after every six months of normal driving or after minor accidents, such as skidding into a curb.

To get maximum tire life, change the wheels together with the tires from one position to another at regular intervals. If your "spare" is in good condition it should be used, taking its turn at the various positions as indicated in Figure 4-42.

The percentages of average wear can be estimated by careful examination of the tires at each position. Never let a good spare remain idle until the other tires are worn out, because it will deteriorate. Tires need to be massaged or exercised in order to keep in good condition. By including the spare, all of the tires at the time of the fifth change will have run the same distance at each wheel position. Since tires are switched at 5000 mile intervals, when your car has gone 25,000 miles, your tires will have had only 20,-000 miles wear.

A few minutes spent on regular inspection and care may save you the trouble of changing tires on the road and will add thousands of miles to tire life. Side walls and tire fabrics slowly accumulate minor damages until at last the blowout point may be reached. And remember, a tire is no better than the tube inside it. It is false economy if you try to use overpatched or badly worn tubes.

Changing a Flat Tire. Here are a number of important and helpful guides to show you the efficient and safe way of changing a tire:

1. Move the car entirely off the traveled surface of the highway. At night, check to be sure the tail light is lit and can be seen to the rear. Put the hand brake on hard and, if the car is on a grade, block one of the wheels with a stone or piece of wood. Remove the spare tire from its compartment.
2. Rest the jack on flat, solid ground, or on a block of wood. Depending on the design of the jack, raise the axle, wheel rim, or bumper. Pry off the hubcap cover with a screwdriver, and then remove the nuts which hold the wheel on.
3. Remove the wheel and put on the spare. Replace and tighten hard all the wheel nuts. Replace the hubcap cover.
4. Place the "flat" in the spare-tire carrier; bolt it down and lock it. Let the jack down, then remove the wheel-block. Put away all the tools.

Fig. 4-36. Misalignment of the front wheels may cause these tire difficulties. (*Courtesy: General Motors Corporation.*)

Fig. 4-37. Care of the exterior finish and interior upholstery is an important part of preventive maintenance, which pays big dividends when the time comes to trade in your car. (Courtesy: "Your Car.")

The Lighting System

Headlights and tail lights must be kept in good condition; otherwise safe and efficient driving at night is impossible. Have your headlights checked periodically to see that they are properly aimed. Even a variation of only one degree will cause the beam to be about five feet out of line at a distance of 300 feet. This amount of error is enough to throw the full intensity of the beam right into the eyes of an oncoming driver, even when the passing beam is used. If the beam is not illuminating the road exactly as it should, you are not getting the full benefit of your lights, and your own safety is in jeopardy. Keeping the lenses clean also aids in providing proper illumination.

Keeping Your Car Neat and Clean

The paint and chromium trim on the outside of your car need regular attention. Give your car a good washing with a hose and water and a light rubdown with a sponge or chamois about twice a month. A good wax polish applied at least twice a year will help keep the body looking shiny and new.

The inside of the car should be cleaned and swept out each time the outside is washed. Careful attention to a small hole or rip in upholstery when it first appears will prevent unsightly damage. The care to the finish and upholstery of your car will pay real dividends when the time comes to trade the car or sell it.

PERIODIC CHECK-UP

At least twice a year a car should get a thorough check-up by a reliable, expert mechanic who is familiar with your make of car. Engine, wheel alignment, universal joints, differential, and transmission should be checked, adjusted and serviced. Brakes, lights, windshield wiper, horn, muffler, and tires should also receive special attention. A regular check-up on a car by a competent mechanic is essential to keeping it in safe and effective operating condition. The modern car is far too complicated to be serviced and maintained by the owner, unless he himself is a skilled mechanic or engineer.

In many states, motor vehicle inspection laws that are designed as an accident-prevention measure require that all vehicles meet a specific safety standard of performance. Periodically, drivers are required to bring their cars to be inspected by authorized mechanics. These laws serve to remind the driver of his responsibility, and they guarantee that careless and forgetful drivers will be forced to keep their cars in better condition.

Repair Shops

There are good and bad repair shops and service stations. You will do well to take considerable pains in selecting a good one. When you find a good reliable service station or garage, stick by it. Look for a shop where a high-grade mechanic will take personal and continuing interest in keeping your car in good condition for a reasonable price.

Fig. 4-38. Momentum is a kind of "bonus," which you can cash in on by letting it take you the last few hundred feet when coming to a stop. (Courtesy: General Motors Corporation.)

DRIVING ECONOMICALLY

The way a person drives makes a big difference on how much his driving will cost. Driving at high speeds, for example, is expensive as well as dangerous. Tests made on certain light cars showed that 18 miles could be driven on a gallon of gas at 30 miles an hour, and only 10 miles at 60 miles per hour. Speeding on turns and corners is particularly hard on tires. In fact, increased speed not only uses more gas, more oil, and more rubber, but increases the strain on the whole mechanism.

In addition to moderate speed, there are other driving tactics that will save gasoline. Racing the engine while starting, or while the car is waiting at a traffic light, wastes gas and oil and causes unnecessary wear. Jack-rabbit starts eat up rubber as well as gas. Acceleration should be smooth and steady. Shift into second gear by the time the car is moving 10 miles an hour and into high by the time it is moving 20 miles an hour. On the highway, frequent speeding up and slowing down uses much more gasoline than maintaining a steady cruising speed. Usually the steady driver will make as good time as the one who drives by "fits and starts."

Sudden stops, like sudden starts, are wasteful. A good part of the energy used in getting under way is stored up in the form of *momentum,* which tends to keep your car rolling even after you

CRUISING SPEED	AVERAGE SPEED	OPERATING COST (1,000 MILES)	DEATH RISK*
35	34	$12.95	45
45	42	$14.51	61
55	48	$16.65	85
65	53	$19.43	160 (ALL SPEEDS OVER 60)

*DRIVERS INVOLVED IN FATAL ACCIDENTS PER 1,000 DRIVERS INVOLVED IN INJURY ACCIDENTS.

Fig. 4-39. High speed is not only more dangerous but much more expensive. (Courtesy: National Safety Council.)

UNDERSTANDING YOUR CAR

Fig. 4-40. Skid marks on the road are particles of rubber that have been scraped off the tires. (Courtesy: National Association of Secondary School Principals.)

take your foot off the accelerator. Plan ahead to let this momentum carry you into the stopping position with a minimum use of the brakes. Thus you will be collecting your bonus on the gas that was required to get your car rolling, instead of using the extra energy to burn up your brakes and tires.

When descending long hills or slowing down from high speed, a continuous, heavy pressure on the brake pedal produces excessive heat within the brakes and causes rapid wear. Use a series of gentle jabs on the pedal. These are some of the more important ways in which you can get your money's worth from your car by driving economically.

PROTECTION AGAINST UNFORESEEN LOSS

Insurance is available to protect the motorist from the financial loss resulting from unavoidable misfortunes. *Comprehensive coverage,* for example, will pay the motorist for any loss or damage caused by fire, theft, falling objects, explosions, earthquake, windstorm, hail, water, flood, vandalism, riot, and the like. This type of coverage, however, does not protect against loss or damage resulting from upset of the car or collision with another object; these are covered by *collision insurance.* Many collision policies are written so that the owner pays for any loss up to 50 dollars and the insurance company pays for all damage in excess of that amount. Collision policies with these deductible clauses provide adequate protection at a relatively low cost. Other types of insurance coverage will pay for *towing and emergency repairs* in the event of a breakdown or disablement or cover the cost of *medical expenses* resulting from injury to the driver or passengers in his car.

Each of the types of insurance coverage mentioned protects the owner of the automobile against direct loss resulting from damage to his car. Another type of insurance, which is discussed in Unit V, Problem Four, protects the owner so that he can fulfill his social and economic obligations in the event his car injures another person or damages property. A smart driver makes sure that he has adequate insurance protection, or other financial arrangements so that he can assume full responsibility for economic obligations.

BUYING A USED CAR

There is but one honest and effective line of advice that can be given to anyone who contemplates buying a second-hand car. Buy it strictly for its operating efficiency, for its value as *machinery*. Do not be influenced by a fine, flashy repaint job, shiny gadgets, or new upholstery. Beware of wonderful bargains. Take a trial drive to assure yourself that the car runs with efficiency and economy. Pay particular attention to the condition of the brakes and other safety devices.

Buy a second-hand car only upon the advice and after the careful inspection of an honest and disinterested mechanic, selected and possibly paid by you to make this inspection and advise you. Insist on a complete change of lubricant in the differential and transmission and a flush of the radiator. Check tires and exhaust system for defects and leakage. See that the frame and the wheels are checked for alignment. Some cars appear on the second-hand market because they have suffered a crash. They can be fixed up to look good, but their frame may be more or less out of line. Whether it be brakes, gears, lights, radiator, engine, or other mechanisms, there are always tricks by which an expert mechanic can conceal defects temporarily. It will take another equally skilled mechanic to discover them. There are, of course, many honest and reputable second-hand dealers who put their cars in reasonably good condition. But even they do not pretend to put them in brand-new condition, and not many will point out to you just what is wrong and how wrong it is. *Caveat emptor,* the old horse-trading motto, now applies to the "gasoline horse." It means: *Let the buyer look out for himself!*

SAFETY INSPECTION
Twice a year (Spring and Fall).

CHASSIS LUBRICATION
Once a month or every 1,000 miles.

CHANGE ENGINE OIL
*Normal Driving—Every 2,500–3,000 miles.
(Be sure engine air cleaners are also serviced.)

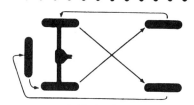

ROTATE TIRES
Every 3,000 miles.

DRAIN AND FLUSH COOLING SYSTEM
Twice a year (Spring and Fall).

RENEW OIL FILTER
Every 8,000 miles to coincide
with an engine oil change.

COMPLETE CAR LUBRICATION
Once a year or every 10,000 miles.

REAR AXLE AND UNIVERSAL JOINTS
Once every two years or every 20,000 miles.

* More frequent oil changes recommended if
your car is operated in dusty areas or at
slow speeds.

Fig. 4-41. Give your car a square deal through systematic maintenance.
(Courtesy: Chrysler Corporation.)

SUMMARY

Good drivers, like expert craftsmen and champion athletes, take pride in keeping their equipment in top-notch condition. Every good driver wants his car to have reliable engine, brakes that hold smoothly and firmly, tires that grip the road securely, lights that illuminate effectively, and steering that is true and dependable. A driver who understands the construction of his car and gives his car a "square deal" through good care, necessary repairs, and efficient operation, will find his driving smoother, more enjoyable, less expensive, and much safer. Moreover, the young driver who can convince his parents that he has developed the mature judgment and sense of personal responsibility to care for a car properly will be more likely to get permission to use the family car or to get a car of his own!

DISCUSSION TOPICS

1. How may good gas and oil mileage be obtained?
2. What specific parts of a car should be given regular inspection? How do these parts affect safe driving?
3. What parts of the car should be inspected occasionally?
4. How can one get maximum service out of brakes?
5. How should brakes be tested?
6. Name several ways to get maximum use out of tires.
7. Is a frozen radiator injurious to an automobile? Why? Does the cooling system function under this condition?

PROJECTS AND PROBLEMS

1. Prepare a check list of the items to be regularly inspected for maintaining safe and efficient car operation.
2. Prepare an automobile inspection blank and try it out on the family car.
3. Prepare a graph indicating the increase in driving costs as speed is increased.
4. Visit a garage and find out how various parts of the car are lubricated. What parts require oil? What parts require grease? Why?
5. Consult a reliable automobile dealer or a good mechanic regarding the items to be considered in buying a used car.
6. Arrange for the class to visit a well-equipped inspection station, follow a car through inspection procedure, and note any defects and maladjustments revealed by the inspection.
7. Debate the statement: "Cars in poor condition are responsible for many traffic accidents."
8. Appoint a committee to prepare a guide book to aid motorists in keeping their cars in safe driving condition.

SELECTED REFERENCES FOR UNIT IV

1. *A Power Primer,* General Motors Corporation. Detroit, 1944.
2. *Automobile Users' Guide,* General Motors Corporation. Detroit, 1944.
3. *Automotive Mechanics,* William A. Crouse. New York: McGraw-Hill, Inc., 1946.
4. *Dyke's Automobile and Gasoline Engine Encyclopedia,* A. L. Dyke. Chicago: The Goodheart-Wilcox Company, Inc., 1943.
5. *How the Wheels Revolve,* General Motors Corporation. Detroit: 1952.
6. *Youth at the Wheel,* John J. Floherty. Philadelphia: J. B. Lippincott Co., 1937.

Valuable information may also be found in booklets, issued by various insurance companies, and in owner's manuals, obtained for different makes of cars from local automobile dealers.

UNIT 5

TRAFFIC LAWS
NATURAL AND MAN-MADE

DEAD
END

R R

PROBLEM ONE
How do the laws of motion and energy affect the car and the driver?

PROBLEM TWO
What are the basic man-made traffic rules?

PROBLEM THREE
How does engineering affect traffic and its laws?

PROBLEM FOUR
What are the laws concerning licensing and liability?

PROBLEM FIVE
How are traffic laws enforced?

Fig. 5-1. Contrary to the cartoon shown to the left, this detonator stopping-distance test demonstrates that you can't stop on a dime. The detonator places one chalk mark on the road at the point at which the driver receives the signal to stop and another at the point at which he applies the brakes. A measurement of these distances from the point at which the front bumper of the car stops indicates reaction, braking, and total stopping distances. (Cartoon—Courtesy: Chrysler Corporation.)

How Do the Laws of Motion and Energy Affect the Car and the Driver?

Nature's laws are constant and automatic. Failure to observe them carries swift and often severe penalties. These laws have such an important effect on driving that it is impossible to drive intelligently without understanding them.

At one time or another one of these situations may have come to your attention: A car goes into a skid and spins out of control off the roadway: a vehicle enters a curve at high speed, fails to make the turn and rolls end over end into a ditch; an automobile traveling at high speed strikes a concrete abutment and is smashed; or the brakes of a truck give out and the vehicle plunges wildly down a steep hill. Did you ever wonder why such things happen? The answer is that motor vehicles involved in such situations were not being driven in harmony with the laws of nature.

FRICTION

A driver can control the motion of a car on the highway in four ways: he can speed up, slow down, maintain constant speed, or steer to either side. It may surprise you to learn that none of these things would be possible without the help of friction. The complete control of a car depends on the amount of friction between the tires and the road—the grip between four contact points, each no larger than the sole of your shoe. As long as this frictional grip is strong enough to counteract other forces acting on the car, the driver has control; but if the force of friction is re-

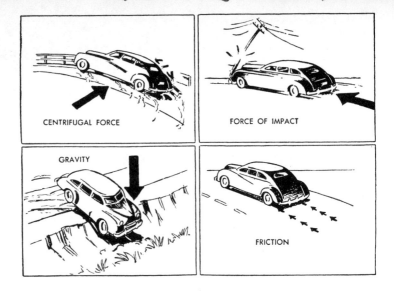

Fig. 5-2. Natural laws affect driving.

duced, or if the other forces acting on the car are substantially increased, then the car may go out of control.

Earlier you learned about the effect of friction on the clutch, brakes, and engine parts. You will recall that friction results from the interlocking of slight bumps or irregularities on surfaces that are rubbed together. When an attempt is made to slide one surface over the other the grip of the rough projections on each surface resists the motion.

Starting on Ice, Snow, Mud, or Sand

Many motorists try to start their cars on snow-packed or icy roads by putting the car into low gear and then racing the engine; the rear wheels spin at great speed, but the car itself does not move. The trick in starting on a slippery surface lies in applying the power to the rear wheels so that they grip gently and gradually. Start in second or high gear, engaging the clutch slowly and evenly to permit the rear wheels to grip and not to spin. If the wheels do spin without moving the car discontinue this method at once, and try some other. When the wheels have dug in, "rocking" will often be the solution. This consists of starting slowly as just described, and then, when the car has moved forward as far as it will go, shifting quickly into reverse to assist the tendency of the car to roll back slightly. When the car has backed as far as it will go, again shift quickly into low and go forward. By repeating this forward and backward process, you may succeed in developing sufficient momentum and traction to move forward.

On ice, or when rocking fails, the best procedure is to provide better friction between tires and road surface by spreading sand, cinders, an old piece of carpeting, or anything else that has possibilities for increasing friction. Make sure that both rear wheels are turning whenever you are attempting to start on surfaces with poor frictional grip. If one wheel has traction while the other wheel has little, spread plenty of friction-increasing material before and behind the wheel that is spinning so that it will be able to get a grip.

Stopping the Car

If friction is important in moving the car, it is even more important in stopping it. Brakes, you recall, are devices for creating friction to use up the energy of the spinning wheels by converting it to heat. This friction between the brake shoes and drums takes hold to stop the wheels; then the friction between the tires and the road pushes against the direction of the car's movement. These two sources of friction working together provide the braking force to stop the car.

Just as a chain is no stronger than its weakest link, braking force can be no stronger than the weakest of its two components— brake friction and road friction. The amount of brake friction varies with the conditions and adjustment of brake shoes, brake drums, and their controls. Road friction depends upon the type and condition of the tires and the road surface. Therefore, the force available to stop a car is dependent upon the condition of brakes, tires, and road surface, and—this braking force will be no greater than the friction produced by the weakest of these three factors. Even if brakes and tires are in excellent condition, not much braking force is available if the road is icy. On the other hand, even the best tires on dry concrete will not develop much braking force if the brake linings are badly worn.

Coefficient of Friction

The amount of grip between two surfaces is expressed as the *coefficient of friction*. It is calculated by dividing the amount of force necessary to pull one surface over another by the amount of force pressing the two surfaces together. For example, if it takes 2000 pounds of force to pull a 3000-pound car (with its brakes set) over a gravel road, the *coefficient of friction* between the tires and the road would be .67. This is how it was calculated:

$$CF = \frac{Fs}{Fp} \qquad\qquad CF = \frac{2000}{3000} = .67$$

In the formula:

CF represents coefficient of friction;

Fs represents the amount of force in pounds necessary to slide one surface over the other; and

Fp represents the amount of force in pounds (weight of the car) pressing the surfaces together.

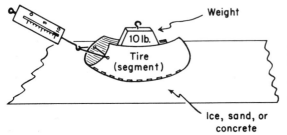

Fig. 5-3. (From Brody and Stack, "Highway Safety and Driver Education," Prentice-Hall.)

The following simple experiment will give you a better understanding of the coefficient of friction between various tire and road surfaces:

Obtain several small cross-section segments of various types of tires, a ten-pound weight, and a spring scale, and arrange these as shown in Figure 5-3. Pull each segment over various types and conditions of road surface. Record the force necessary to pull the segment in each test. Divide this amount by the total weight of the segment plus the ten-pound weight. Compare your findings with Chart 1.

Several factors affect the gripping efficiency of a road surface. As Chart 1 indicates, the material of which the surface is made is important. Also, dry surfaces have a much greater gripping efficiency than wet. Sand, loose gravel, mud, or wet leaves on a pavement tend to lower this efficiency. Ice and snow, of course, provide very little frictional grip, and melting ice and snow at a temperature of about 32°F. have only about half the frictional grip of hard frozen ice or snow at a temperature of about 0°F.

Many drivers fail to realize that bumpy, washboard roads also greatly reduce the frictional grip of tires on the road. A driver, therefore, should be just as cautious on bumpy roads as he would be on a wet or icy pavement.

202   TRAFFIC LAWS

CHART 1

**Coefficient of Friction for Good Tires
on Various Road Surfaces**

Type of pavement	Dry	Wet
Concrete	.90	.60
Asphalt	.85	.65
Brick	.85	.65
Oiled Gravel	.90	.65
Gravel, Cinders	.65	.65
Packed Snow	.45	.45
Ice or Sleet	.20	.20
Mud on Pavement	.20	.30

National Safety Council

Skidding

As long as a car maintains the frictional grip on the roadway the driver is in a position to control it. Once that grip is broken, however, the driver no longer has much control. A skid occurs when your tires lose their rolling grip on the pavement and start to slip as sled runners do. When this happens, the engine loses its pulling effect, the brakes lose their braking effect, and the wheels lose their ability to hold the car in line. They no longer track, and consequently the car is just as likely to travel sideways or backward as it is to go straight ahead. Sudden increases either in braking force or engine pull cause one type of skid. Another type is the sideslip, caused by turning a curve or corner. A third type of skid is produced by an unequal grip of the brakes or tires. For example, one brake drum may grip harder, and the car tends to swing or pivot around that wheel and skid.

Speed is one of the most important factors in increasing the possibilities of a skid. Therefore, one secret of avoiding skids is to reduce speed when the road is slippery or when turning and to keep tires and brakes in good condition. The way the brakes are applied is also important. A detailed explanation of the recommended method of pulling out of a skid is given on page 306.

Slowing Down and Stopping on Slippery Roads

Under slippery road conditions, brakes must always be applied with extreme caution. Apply the brakes gently and intermittently, instantly releasing the pressure on the brake at the first hint that the wheels are starting to slide. Keep the clutch engaged until the car is almost at a halt.

In some situations, a driver may use second gear to slow the car

Fig. 5-4. Winterized tires helped to bring this car to a stop from 20 miles per hour in 188 feet. This distance was 21 feet shorter than the stopping distance with conventional tires. (*Courtesy: National Safety Council.*)

down to a speed at which it is safe to use the brakes. In general, it is best to "drive well ahead" of the actual position of your car and anticipate the need for having to slow down. If you do this, you can slow down gradually, in many cases without having to use the brakes very much, and thereby reduce the chances of a skid.

Stopping Distances on Slippery Surfaces

Experiments have shown that it often takes as much as ten times the distance to stop a car on an icy pavement as it does on the same pavement when it is dry. Consider what would happen if you were driving in the rain at 40 miles an hour over a road on which you can normally stop in 124 feet (reaction distance plus braking distance). On this wet road, the coefficient of friction between tires and road is perhaps 50 per cent less. Suddenly a car pulls out of a driveway 150 feet ahead. You jam on your brakes. Ordinarily, your car would come to a halt with a 26-foot margin of safety. But this time it will either strike or pass the car ahead. Whenever you operate a motor car, remember that *the more slippery the road*—whether from rain, sleet, snow, ice, wet leaves, or from any other cause or combination of causes—*the slower you must drive!*

Tires and Chains

During the past several years, a variety of specialized tires have been developed to improve the frictional grip of the car on the road. Generally, these tires might be classified into four groups:

Lacerated tread tires: essentially conventional rib-type tires with fine cuts or lacerations in the tread.

Winterized tires: lacerated tread-type tires, with minute particles such as salt, sawdust, or other materials imbedded in the tread.

Mud-Snow tires: generally characterized by a special tread design— deep tread, studs, or knobs.

Winterized Mud-Snow tires: a mud-snow tire that has been given the winterizing treatment.

All of these special types of tires tend to reduce skidding and improve traction. Tire chains also improve traction and reduce stopping distances, especially under snow or icy road conditions. Figures 5-5 and 5-7 show comparative stopping distances on various road surfaces, using different types of tires or chains.

CENTRIFUGAL FORCE

Centrifugal force is another natural phenomenon that has an important effect on driving. This phenomenon was first recognized by Newton, who stated the law somewhat like this: *Moving objects tend to travel in a straight line and can be prevented from doing so only by the application of force.* If you tie a stone on a string and swing it in a circle, you will note that the stone exerts a pull on the string. This pull away from the center of the circle is called *centrifugal force.* The same thing happens when a car is rounding a curve, only in that case the opposing force is not the pull of your hand on the string but the frictional grip of the tires on the pavement.

You would find that, if you increased the speed of the stone, a point would be reached where the centrifugal force became so great the string would snap, and the stone would go flying off on a tangent to the circle. In the same way, if a car enters a curve too fast, the centrifugal force is strong enough to "snap" the gripping hold of the tires on the pavement, and the car goes careening off the road.

There are several practical conclusions to be drawn from these facts:

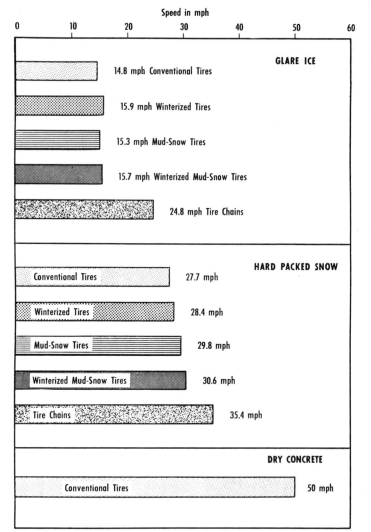

Fig. 5-5. Equivalent speeds on glare ice and hard-packed snow to provide stopping performance equal to that obtained at 50 mph on dry concrete. (Courtesy: National Safety Council.)

Speed in mph

GLARE ICE

14.8 mph Conventional Tires

15.9 mph Winterized Tires

15.3 mph Mud-Snow Tires

15.7 mph Winterized Mud-Snow Tires

24.8 mph Tire Chains

HARD PACKED SNOW

Conventional Tires   27.7 mph

Winterized Tires   28.4 mph

Mud-Snow Tires   29.8 mph

Winterized Mud-Snow Tires   30.6 mph

Tire Chains   35.4 mph

DRY CONCRETE

Conventional Tires   50 mph

USE TIRE CHAINS *on* ICE *and* SNOW

Fig. 5-6. On snow, ice, mud, or sand, tire chains help keep you going. On ice and snow, chains help you stop. Take the trouble to put them on when you need them.

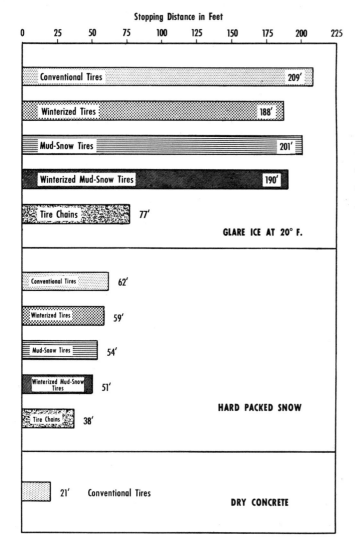

Fig. 5-7. Stopping distance from 20 mph on various road surfaces. (Courtesy: National Safety Council.)

1. Before entering a curve you should reduce your speed to a point where centrifugal force can be safely overcome by the grip of the tires on the pavement.

2. The sharper the curve, the greater the centrifugal force, and consequently the slower you will have to drive to get around it safely.

3. The grip of the tires will depend on the condition and contour of the surface. If the road is wet or icy it will have less grip on the tires, and the safe speed for rounding the curve will be reduced. If the curve is banked, that is, if the outside edge is tipped up, this will counteract some of the tendency of the car to leave

LAWS OF MOTION AND ENERGY   207

the road; therefore, a banked curve can be taken at higher speed. When curves are banked, the allowable speed is often indicated by a sign. It is not safe, however, to assume that curves will be banked. Many of them are flat, and old-fashioned roads which are crowned—high in the middle—slope down on the outside, which is just the opposite of being banked.

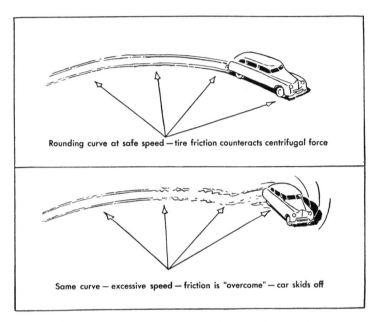

Rounding curve at safe speed—tire friction counteracts centrifugal force

Same curve—excessive speed—friction is "overcome"—car skids off

Fig. 5-8. On curves, low speeds are safe speeds.

MOMENTUM

Momentum is the force that keeps a car rolling even after you remove your foot from the accelerator. The momentum, or kinetic energy, of a moving body increases with its speed. In order to stop a moving vehicle, friction must be applied to use up its kinetic energy, and the greater the kinetic energy of the car the greater the distance required. This can be demonstrated mathematically.

To simplify matters, we will express speed in feet per second:

$$\frac{\text{Number of miles per hour} \times 5280}{3600} = \text{number of feet per second}$$

$$1 \text{ mile} = 5280 \text{ feet}$$
$$1 \text{ hour} = 3600 \text{ seconds}$$

TRAFFIC LAWS

A quick way to estimate the number of feet that a car travels per second at various speeds is to take the number of miles per hour and add half to it. For example, a car traveling 20 miles per hour travels approximately 20 plus ½ of 20, or 20 plus 10, which is 30 feet per second.

The kinetic energy of a moving object varies in relation to the "square" of the speed. That is:

$$KE = \frac{1}{2} MV^2$$

where

KE represents kinetic energy of the object in foot-pounds;

M represents the mass of the object

$$\frac{\text{weight in pounds}}{\text{acceleration of gravity (32.2)}}; \text{ and}$$

V represents velocity or speed in feet per second.

A 3220-pound car, traveling at 20 miles per hour, develops about 45,000 foot-pounds of kinetic energy.

$$KE = \frac{1}{2} MV^2$$
$$KE = \frac{1}{2} \times \frac{3220}{32.2} \times (30 \times 30) = 45,000$$

This is enough energy to lift a 1000-pound elevator about three stories!

Thousands of tests at automobile proving grounds have indicated that a car with good brakes and good tires can be stopped in approximately 20 feet from a speed of 20 miles per hour on a clean, dry, concrete pavement. This means that, in the previous illustration, the 45,000 foot-pounds of energy could be used up by applying frictional force (of the brakes and of the tires on the road) for a distance of about 20 feet. This braking distance would be about the same for a heavier car or truck that develops a greater amount of kinetic energy, because such vehicles are equipped with correspondingly more powerful brakes.

Many drivers make the mistake of thinking that when they double their speed they merely double the braking distance. Since braking distance depends directly upon the amount of kinetic energy developed by the car, when the speed is doubled kinetic energy and braking distance are increased four times. For example, our 3220-pound car traveling at 40 miles per hour develops, not twice as much kinetic energy (90,000 foot-pound), as might be expected, but four times as much (180,000 foot-pounds).

$$KE = \frac{1}{2}\ MV^2$$

$$KE = \frac{1}{2} \times \frac{3220}{32.2} \times 60 \times 60 = 180,000 \text{ foot-pounds}$$

Twenty feet were required to use up the kinetic energy developed by the car traveling 20 miles per hour. Since the car has developed four times as much kinetic energy at 40 miles per hour, the braking distance is therefore four times as great, or 80 feet.

At 60 miles per hour, nine times as much kinetic energy is developed by the moving car as at 20 miles per hour.

$$KE = \frac{1}{2}\ MV^2$$

$$KE = \frac{1}{2} \times \frac{3220}{32.2} \times (90 \times 90) = 405,000 \text{ foot-pounds}$$

Therefore, at 60 miles per hour it takes 180 feet braking distance to use up the kinetic energy, or nine times the distance required at 20; yet the speed has only become three times greater. It must be remembered also that all of the braking distance mentioned apply only to ideal conditions; adverse conditions would increase braking distance substantially.

An easy way to figure the minimum braking distance of a car from any given speed is to follow this procedure:

1. *Take the first digit in the rate of speed* (expressed in miles per hour). At 30 miles per hour, for example, this would be 3.
2. *Divide this by 2.*
   Example: $3 \div 2 = \frac{3}{2}$
3. *Multiply this result by the whole number,* to get the minimum braking distance.
   $30 \times \frac{3}{2} = 45$

Therefore, the minimum braking distance at 30 miles per hour is 45 feet.

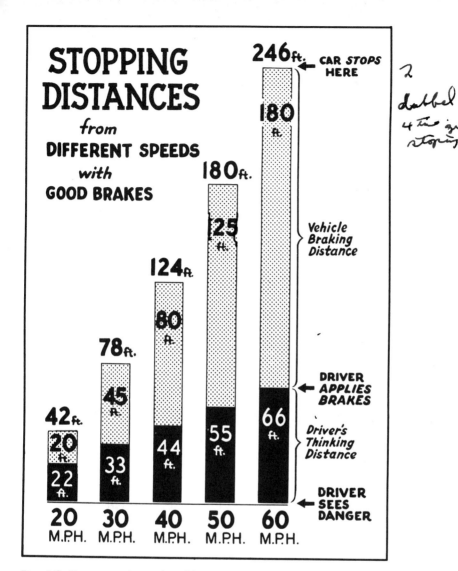

Fig. 5-9. You must always be able to stop in time to avoid hitting something ahead. It usually takes longer than you think. (*Courtesy: American Association of Motor Vehicle Administrators and National Safety Council.*)

Reaction and Braking Distances Determine Stopping Distance

The minimum total distance, under ideal conditions, in which you can stop your car in an emergency depends on two basic factors: (1) your reaction time, and (2) the distance the car will continue to travel after the brakes are applied. Figure 3-15 on page

129 shows the distances a car will travel at varying speeds before drivers with different rates of reaction time, confronted by an unexpected situation, will begin to move their muscles to meet the emergency. The normal driver's reaction time is assumed to be three-fourths of a second. You will note that the distance a car travels in three-fourths of a second at speeds in multiples of 10 miles per hour is very easy to figure. For example, at 20 mph it is 22 feet, at 30 mph it is 33 feet, at 40 mph is 44 feet, and so on. Using this technique to figure reaction distance, and the method previously described for calculating braking distance, you can determine the approximate minimum stopping distance at any given speed.

STOPPING:
Reaction + Braking = Stopping Distance

Speed greatly extends braking distance, so ~ START STOPPING SOONER !

(Courtesy: Transit Casualty Company, St. Louis, Missouri.)

You can either use a commercial detonator or perform the following experiment to test reaction time and braking distance:

Select a quiet street or, preferably, an off-street parking area. Two or more drivers can test one another. The first takes his place behind the wheel, with the tester sitting behind with his left arm out the window. In his hand he carries a small paper bag containing a little flour or lime. A spotter stands at the side with chalk and tape measure.

Drive at 20 miles an hour.* The tester then gives various commands, and finally calls "brakes." At the same time, he throws the bag to the pavement near the rear wheel.

The distance from the flour to the skid mark is the reaction distance. From skid mark to the stopping point is the braking distance. The stopping distance is the reaction plus braking distance. At 20 miles per hour on dry concrete, reaction distance averages 22 feet, braking distance 22 feet. (To get your complex reaction time, divide your reaction distance at 20 mph by 22 and multiply by .75 seconds.)

---

* Warning: This is a very good demonstration at 20 mph, but at higher speeds it can be dangerous!

Reaction distance and braking distance are physical factors, for which you must always allow in driving. Do not merely memorize these figures, but learn to sense, under all conditions, the varying distances that you will need to bring your car to a halt. Drive so that no emergencies will arise calling for you to stop within a shorter distance. If speedometers indicated stopping distances in feet instead of speed in miles per hour, we might all drive a lot slower. When it got up to 180 feet, over half the length of a football field, we would be much more cautious to be certain we had this "assured clear distance ahead." The next time you hear somebody confidently say that he can "stop his car from 60 miles per hour on a dime," you can tell him that the dime will have to be at least 246 feet wide.

GRAVITY

The force with which a car presses against the road is, of course, known as its weight. Weight is caused by the pull of the earth—gravity—on all objects around its surface. Gravity has its most important effect on driving techniques when a driver is descending or ascending a slope; it makes braking necessary for descending a hill and more power necessary for climbing a hill.

Descending Hills

When you come to the brink of a hill you should, so far as possible, survey it over its whole length before you start down. If the bottom of the hill is hidden by a curve or by any other obstruction, assume that you may meet driving difficulties beyond that point. Plan your descent so that as the slope of the hill unfolds to view, you will be able to meet any emergency.

On slight downgrades, merely releasing pressure on the accelerator may reduce speed sufficiently so that you will drive down the hill safely, the engine acting as a brake. On slightly steeper grades, you will have to help the braking effect of the engine by applying the foot brakes. On steep downgrades you should shift into second and sometimes even into low gear before starting the descent. This utilizes the maximum braking-force of the engine, and will save wear on your brake linings. Determine the gear you will use in descending a hill, and shift into that gear before you start down. Once you have started down a steep grade and find that your foot brakes lack the power to slow your car sufficiently, you may find it difficult or impossible to shift to a lower gear. The length and steepness of the descent will be your guide in determining what gear to use. In general, the same gear should be used in descending that is needed for ascending.

Coasting

Some motorists have the habit of pressing the clutch down or putting the shift lever in neutral and permitting the car to coast, or "free-wheel," downhill. This is a dangerous practice, and most states have made it illegal! When you coast, you are failing to make use of the braking effect of the engine, and you may find in an emergency that the foot brakes alone are unable to stop or slow down the car sufficiently. The safe thing to do is to keep the engine in gear and your foot off the clutch pedal when descending a hill.

Climbing Hills

Speeding uphill was no problem in the old days. You were lucky to creep over the top in third gear. But modern cars can take you up many grades at 50 or 60 miles an hour. Slowing down while going upgrade may sound silly, but suppose you should overtake a slow-moving vehicle that is just out of sight over the hill? Oncoming traffic would prevent you from going around it to the left. A guard rail or soft shoulder might keep you from going around it at the right. Your only chance would be to stop behind the vehicle.

Keep well to the right and slow down when approaching the crest of a hill; there is no way of telling what may be in your path. The limited sight distance, coupled with the fact that, as the slope decreases at the crest, less power is needed to maintain a reasonable cruising speed, make slowing down essential. Extra caution should be the watchword in hilly country.

THE INFLUENCE OF SPEED ON TRAFFIC SAFETY

You have probably noticed that as speed increases all of the harmful effects of nature's laws are magnified. The faster a wheel spins, the less frictional grip it has on the road. The greater the speed at which a car travels, the farther it takes to stop. Every traffic accident may be attributed to motion, and hence to speed. Of course, this fact is ridiculously obvious. But, there are many indications that speed "too fast for conditions" is a basic element in both the frequency and severity of traffic accidents. *Accident*

Facts, the annual summary of accident statistics published by the National Safety Council, lists "speed too fast for conditions" as primarily responsible for at least 25 per cent of all fatal accidents. Moreover, speed is probably the underlying cause of many other accidents, such as those attributed to driving off the road, skidding, and the like. Let us examine how three vital factors—perception, reaction time, and force of impact—vary in relation to speed.

Perception

Visual acuity, as described in Unit III, is the ability to distinguish at a distance the sizes and shapes of various objects. If the object and the observer are both stationary, the object will be readily distinguished. However, if either the object or the observer is moving with respect to the other, the task immediately becomes more difficult.

This can be easily demonstrated in a group by holding up two objects, of different shapes but of the same size, sufficiently small to be just within easy visual range of the group. The group can distinguish one shape from the other when both are stationary; but if the instructor moves first one and then the other quickly across the group's line of sight, they will be unable to discriminate one from the other. A similar reduction in visual attention is experienced by the driver of a moving vehicle as he increases his speed. For example, nearly every driver has had the experience of being too far from a road sign to read it; and, when the distance was sufficiently reduced to see the letters, the car passed the sign before its message could be read.

In addition to reducing visual attention, increased speed causes the driver to focus his eyes farther ahead down the road. Studies show that at 45 mph the average focal distance is about 400 yards, but at 65 mph the driver is forced to strain to see as far as possible down the road. As the focal distance increases, the driver's visual attention is reduced considerably. At 60 mph, for example, the field of vision is only half as great as at 20 mph. Thus speed tends to give all drivers "tunnel" vision. It is, therefore, apparent that because of visual limitations drivers cannot see clearly enough, quickly enough, or widely enough to operate safely at high speeds.

Reaction Time

While the importance of reaction time is well recognized, it is

Fig. 5-10. Speed increases the destructive force of a crash. At 60 miles per hour a car would strike a stationary object with the same force it would strike the ground if dropped from the top of a nine-story building.

20 M.P.H.
Height 13.5 ft.

40 M.P.H.
Height 54 ft.

60 M.P.H.
Height 121.5 ft.

not generally known that reaction time changes with increased speed and varying emergency situations. Traffic specialists recognize that in an extreme emergency stop driver reaction time (0.50 to 0.75 sec.) probably approaches the so-called simple reaction time as closely as may be found in practical situations. Complex reaction time (as discussed in Unit III) is the time necessary for interpreting the situation and making a decision plus simple reaction time. Laboratory experiments, under controlled conditions, have shown that the overall reaction time increases as the number of choices or the number of factors to be perceived becomes greater. It is obvious that in traffic situations or at high speeds the number of things to be perceived and evaluated in a given period of time increases. Complex reaction time will, therefore, be longer than was determined in simplified classroom measurements. The American Association of State Highway Officials estimates that complex reaction time varies from two seconds at 30 miles per hour to three seconds at 70 miles per hour.

Forces of Impact

The force with which a moving vehicle hits a stationary object or another vehicle is difficult to imagine. Viewing a wrecked car is evidence of the destructive forces, but the observer, as a rule, has no way of knowing the speed of the vehicle before the impact. When force is applied to stop a vehicle, the work done equals the amount of force multiplied by the amount of distance taken to stop (Fd). If the kinetic energy of the vehicle is used up over a considerable distance, such as in braking to a gentle stop, the force is very small. But if the energy is used up in a very short distance, such as a crash into a concrete wall, the force is tremendous. And the greater the kinetic energy the greater the force. Figure 5-10 shows the relationship between speed and force of impact.

Regulating Speed in Accordance with Nature's Laws

In addition to perception, reaction time, and force of impact, many other factors are also affected adversely by increased speed. As speed increases the driver is forced to make more rapid decisions and reactions. He is perceptually handicapped in making these decisions and responses, and the results of wrong decisions or improper responses become increasingly serious.

You will frequently be driving under varying conditions of road surface, gradient, curvature, weather, visibility, and obstructions to visibility. In the early stages of your driving experience, you may not always be able to determine the maximum speed at which you can drive safely when one or more of these factors are present in a hazardous degree. That is why it is wise always to drive *under* the maximum safe speed. Develop the habit of always slowing down when approaching potential hazards.

The laws of motion and energy have established speed limits above which even the best driver, in the finest car on the most modern road, cannot operate with safety. A driver who attempts to break these speed limits is flirting with an accident and sudden death. Since the frequency and severity of accidents greatly increases at speeds above 50 mph, it is recommended that drivers do not exceed this limit under any condition. The most economical and efficient operating speed varies between 35 and 45 miles per hour, depending on the vehicle.

Speed Invites Sudden Death

The results of accidents that occur at high speeds are particularly severe. In his famous magazine article, "Sudden Death," J. C. Furnas pictured such an accident:

To describe the scene of a high speed traffic accident in words alone is a difficult task . . . because that picture will need to include motion and sound. We would need to see the flopping, pointless efforts of the injured in their attempts to stand up. The queer, grunting noises and labored, panting, groaning of a human being realizing his pain as the first shock wears off. This picture should portray individually the expression on the face of a man coming out of this first shock, looking at the Z twist of his broken leg. This picture should bring to your ears the sounds of a hysterical woman with her screaming mouth opening back to her ear showing the raw ends of bones and teeth while the blood drips off her chin. Some of the minor details would show what raw flesh and bones look like where clothes and skin were torn off together.

This accident picture is one which would challenge the best artist—shock even the strongest men. But, this picture is repeated daily along roadsides of our nation.

Yes, this picture is shocking! However, lest we have the nerve to risk our lives and the lives of others by driving too fast and taking chances, we ought to have the nerve to learn what has happened to other people who drove fast, took chances, and defied the uncompromising laws of nature.

DISCUSSION TOPICS

1. What are the laws of nature that influence driving? Describe the beneficial and harmful effects of each.
2. What is the recommended technique for starting on a slippery surface? When is "rocking" used?
3. What are the relative effects of ordinary tires, chains, snow and mud tires, and winterized tires on braking distance? On traction?
4. What factors influence the amount of centrifugal force acting on a car rounding a curve? What can the driver do to control these factors?

5. Describe the relationship between the following:
   a. speed and kinetic energy
   b. kinetic energy and braking distance
   c. braking distance and friction
6. What are the effects of speed on the driver?

PROJECTS AND PROBLEMS

1. Draw schematic diagrams showing the forces of nature acting on a motor vehicle in the following situations:
   a. starting
   b. stopping
   c. driving around a curve on a
      (1) level road
      (2) crowned road
      (3) banked road
   d. driving uphill
   e. driving downhill
2. If the braking distance for a car is approximately 20 feet at 20 mph, calculate the approximate braking distance at 15 mph, 30 mph, 40 mph, 50 mph and 60 mph. Explain the significance of your results. Assuming reaction time to be ¾ second, what is the total stopping distance at these speeds?
3. As a result of your previous findings, what maximum safe speed would you recommend for the following conditions:
   a. any place where the driver's view is obstructed, such as at corners, crowded intersections, and so forth.
   b. thickly settled areas where obstructions are likely to appear as close as 50 feet ahead without warning.
   c. open highways where obstructions may develop as close as 200 feet ahead without previous warning.
   d. open highways at night (assume that headlights clearly illuminate the road for about 150 feet ahead).
4. Cut a block of wood ten inches high, with a base two inches square. Stand this block on a level spot on the floor of the car. Drive at various speeds around several curves and determine the maximum speed at which you can drive around each curve without upsetting the block. This maximum indicates a safe and comfortable speed for each curve.
5. Write a short essay on your recommendations for the speed at which motor vehicles should be operated under various driving conditions. Support your recommendations with facts.

Fig. 5-11. The work of traffic policemen is to protect highway users. Co-operate with them. The life they save may be your own. (*Courtesy: Scholastic Magazines.*)

TRAFFIC LAWS

What Are the Basic Man-Made Traffic Rules?

Driving rules were not invented; they grew quite naturally from customs and habits of the horse-and-wagon period. With the coming of the automobile, these ways of doing things became still more important. Some of them became established in law. The specific traffic laws that exist in your area can be found by consulting your state driver's manual and city traffic ordinances. Not all of our driving rules, however, are to be found in the state codes and city traffic regulations. *A great deal of the skill and safety of driving depends on expert practices and good judgment which cannot be put into legal restrictions.* These systems of tried and proven practices, partly fixed by law and partly enforced by our own common sense, have become the basis for good driving.

Traffic rules have been established for several reasons:

1. To promote uniform driving practice.
2. To give some assurance of controlled power on the highways, particularly when it is in the hands of discourteous, irresponsible drivers.
3. To serve as guides for all those who want to do the right thing.

Without rules, the use of the highways by millions of people

BASIC MAN-MADE TRAFFIC RULES 221

would lead to utter chaos and confusion. These traffic rules promote a smooth, efficient flow of highway traffic.

BASIC RULES

In the various state and city regulations that grew out of driving experience, there is a fairly simple and uniform body of customs that are based on common sense. If we understand these *basic* rules we shall have little trouble in grasping the other rules, which developed as traffic grew more complex. It must be remembered, however, that these general rules should be interpreted in terms of your local and state traffic laws. If you find in the following set of general rules anything that seems to conflict with the regulations of the city and state in which you are driving, follow your local rules. They are binding for your community. Each citizen, however, should urge his state and community to bring their local laws into general agreement with the Uniform Vehicle Code and the Model Traffic Ordinances, which have been developed by the National Conference on Street and Highway Safety as standard guides.

The most important and widely accepted driving rules may be summarized as follows:

Signaling

1. Give clear warning well in advance of your intention to cause any interference with the normal flow of traffic (by hand, by mechanical device, by "position shift" of car).
2. Observe and take warning from the signals and the significant movements of others (cars, pedestrians, bicyclists, and animals).
3. Observe and obey the authorized signs and automatic signals that are provided to guide and control traffic.

Rules 1, 2, and 3 cover the essentials of signaling. There is, however, no universal or nationally adopted code of driver signals. This lack of uniformity is unfortunate, because signaling should be one of the driver's most ingrained and unfailing habits.

The sudden and unexpected actions of drivers are responsible for a large proportion of traffic accidents. We can avoid most dangerous situations if we know that they are coming. Yet even in those states where the law requires them, hand signals are largely neglected. This matter of signaling, therefore, is one that needs more attention, and there should be a country-wide effort to secure standard practice and more widespread observance.

Fig. 5-12. Arm signals for stops and turns. When other drivers may be affected, show your intention to stop or turn by arm signals. (*Courtesy: American Association of Motor Vehicle Administrators and National Safety Council.*)

Hand Signals

The nearest approach to standard practice is the hand signals set up in the Uniform Vehicle Code, Act V, Section 78. These are:

Left Turn—Hand and arm extended horizontally.
Right Turn—Hand and arm extended upward.
Stop or Decrease Speed—Hand and arm extended downward.

These are by no means universal, and your own state and city regulations are, of course, the ones that you should follow. It is possible, however, to obtain practical agreement everywhere if these rules are carried into effect as follows:

Left Turn. Left turns are indicated by extending the left arm horizontally out of the window. This signal should be used also when you move from the curb into a stream of traffic, or when, on multiple-lane highways, you move from a right to a left lane to pass another car.

Right Turn. The standard signal for a right turn is usually made by extending the left arm out of the window and bending it sharply upward. In a few states a right turn is indicated by moving the arm or hand in a rotary motion, as though beckoning those behind to "come on!" Since cars from one state today go everywhere, it is important that both kinds of signals should be understood by all drivers.

Stop or Decrease Speed. The stop signal, which is used also as a slow-down signal, is given by extending the left hand and arm downward out of the window, the palm of the hand being open and facing backward.

BASIC MAN-MADE TRAFFIC RULES

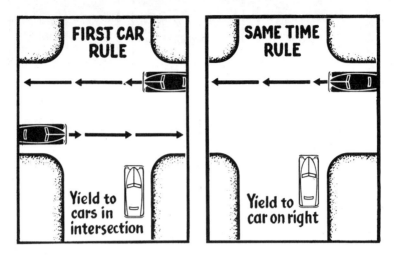

Fig. 5-13. Right of way at intersections:
A. *First car rule.* If you are driving the white car, give right of way to the black ones, because they are in the intersection first.
B. *Same time rule.* When you reach the intersection at about the same time as another car, let him go on first if he is coming from your right. (*Courtesy: National Association of Motor Vehicle Administrators and National Safety Council.*)

False Signals. Drivers should beware of driving with the arm out of the window, of pointing out the window to objects in the landscape, and of flicking off the ashes of cigars and cigarettes. There is a very real danger that these motions may be interpreted as signals. A false signal is worse than none. Take pride in signaling clearly; avoid the use of half-hearted or sloppy gestures. Let there be no doubt as to what your hand signals mean. Even use them to supplement electrical directional signals.

Shift-of-Position Signals. Shift-of-position signaling is quite generally used. It is a natural and easy habit to acquire. After giving the necessary hand and mechanical signals, the driver gradually shifts the position and adjusts the speed of his car to indicate what he is going to do. (By slowing up and moving near the center of the road, for example, he indicates that he intends to make a left turn.) *The use of position-signaling, however, will not justify omitting other signals, required by law.* In case of accident, any failure to give a required hand or mechanical signal will prove damaging evidence against a driver who is involved.

Signaling Devices. Signaling devices that warn of stops and turns are installed as standard equipment in some makes of cars. These

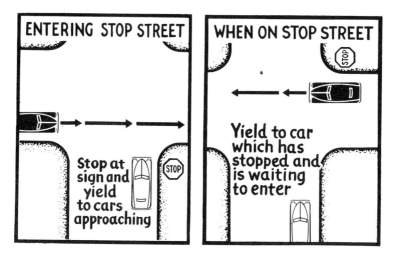

Fig. 5-14. Right of way at stop streets.

A. *Entering the stop street.* If you are entering or crossing a stop street, you must bring your car to a full stop at the stop sign or a marked line, and you must yield the right of way to any car on the cross street that is in the intersection or so close to it as to be dangerous if you entered in front of it. After that you may proceed; other drivers are required to yield to you.

B. *When on stop street.* If another car has stopped at a stop sign, and has been waiting to enter a through street, yielding the right of way to cars that are approaching, and if it then enters the intersection, you must yield the right of way to him even though you are approaching the intersection on the through street. (*Courtesy of the National Association of Motor Vehicle Administrators and National Safety Council.*)

devices may prove to be the answer to our present bad signaling situation. In some states such devices are now legally required.

Rules for Passing

4. Drive on the right side of the roadway.
5. Pass to the right of those approaching you.
6. Pass to the left of those whom you are overtaking, except when driving on highways having two or more lanes for traveling either direction, where signs indicate that passing on the right is permitted.
7. Give way to those who seek to overtake you.
8. Overtake and pass other cars only when the view ahead is unobstructed and shows ample room for the passing maneuver.

The first three of these rules for passing are based simply and arbitrarily on custom. Some fixed rule is needed, and in this country we follow the starboard or right-hand rule of the sea. In England, however, the reverse of this rule is standard practice. Rule 7 is, or should be, universal. It is based on our need for good will and co-operation. When you observe another driver overtaking you, move over promptly and let him pass without waiting for him to blow his horn. This courtesy helps to reduce the nervous strain of driving. Often another driver makes your good sportsmanship more pleasant by acknowledging it with an appreciative wave of the hand. Rule 8 has some very important special applications which will be fully described in the problem dealing with skills on the highway.

Crossing Traffic

Cross-traffic is one of the most direct and dangerous types of interference that drivers encounter. Crossing the path of another vehicle is much more dangerous than simple passing. The parallel passing of cars does not require that you block or stop the other car. But when one car closely crosses the path of another there is an immediate and direct risk of collision, unless one of the cars checks its speed or stops. The most dangerous crossings are likely to be controlled by fixed stop signs or signal lights. The law requires the motorist to obey these special signs in preference to any general crossing rules. But at many intersections, in both city and country, no special traffic control devices are provided. This interference problem has resulted in four fairly widespread customs, which have been expressed in laws in various ways, but which are all based on the same ideas.

9. A car moving on a highway or street of major importance should be given the right of way by cars crossing or entering from minor roads or private driveways; cars crossing or entering from minor roads or private driveways should come to a stop before entering a thoroughfare.
10. A car approaching an intersection shall yield the right of way to any car which has already entered the intersection from a cross street.
11. If two cars approaching on different streets reach a non-signal intersection at the same time, the car on the left must yield the right of way to the car on the right.
12. The driver of a car must yield the right of way to all pedestrians.

It should be clear that these right-of-way rules govern only the crossings not controlled by fixed signs or signal lights. The safest approach to right of way problems, when in doubt, is to allow the other driver to proceed first.

Turning

13. A car making a left turn must approach and start such turn from the center lane or left side of its half of the roadway.
14. A car making a left turn must yield the right of way to all opposite-moving cars, which such a turn might block or hinder.
15. A car making a right turn must approach and start such turn from the curb lane or right side of its half of the roadway.

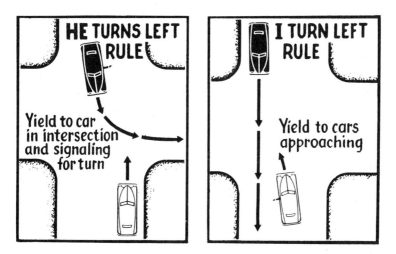

Fig. 5-15. Left Turn Right-of-Way.
A. *He-Turns-Left Rule*—To let any car turn left ahead of you if it is waiting in the intersection and the driver is giving a left turn signal when you come up.
B. *I-Turn-Left Rule*—If you want to turn left, give the right-of-way to any other car in the intersection or so close to it that it would be dangerous if you turned in front of it. (*Courtesy: American Association of Motor Vehicle Administrators and National Safety Council.*)

Parking

16. Park your car off the traveled way, where it will not interfere with the normal flow of traffic or obstruct the view of other drivers.

There is a general parking custom, one of good manners rather than of law or safety, which might be expressed as follows: "The stopping and parking of a car should be done with the least

BASIC MAN-MADE TRAFFIC RULES   227

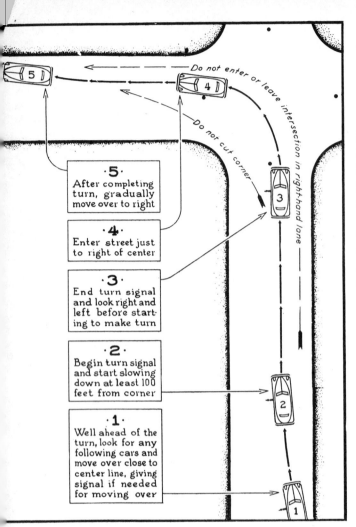

Fig. 5-16. How to make a left turn. There are five things to remember in making a left turn. Take care to keep close to, but not to cross, the center line. (*Courtesy: American Association of Motor Vehicle Administrators and National Safety Council.*)

possible interference to traffic and inconvenience to others." The observance of this is a great help in city shopping sections and crowded streets. There are a number of other parking rules, such as those regulating double and diagonal parking and those specifying the time during which a parking space may be used. These rules, however, vary greatly in different cities and states.

Speed Regulation

17. Drive your car at such speeds as are *reasonable* and *prudent* under existing circumstances.
18. Drive at all times, especially at night, at such speeds as will permit you to stop before reaching the limit of your Assured Clear Distance Ahead.

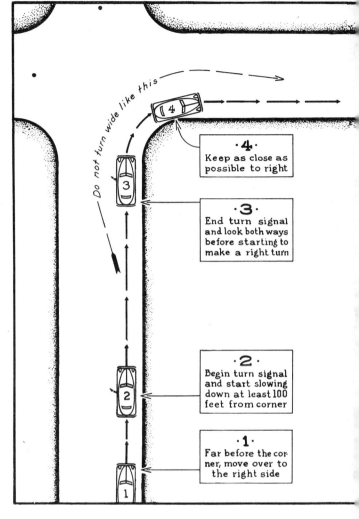

Fig. 5-17. How to make a right turn. There are four things to do in making a right turn. Be careful not to swing to the left before or after making the turn. (Courtesy: American Association of Motor Vehicle Administrators and National Safety Council.)

Do not turn wide like this

·4·
Keep as close as possible to right

·3·
End turn signal and look both ways before starting to make a right turn

·2·
Begin turn signal and start slowing down at least 100 feet from corner

·1·
Far before the corner, move over to the right side

Rule number 17 is quite general; its successful observance depends upon the judgment of the individual driver—or the traffic officer. Rule number 18 sets a more definite standard. It seeks to limit our speed by our assured clear distance ahead. Both of these rules are expressions of "prima facie" laws. In the event a traffic officer apprehends a driver for speeding where such laws apply, the burden of proof of guilt or innocence falls upon both the driver and the arresting officer. This may be a fair and reasonable law as far as the individual driver is concerned but it is difficult to enforce. To overcome this difficulty many states have adopted "absolute speed limits" above which it is illegal to drive. This has disadvantages because it is plain that there is a need for special speed limits in various areas. Some states have adopted a combination of these two types of speed laws in order to utilize the advantage and overcome the disadvantages of each. Which system does your state use?

Although excessive speed is our greatest driving hazard, driving too slowly is also dangerous. The normal flow of traffic must eddy around the obstruction that a slow driver offers, producing, especially on two-lane highways, serious dangers. Some states, therefore, are following the recommendations of the Uniform Code, which advises that "No person shall drive at such a slow speed as to impede or block the normal movement of traffic." If for any reason you are forced to drive very slowly, stay close to the right side of the road, and be helpful in making it easy for others to pass you.

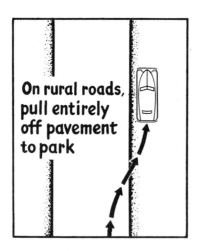

On rural roads, pull entirely off pavement to park

Fig. 5-18. Park off the pavement. Outside of a business or residential district, if there is no curb and if you can pull your car entirely off the roadway, you should never park it or leave it standing on a paved or main-traveled part of the road. (*Courtesy: American Association of National Motor Vehicle Administrators and National Safety Council.*)

Responsibility for Others

19. A car must be so driven and controlled as to enable the driver to avoid the normal actions and mistakes of other drivers and pedestrians.

Driving, by its very nature, requires us to accept a personal responsibility for others. Our skill and control must be equal to dealing with the frequent faulty performances we meet every day. Human nature is full of faults. If we choose to drive, we must be able to adapt ourselves to deal with these faults, and we must accept personal responsibility for others. Whenever an accident occurs, the courts and the public ask, "*Who had the last clear chance to avoid this accident?*" The person who made the first mistake is not excused. But if the other person involved had a chance to avoid the effects of the first mistake, and either refused or neglected that chance, he is held also to be at fault. This responsibility of the driver is particularly strong when pedestrians are involved, for they are easily hurt and often helpless in trying to avoid a swiftly moving car. The best way to meet this responsibility is to expect always that other drivers or pedestrians may do the wrong thing, and be ready for such an action. When you can avoid other people's errors with foresight, you have put yourself in the expert class.

Fig. 5-19. Power under control is a faithful servant, but like other good servants, out-of-control power can be a cruel master.

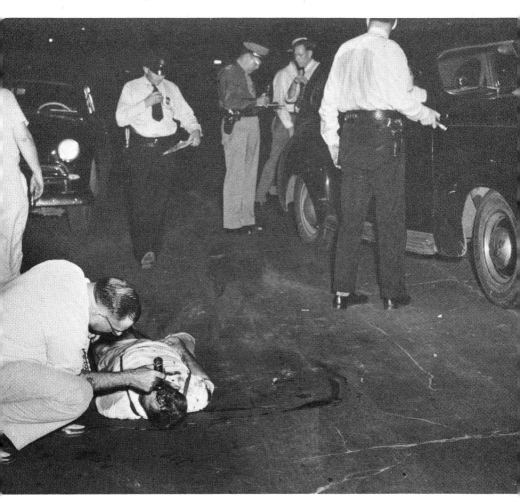

Passing School Busses

Most states require that the driver come to a stop upon approaching, from either direction, a school bus that is taking on or discharging children. Even though the laws in some places do not demand this, it is recommended that drivers always stop until the school bus has moved away and there is assurance that the road is clear.

Making Way for Emergency Vehicles

When you hear the familiar siren or bell of a fire engine, a police car or an ambulance, pull over to the right as far as you can and slow down or stop until it passes safely. Because these vehicles are on emergency errands, often involving matters of life and death, they must travel as fast as possible and, therefore, have a special right of way. Give them a clear way, as you would want it given if they were coming to help you.

SUMMARY

Our man-made traffic rules require us to accept personal responsibility for the security and safety of other users of the streets and highways. The basis for good driving is the spirit of co-operation. Traffic rules are designed to keep order in the traffic pattern and to avoid trouble on the highways. When followed, they serve to protect both walkers and drivers from dangerous practices and confusion. The success of any set of rules, however, depends on the good will and sportsmanship of the players. Drivers, like athletes, find it to their advantage to follow the rules.

DISCUSSION TOPICS

1. Describe how the traffic laws in your state originated. Who is responsible for putting them into effect?
2. How has custom affected the development of rules of the road? What has been the influence of natural laws?
3. What is the meaning and significance of uniform regulations? What is being done by national, state, and private agencies to encourage uniform traffic legislation?
4. What general driving regulations are in effect throughout the United States?
5. What is the legal interpretation of the "right-of-way"?
6. Explain the basic rules of the road.
7. What are the specific regulations of your state and community affecting driving?

8. Explain what is meant by the principle: "The motorist who is to blame is the one who had the last clear chance to avoid the accident."

PROJECTS AND PROBLEMS

1. Make an analysis of local traffic ordinances in your community. Offer recommendations for their improvement. Indicate what changes would be made if your community adopted the "Uniform Vehicle Code" and "Model Traffic Ordinance."
2. By means of diagrams, illustrate an accident situation or a near-accident situation. Show the relationship between poor driving practices, traffic rule violations, and accidents.
3. Using models, demonstrate correct and incorrect procedures in various traffic situations.
4. Secure copies of your State Motor Vehicle Code and prepare a brief statement of the regulations that have to do with "right-of-way."
5. Make a comparison of state regulations for hand signaling in your state and surrounding states. Secure copies of the motor vehicle code from several states.
6. Debate the subject: "Uniform Traffic Laws conflict with our American policy of States' rights."

Fig. 5-20. Effective engineering facilitates traffic control and aids highway safety. (*Courtesy: "Your Car" magazine.*)

How Does Engineering Affect Traffic and Its Laws?

By providing better highways and vehicles and by improving traffic operations, engineers are constantly attempting to reduce the number of hazardous situations that confront highway users. However, it is up to us, as drivers and pedestrians, to learn to use traffic facilities with intelligence comparable to that used in their design and construction. The most carefully planned and executed engineering measure can prove a complete failure if driver and pedestrian behavior fails to meet expectations.

Automotive engineering, highway engineering, and traffic engineering make up the engineering team that attempts to apply the technical assistance of science to the construction and operation of traffic facilities. Automotive engineering is concerned primarily with the design and construction of more efficient cars; highway engineering, a profession as old as road building itself, deals with the fundamental problems of highway design and construction; and traffic engineering has as its basic function promoting the most effective operational use of existing traffic facilities. Even though the development of new major traffic facilities is primarily the task of the highway engineer, there is an increasing tendency for traffic engineers to assist in planning such projects in terms of the future operation of vehicles on these roadways.

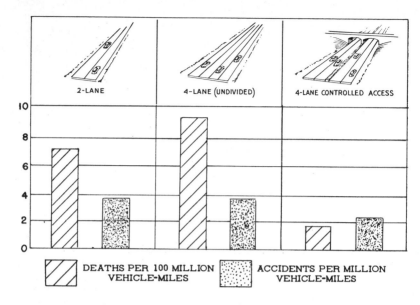

Fig. 5-21. Safety record of modern road design.

Since we have already considered the improvements that have been made in the design and construction of motor cars and highways, let us now consider what the traffic engineers are doing to promote the safer and more effective use of these existing facilities.

Fig. 5-22. How fast will our highways wear out? (*Courtesy: Scholastic Magazines.*)

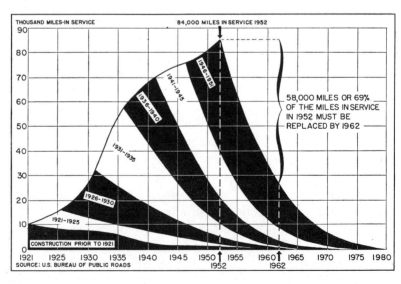

TRAFFIC ENGINEERING

Within the last decade the traffic engineer has emerged as one of the most important figures in the traffic picture. In traffic as in industry, once the plant and machines have been constructed there still remains the problem of operational control. When the operation of motor vehicles on highways first began to create problems, the police were given the responsibility for traffic operation and control. However, as the complexity of traffic increased the need for technical assistance also increased. This assistance was obtained from traffic engineers.

Fig. 5-23. Enforcement uptrend reduces accidents. (*Courtesy: FBI Cartographic Section.*)

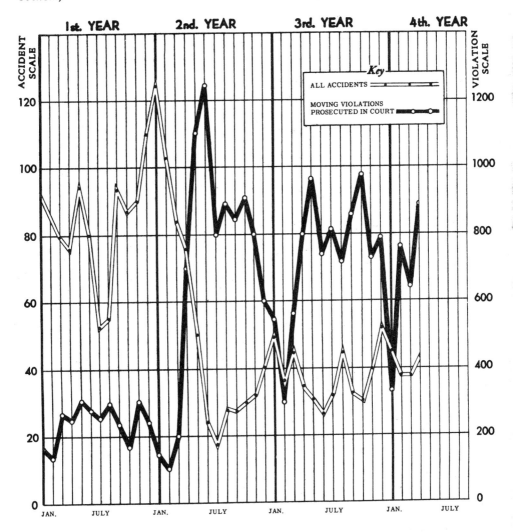

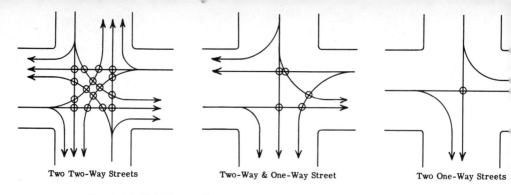

| Two Two-Way Streets | Two-Way & One-Way Street | Two One-Way Streets |

Fig. 5-24. Vehicle conflict points at intersections. (*Courtesy: FBI Cartographic Section.*)

EFFECTIVE USE OF EXISTING FACILITIES

The major problem facing most traffic engineers today is that of achieving the greatest possible use out of existing roadways. This involves the installation and operation of traffic control devices, the application of traffic control measures in accordance with the law, and structural changes at specific locations of streets and highways.

Getting the Facts

Many of the present day weaknesses in our highway transportation system can be traced directly to decisions based upon opinion rather than upon facts. Traffic engineering is based on the principle that decisions must be guided by facts. These facts are obtained through comprehensive studies and surveys dealing with such factors as the following:

Vehicle and pedestrian volume
Origins and destinations of vehicles
Speed
Accidents
Congestion and delay
Parking
Economic loss caused by existing traffic facilities

The analysis and interpretation of these facts provides the basis for deciding on the operational measures that will promote the most efficient use of existing facilities.

TRAFFIC CONTROL MEASURES

Traffic control measures are basically the application of engineering techniques and control devices to promote the safe and efficient movement of traffic. To be effective, these control measures should be used only when found needed as a result of engineering study and analysis. Improper use may readily lead to disregard of regulations or may create problems at other locations.

Regulations

Stop regulations. Traffic on through streets naturally deserves the protection provided by requiring traffic on cross-streets to come to a stop before entering. In addition, there are many intersections where traffic signals are not necessary but where stop signs are placed as a practical measure to protect both the pedestrian hand motorist from such hazardous conditions as high approach speeds and restricted visibility.

Turning regulations. Control of turning movements, by restriction or prohibition, is rapidly increasing, for turning movements result frequently in conflict, congestion, and accidents. In some instances, conditions necessitate the prohibition of turning movements during rush hours and other periods of heavy traffic. Left turns have the most serious effect on efficient operation, and in many situations, such as on high-speed, high-capacity highways, it is considered essential to prohibit them at all times. The volume of pedestrian traffic also may justify the prohibition of right turns at all times, unless a special timing interval is provided in the traffic signal for the pedestrian. U-turns are a serious hazard and a source of interference with other traffic, and are ordinarily not permitted at intersections or within business districts.

Fig. 5-25. *Special speed limits set for some locations.* Special speed zones tell you when you must go slower or may go faster than the ordinary speed limit. *(Courtesy: American Association of Motor Vehicle Administrators and National Safety Council.)*

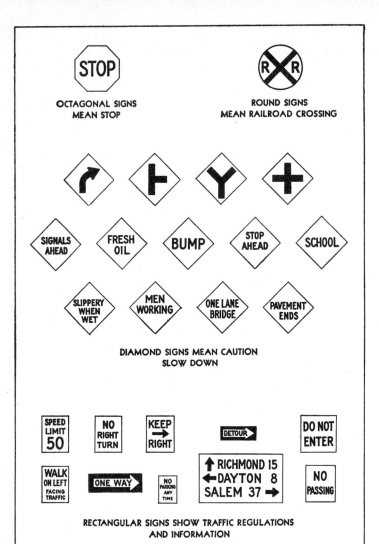

STOP

OCTAGONAL SIGNS
MEAN STOP

R✕R

ROUND SIGNS
MEAN RAILROAD CROSSING

SIGNALS AHEAD · FRESH OIL · BUMP · STOP AHEAD · SCHOOL

SLIPPERY WHEN WET · MEN WORKING · ONE LANE BRIDGE · PAVEMENT ENDS

DIAMOND SIGNS MEAN CAUTION
SLOW DOWN

SPEED LIMIT 50 · NO RIGHT TURN · KEEP RIGHT · DETOUR · DO NOT ENTER

WALK ON LEFT FACING TRAFFIC · ONE WAY · NO PARKING ANY TIME · RICHMOND 15 DAYTON 8 SALEM 37 · NO PASSING

RECTANGULAR SIGNS SHOW TRAFFIC REGULATIONS
AND INFORMATION

Fig. 5-26. Typical Standard Signs.

One-way streets. Properly planned and controlled one-way streets can greatly improve traffic conditions by increasing the street capacity, speeding traffic flow, and reducing potential conflicts at intersections. Perhaps the greatest single factor effecting the widespread adoption of one-way streets has been the need for increasing the traffic capacity of existing streets.

Speed regulations. The basic speed rule of the road is that a vehicle should never be driven at a speed greater than is reasonable and prudent under existing conditions; however, it is difficult for even an experienced driver to determine what speed is ap-

Officer Directing Both Streams
of Traffic to Proceed

Officer Signalling Traffic to Stop

Officer Signalling Traffic
from Right to Start

Officer Directing Left-turning Traffic
to Proceed while Stopping Crossing Stream

Fig. 5-27. Signals used by traffic officers. (*Courtesy: FBI Cartographic Section.*)

propriate for all conditions. Because of this, speed limits are normally set for average road and traffic conditions and for favorable weather conditions. The practice of establishing specific speed limits for certain areas is known as speed zoning. This permits safe speed limits to be established for potentially hazardous locations without unduly restricting drivers elsewhere.

Parking regulations. Undoubtedly one of the most critical traffic problems facing most cities is that of providing adequate parking facilities. Curb parking is a major cause of congestion in business districts and a frequent contributing factor in accidents. *Basically,*

EFFECT OF ENGINEERING 241

streets were developed for the purpose of moving traffic, not for storage. However, effective transportation is not only dependent on the ability to go places, but also requires parking or standing space near the destination. Therefore, it is only reasonable that where curb parking does not interfere with safe and convenient movement of traffic, it. should be permitted for a reasonable period. Where the demand for parking space has surpassed the supply, it is necessary to establish regulations to limit the length of time that any car can occupy a given space, and to increase the amount of off-street parking space.

Traffic Control Devices

Traffic control devices consist of signs, signals, and pavement markings. They are mechanical aids to traffic regulation that make regulations effective and enforceable and serve as warnings or guides for motorists and pedestrians.

Signs. Signs are placed at specific locations where special regulations apply or where certain hazards are not clearly evident. They also provide the driver with information on directions, routes, and destinations. The standard shapes and colors of these signs give the driver an idea of what is ahead even before he is close enough to read the wording. An eight-sided sign means "Stop." Diamond-shaped signs give a warning to "Slow Down"; they indicate dangerous situations, such as hills and curves. A round sign warns the driver that he is approaching a railroad crossing. Square or rectangular signs indicate special regulations and give information.

In order to make them visible at night, many signs are equipped with reflector buttons, or have coatings that illuminate the signs when they are struck by a beam from approaching headlights. Reflectors have also been installed along the sides of the road, on guard rails, at sharp curves, and similar places, to increase visibility and warn of hazards at night.

Signals. The introduction of electrical stop-and-go signals has enabled us to develop more efficient use of our street system. We are all familiar with the standard automatic stop light with three colors. While the green light is lit, traffic flows across steadily. When the green changes, the signal shifts to an intermediate amber light, which stays lit long enough to permit all closely approaching cars and pedestrians already in the street to clear the intersection. Then the red flashes, and all movement in that direc-

Fig. 5-28. Traffic engineers devised these signs to warn motorists of traffic conditions ahead. (*Courtesy: New Jersey Turnpike Commission.*)

Fig. 5-29. Adequate illumination is an important engineering factor.

Fig. 5-30. Traffic engineers are also concerned with such factors as prompt and adequate snow removal.

Fig. 5-31. Structural changes to an intersection increase the efficiency and capacity of all streets involved.

ENFORCEMENT

General Enforcement

Accident Investigation

Public Education

Checking Drivers

Pedestrian Control

Control of Movement of Traffic (Intersection)

EDUCATION

Pamphlet Distribution

Classroom Instruction

Radio

Public Meetings

Driver Instruction

ENGINEERING

Road Design

STOP KANSAS U S 56

ONE HOUR PARKING

Signs, Signals, Markings

Studies and Surveys

LEGISLATION

ADMINISTRATIVE RULES AND REGULATIONS

STATE TRAFFIC CODES

Municipal Ordinances

- Uniformity Must Be Kept Current
- Uniformity in States
- Municipal and State

CHARTED
April 15, 1946

Fig. 5-32. Basic components of a balanced traffic safety program. (*Courtesy: FBI Cartographic Section.*)

tion stops. Meanwhile, the other set of lenses, at right angles, has been giving just the opposite control orders. The standard arrangement has the red, or "stop," light at the top, the amber in the middle, and the green, or "go," signal at the bottom.

Lights flashing red, meaning *stop* and proceed when safe, or flashing yellow, meaning *caution,* often are used to call attention to dangerous intersections. The good driver takes the necessary precautions to meet the special conditions for which they give him warning.

Synchronized traffic lights are the foundation of traffic control in large cities. They allow traffic to move more quickly on the main street by giving it longer intervals on green than are given to the less important cross-flow from side streets. In some places the lights go on and off simultaneously at all points on the street. In the progressive system, now being widely adopted, the lights are timed so that a vehicle going at a normal speed can travel through without stopping. Cross-traffic moves across between waves of through traffic. In some places, because of irregular street layout, such a system is not possible.

The trend toward the use of special pedestrian signals, such as "Walk"—"Don't Walk," is rapidly gaining popularity in cities as an effective means of providing additional protection for pedestrians and enforcing pedestrian regulations.

Road Markings. Lane markings, almost unknown 15 years ago, now are almost universal; they have proved to be exceedingly valuable. Double solid lines marking the center of the pavement must not be crossed in either direction. When one of the lines is broken, however, the lines may be crossed from the broken side but not from the solid side. This system of marking no-passing zones is particularly valuable on hills and blind curves. In some states these distinctions are indicated by the use of colors.

Structural Roadway Changes

Structural changes in the roadway, varying in size from small- to large-scale projects, are engineering measures taken to increase the efficiency of the existing street and highway networks. When properly designed, they contribute generally to increased traffic capacity and efficiency. (See Figure 5-31.)

SIGNIFICANCE TO DRIVERS

Engineering has an important effect on traffic and its laws. It is attempting to make driving easier, safer, and more enjoyable. Drivers and pedestrians, however, must learn to use automobiles and highways with an intelligence comparable to that used in their design and construction. The most carefully planned and executed engineering measure can prove a complete failure if driver and pedestrian behavior fails to meet expectations.

Fig. 5-33. Failure to follow the rules, whether in basketball or in traffic, results in penalties. (*Courtesy: New York University.*)

TRAFFIC LAWS

What Are the Laws Concerning Licensing and Liability?

Since improperly driven motor cars cause property damage, injury, and death, the losses must be met in some way. Justice demands that the person responsible for an accident shall be identified and that, as far as possible, he shall be made to compensate his victims for their losses. Therefore, laws concerning licensing and liability have been established for this purpose.

Most states will not issue a license to a driver until he has proved his skill and fitness to operate a car by passing certain tests. The requirements in regard to manual skill and mental qualifications vary greatly in different states. Anyone can easily obtain, from local police headquarters or the nearest office of the State Motor Vehicle Department, a state driver's manual that gives exact information regarding procedures for applying for the privilege. Most states now require an applicant to pass successfully a test for vision, a road skill test involving basic driving maneuvers, and a test (either written or oral) covering driving rules and safe driving methods.

The purpose of driver license laws is primarily to make the driver responsible. His license to drive is not a right, but a privilege subject to forfeit if it should be found later that he is not qualified. Without driver's license laws, we should have our streets filled with drivers who are physically, mentally, or morally unfit —types of persons who never should be allowed to assume the responsibility for driving a car. Much still needs to be done in most states to raise the standards for such laws.

RESPONSIBILITY IN CASE OF ACCIDENT

Since improperly driven motor cars wreck other vehicles, damage property, and cause death or serious bodily injury, the losses must be met in some way. Justice requires that the responsibility for each accident shall be established and that, as far as possible, the persons who were at fault shall be made to pay. When a car is damaged there are repair bills; when a person is injured there are doctor's bills and hospital bills. If a working man is injured, he may lose his wages while he is being treated; the loss of an arm, a leg, or an eye may greatly reduce his earning capacity. It is only fair that whoever is responsible should make amends by paying for repairs, for the cost of medical service, for the wage loss, and for any decrease in earning ability.

LIABILITY

Both the English law and the American law require that one whose negligence is responsible for damage must pay for it. In some states, an employer who has neglected to guard dangerous machinery can be made to pay the cost of injuries sustained because of such negligence.

Liability in Automobile Accidents

The same principle applies to the actions of motorists. If they cause accidents solely by their negligence, they are liable under the law. They can be sued for the cost of repairs and for loss sustained because of bodily injury. The courts will enforce such payment. Passing another car on a curve or at the crest of a hill, driving too fast for road conditions, driving on the wrong side of the street, violating traffic signals and stop signs, cutting in, failing to give signals and parking improperly are all actions that indicate negligence.

In most states the owner of the vehicle involved in an accident shares under certain conditions the liability even if another person was driving. A company is legally responsible in all states for the operation of its vehicles by employees in line of business; in some states an automobile owner may be liable for the property damage or bodily injuries caused by the negligence of anyone who uses his automobile with his permission.

In individual cases, placing responsibility on the owner may appear unfair; it is more just, however, than allowing the victims of negligence to suffer. For example, a high school girl, using her father's car, had a serious collision. Witnesses agreed that the accident would not have happened if she had been driving at a reasonable speed, and if the car had not been overcrowded. The victims of the accident sued her father for damages and won awards totaling 25 thousand dollars. Her family had to sell their car and their home, and the savings of her parents, earned by a lifetime of hard work, were wiped out. Someone had to pay the cost of the bad driving.

The doctrine of liability is a stern one. Anyone who owns or uses a machine with such potentialities for doing damage as the motor car must realize, and must be prepared to assume, the heavy responsibilities that go with such use.

Contributory Negligence

In most states, an injured person cannot collect damages as a result of an accident if he was partly to blame; such a person is guilty of contributory negligence and loses his position of advantage. For example, in a head-on collision between two cars, each of which had been trying to pass another car near the top of a hill, neither driver could force the other to pay, for each would be partly to blame. This type of problem also involves the doctrine of "last clear chance." If you were involved in an accident resulting from another driver's negligence, and if you had the last clear chance to avoid the accident and neglected to do so, you would be held to be partially responsible. Therefore, you would probably be unable to force the other driver to pay for the damages.

The purpose of civil suits is not to determine the criminal guilt or innocence of the driver; that is handled in traffic courts or in criminal courts. Civil suits are designed to help the victims of an accident by forcing the person who caused the damages to pay for them. Hence, if your negligence is partly the cause of an accident, you cannot expect to force the other driver to pay for your losses.

Paying for Accidents

If the injured person wins a judgment for damages, the courts will enforce payment. If the person responsible has sufficient available funds, he may be able to pay without undue pressure on his finances. However, if he does not have the money in cash or is not insured, he may be forced to sell his home, his automobile, and any other of his possessions, except his clothing, household furniture, or the tools of his trade. A person who has been awarded damages wants his money; he often needs it badly. If the damages cannot be paid in a lump sum, the wages or salary of the person legally liable may be "garnisheed"—that is, the claimant will be given a legal right to a part of the wages. This right will run until the total amount due has been paid.

INSURANCE

Let us briefly consider what we may do to protect ourselves against the economic consequences of accidents and the other misfortunes that sometimes happen to the most careful and skillful drivers. Insurance will protect us against the financial costs of all of these misfortunes.

Insurance for Automobile Owners

Insurance covers two quite different types of loss: (1) a loss that falls directly on the car owner, such as the theft of the car, its injury or destruction by fire or collision, and bodily injury to the owner of the car; and (2) a loss that the owner sustains when the automobile has caused injury to another person or his property.

In the first type of insurance (discussed in Unit IV) only two parties are involved—the owner of the car and the insurer. In the second type of insurance a third party is involved—the person who sustained the property loss or the bodily injury. This type of insurance is often called "third party insurance."

Liability or "Third Party" Insurance

The two basic types of third party insurance cover bodily injury and property damage. Bodily injury liability insurance protects the automobile owner against claims for bodily injury produced by the ownership, maintenance, or use of his car. As a practical matter, this means that the insurance company will undertake either to settle the claims or defend them in court if suits are brought. It will have to pay the judgment if the case is lost, provided the amount called for is not larger than the maximum amount named in the policy. If the total of the court award is larger than the maximum named in the policy, the insurance company will have to pay the claim up to the amount so named. In a similar manner, property damage liability insurance protects the automobile owner against claims for property damage.

It should be clearly understood that bodily injury liability insurance and property damage liability insurance protect the insured person only against claims for damage that his car has done to the person or property of another. These forms of insurance do not protect the owner of a car in case of injury or loss that he may suffer.

Safety Responsibility Laws

It is highly desirable that definite provision be made so that if a person sustains an injury or property damage in an accident for which he is not to blame, he may be able to recover his losses. For this reason many states have established financial responsibility laws. While these laws vary in detail from one state to another, their general purpose is to require any owner or driver of a motor vehicle that is involved in an accident to furnish evidence of ability to pay for the damages caused. Failure to furnish such proof results in suspension of his driving privilege until he has deposited sufficient security with the proper state authority to cover the cost of claims that are likely to result from the accident, settled such claims, or has been found to be free from blame by a court. In most states, such suspension also extends to the ownership of the vehicle. Usually these laws do not apply to accidents of $50 or less, but they do apply to an accident that has caused any degree of bodily injury.

The possession of an automobile liability policy is sufficient evidence of financial responsibility under these laws. One commonly recommended coverage assures a maximum of $10,000 for bodily injury to one person, $20,000 for bodily injury to more than one person, and $5000 for property damage.

Thus, while these laws do not compel a driver or owner of a motor vehicle to carry such insurance, they protect the public against the economic consequences of an irresponsible driver and afford the driver a specific means by which he can protect his own economic security as well as his driving privilege.

Insurance as Prevention

The primary function of insurance is protection. Insurance, however, has a secondary function: prevention. Because of their ability to pool the premiums of their many policy-holders, insurance companies can undertake important work of a preventive nature that would be quite beyond the resources of a single individual; in fact, the "preventive" function of insurance may be as important as its "distributive" function. For example, in the automobile field, insurance companies are carrying on much work of a preventive nature, such as the promotion of safety education, the development of traffic engineering, work with the police on enforcement problems, and the supervision of commercial motor vehicle fleets.

This is not the place to discuss the question of insurance costs, except to the extent that they may contribute to community safety. In a sense, insurance rates are made by the public, for the premium rate depends upon the amount paid out by insurance companies in claims. This, in turn, depends (1) upon the number and severity of accidents, and (2) upon the way in which cases are treated by judges and juries. Both of these factors are within the control of the community. If a community has the courage and is willing to discipline itself by enforcing its traffic laws and educating its citizens in safe driving habits, and if its judges and juries are fair in awarding damages, that community can have low insurance rates. On the other hand, if a community has no respect for traffic laws, if it is possible for a driver to evade punishment for traffic violations, and if judges and juries make excessive or unwarranted awards for damages, that community has only itself to blame for its high accident record and high insurance rates.

IN CASE OF AN ACCIDENT

If you are involved in an accident, stop instantly, identify yourself, and do all you can to help, whether you were at fault or not. In the first confusion and shock that an accident causes, there may be a temptation to run away. But that is a cowardly act that brings both legal punishment and the contempt of all decent people. It is also stupid, because it goes far to establish that you were at fault. Your attitude and behavior at the scene of an accident will have an important effect on any legal action that may follow. The following points are guides of what to do in case of an accident:

1. The first thing to do is to take precautions to prevent other cars from crashing into the damaged cars. This is particularly important at night.

TRAFFIC LAWS

Fig. 5-34. Report accidents. If you are involved in any accident that injures anyone or does damage, you must report it. Notify the police immediately, and later send in a written report to the state motor vehicle department. (*Courtesy: American Association of Motor Vehicle Administrators and National Safety Council.*)

If possible, see that watchers are posted to slow down oncoming traffic from both directions.

2. See that injured persons are protected or helped so that no further injury will occur. Be most careful, however, not to move an injured person in such a way as to affect the injury. This is particularly important in the case of fractures. More harm is done by moving injured persons ignorantly or clumsily than simply by making them as comfortable as possible where they are lying. Do not pick up a seriously injured person and take him to a hospital in a car—it may kill him. (You should also be aware of the fact that if you take the responsibility of signing an injured person into the hospital you may be held liable for his hospital expenses.)

3. Send someone, or go yourself, to the nearest telephone and summon the state or city police, requesting an ambulance if that seems best. If it seems necessary or advisable, summon medical aid. It is better to have too much help rather than too little.

4. First aid should be applied, but only up to the point at which you are sure that you are acting properly. Be sure that even the simplest remedies are known to be correct. Arterial bleeding, occurring in spurts, is something that must be stopped, either by tourniquet or pressure on the heart side of the wound. Suffocation or monoxide poisoning in its early stages will yield to artificial respiration. Some conditions such as spasms and unconsciousness are beyond ordinary experience and should be dealt with only by specialists.

5. It is always important, whether you are directly concerned or only acting in a helpful way, to get the names and addresses of all available witnesses.

6. Stay as long as you are needed, and do not try to avoid being summoned as a witness; you have a duty to perform as a citizen.

These points are important guides, not only for accidents in which you might be involved, but also for accidents you may see or may come upon shortly afterward. In such cases if it seems probable that you can be of assistance, by all means do what you can to help. But do not stop merely out of curiosity. A traffic jam on the highway after an accident is often the cause of an additional accident and always interferes with traffic. If you find that you can be of help, it is essential that you keep cool and do not let excitement lead you into hasty and unconsidered action.

Reporting Accidents to Authorities

The legal requirements with regard to the reporting of accidents differ from state to state and from city to city. If you and your car are directly involved in an accident, you should immediately acquaint yourself with the detailed requirements and submit the necessary statements to the proper authorities. A full and intelligent report will not only fulfill your legal obligation but will contribute materially to getting the facts about the causes of accidents that are so necessary for effective preventive action. In most places, making a report to the state authorities on the required form, if there is one, or by letter, is the most important thing to be done, and in some localities that is all that is required. A report of the accident should also be made to your insurance company or agent. Many drivers make it a practice of carrying a copy of these report forms in their cars at all times.

Such a report will usually call for such information as the following:

Time and place of accident
Nature of road location and road surface
Weather conditions
Nature of accident, with all conditions given in full detail
Names and addresses of persons injured; nature of injuries
Name and address of operator; operator's license number ⎫
Name and address of owner ⎬ To be given not only for the car of the driver reporting, but, if possible, for each other car.
Make, type and registration number of car
Speed; damage sustained ⎭

SUMMARY

Motor vehicle licensing and registration laws are designed to facilitate the identification of both the driver and the car. Their basic purpose is to provide a means by which drivers and operators of motor vehicles can be held responsible for their actions and the actions of their vehicles.

Certain rules make the owner of a motor vehicle liable for damages to person or property caused by his negligence or by the negligence of anyone who uses his car with his permission. If the injured wins a judgment for damages, the court will enforce payment. Protection against the economic consequences of accidents can be had through certain kinds of automobile insurance. Insurance rates are based upon the number and severity of accidents and the amount of money paid out locally in claims. Enforcement of traffic laws and the promotion of safer driving can produce lower insurance rates by reducing the number and severity of accidents.

DISCUSSION TOPICS

1. What is the basic purpose of laws concerning driver licensing and vehicle registration?
2. What are the procedures to be followed in your state when an accident occurs? How should it be reported?
3. What are the important details to be taken care of at the scene of an accident?
4. What should a driver know about accident and liability automobile insurance?
5. What is the purpose of financial responsibility laws? How do they operate?
6. In case of an accident involving a teen-age driver, what are the legal implications of the young driver? His parents? The owner of the car?
7. What is meant by contributory negligence? Give typical examples.

PROJECTS AND PROBLEMS

1. Prepare brief dramatizations to illustrate the procedures for (1) securing a driver's license, (2) registering a motor vehicle, (3) behavior at the scene of an accident, (4) reporting an accident.
2. Interview an insurance agent and find out what the insurance rates are in your community. What factors influence these rates?
3. Write a 500-word report on the protective and preventive functions of insurance.
4. Attend a session at a court in which claims for automobile damage are being heard. Prepare a brief summary of the arguments of the plaintiff and the defendent. Do you agree with the judgment rendered by the court? Explain.

Fig. 5-35. The principles of science are being used to provide more adequate traffic law enforcement. Here a patrolman uses radar to check the speed of oncoming vehicles. (*Courtesy: New Jersey Turnpike Commission.*)

TRAFFIC LAWS

How Are Traffic Laws Enforced?

Traffic rules are designed to protect highway users and promote the smooth, efficient flow of traffic. A person's failure to observe these rules results in danger and inconvenience to others. Enforcement officers in traffic are like referees in sports: their job is to see that activities are conducted according to the rules and that no one endangers or takes unfair advantage of anyone else. The good driver, like the good athlete, observes the rules and co-operates with the officials.

In a democratic society, every privilege carries with it certain responsibilities. Anyone who claims the privilege of driving an automobile must also accept the responsibility it entails: the duty to safeguard the lives and property of his fellow citizens. Voluntary observation of traffic regulations, therefore, is the sign of a good driver and a good citizen.

CO-OPERATION WITH TRAFFIC OFFICERS

The function of traffic officers is simply to protect drivers and pedestrians, and to help them to get to their destination quickly and with safety. They are not there to hinder or to harass drivers; on the contrary, they protect motorists from those who use the highways improperly. In order to keep traffic running smoothly according to the rules, they must direct traffic, apprehend violators, issue warnings and summonses, and give assistance to drivers.

The only drivers who resent or fear traffic police are those

ENFORCEMENT OF TRAFFIC LAWS

whose irresponsible actions endanger themselves, their passengers, and everyone else on the road; every intelligent person realizes that traffic police deserve our respect and co-operation at all times.

ENFORCEMENT AGENCIES

Enforcement deals with putting into practice the codes of good driving that have been established on a basis of custom, ordinance, or law. Although in many communities there is still much to be done in the formation of such codes and their translation into law, there is still more important work to be done in effectively enforcing the laws that now exist. The principal enforcement agencies are the police, the courts, and the motor vehicle departments.

The Police

The city police operate on the streets within each community; the state police operate on the highways throughout the state. Both have the power to arrest for violations of traffic laws and regulations. The work of the police must be supplemented by courts in which the cases that develop can be tried.

Fig. 5-36. Traffic police studying advanced methods of traffic control. (Courtesy: Northwestern University Traffic Institute.)

TRAFFIC LAWS

Fig. 5-37. Teletype machines provide rapid communication between law enforcement agencies. (*Courtesy: Scholastic Magazines.*)

The effectiveness of enforcement procedures depends on many factors, including the adequacy of the size of the police force, the quality of training for the work, the means by which accidents and violations are investigated and prepared for trial, and the way in which the cases are tried. There is all the difference in the world between good and bad enforcement.

Ticket "Fixing." The most flagrant abuse in the field of enforcement, and the most serious threat to effective dealing with the traffic problem, is the setting aside of summonses for traffic law violations by authorities who have yielded to favoritism. A system of political favoritism in a community strikes at the very root of effective enforcement, for an officer will not continue to subject himself to the unpopularity that comes from making arrests if he knows that they will be "fixed."

Many communities have eliminated ticket fixing entirely, but in a few it is so rampant that it completely demoralizes the work of the enforcement agencies. Communities that have eliminated this evil testify that the job can be done if it is done completely. Authorities are only too glad to refuse such improper requests if they are assured that no one else can and will grant such favors.

ENFORCEMENT OF TRAFFIC LAWS   259

Vigorous enforcement, combined with an adequate education policy, will help achieve the goal of real enforcement, which is self-enforcement. Under such a system the traffic police will be free to confine their activities mainly to accident prevention and the control of chronic offenders.

The Courts

One of the serious problems before our courts today is over-crowding. Cases often do not come to trial for months or years after they were entered on the docket. The traffic situation is largely responsible for the condition because of the great number of cases of both minor and major importance that have to do with either accidents or traffic law violations. One way to relieve the situation in large cities is by establishing special courts to deal with traffic violations. In small cities, the cases should be tried by one specially assigned judge.

A still more serious factor in the court situation is the general laxity with which certain traffic violations have been handled in some places. The courts of the country cannot be maintained at a higher level than that indicated by the interest and concern shown by the public. The courts reflect public opinion, and they must depend for their support upon the force of public opinion. The same strengthening of moral purpose on the part of the general public that is needed in the case of ticket fixing should express itself also in the courts. Many outstanding judges, with the support of their communities, have dealt with the traffic problem in a highly forceful and intelligent way. Their work has indicated that the courts can play an important role in the control of accidents. When such an attitude becomes more universal, we shall begin to make substantial progress in traffic law enforcement.

Motor Vehicle Departments

In most states, motor vehicle departments handle the functions of issuing, revoking and suspending licenses, registering and inspecting motor vehicles, and the general supervision of traffic within the state. This agency usually carries on both enforcement and educational functions throughout the state and co-operates closely with state and local police, courts, traffic engineering departments, and driver education programs.

TRAFFIC LAWS

SUMMARY

The task of enforcing traffic laws and preventing accidents is worthy of the dynamic energies of every American. To achieve a heartening progress in accident reduction will require co-operative, continuous effort and unwavering self-enforcement of traffic laws. It demands aggressive leadership by public officials, participation by concerned private agencies, and the wholehearted support of every individual. What role will be played by the two million high school students who reach legal driving age each year? Will you play the part of the safe and responsible driver?

Fig. 5-38. This helicopter is used to supervise traffic from the air. The principles of science applied to law enforcement expedite the smooth flow of traffic. (*Courtesy: The Port of New York Authority.*)

DISCUSSION TOPICS

1. What are the major traffic law enforcement agencies operating in your state? What is the specific function of each?
2. What is meant by "self-enforcement?"
3. What is the effect of ticket fixing on adequate enforcement?
4. How does a bad court situation affect enforcement of traffic laws?
5. What is the responsibility of the general public for improving enforcement procedures?
6. What should be our future goals in the area of traffic law enforcement?
7. You are driving alone on an open highway on a clear night. The special limit is 45 mph. There are very few other cars on the road. Would it be permissible to drive at speeds in excess of 45 mph under these conditions? Explain.

PROJECTS AND PROBLEMS

1. You are judge in a traffic court. A man is brought before you charged with driving at excessive speed. The evidence against him is thin and he tells a convincing story in his own favor. However, his past record shows repeated "minor" violations of the traffic laws. Under the law you can acquit him or find him guilty and sentence him as follows: (1) fine him $100; (2) revoke or suspend his driver's license; (3) suspend sentence with a warning; (4) sentence him to the Police Department Traffic School for a course on good driving. What would you do? Write a brief statement explaining your action.
2. Set up a model traffic court and hold a mock trial of several students accused of various traffic offenses. Have evidence presented by student officers representing a model police accident investigation squad. Have the student judge explain reasons for his judgment.
3. Interview a member of your local police department. Find out what particular problems the department faces in carrying out their traffic law enforcement functions. What can drivers, pedestrians, and citizens do to help reduce these problems?
4. Visit an office of your state Motor Vehicle Department. What is their function in the total enforcement picture?
5. Plan a clinic for traffic violators. What specific recommendations would you offer to rehabilitate accident and violation repeaters?
6. Visit a traffic court session. Make a short written report on the case. What was the case about? What points of law were involved? What was the decision? Do you agree or disagree with the judgment? Explain.

SELECTED REFERENCES FOR UNIT V

1. *Accident Investigation Manual,* Northwestern University Traffic Institute, Evanston, Illinois: 1941.

2. *Digest of Motor Laws*, American Automobile Association. Washington, D. C.: annual publication.
3. *Enforcement for Traffic Safety*, National Safety Council. Chicago: 1938.
4. *Engineering for Traffic Safety*, National Safety Council. Chicago: 1937.
5. *Manual on Uniform Traffic Control Devices on Streets and Highways*, U. S. Public Roads Administration. Washington, D. C.: Government Printing Office, 1948.
6. *Model Traffic Ordinances*, U. S. Public Roads Administration. Washington, D. C.: Government Printing Office, 1946.
7. *Motor Carrier Safety Regulations of the Interstate Commerce Commission*, Interstate Commerce Commission, Washington, D. C.: Government Printing Office, 1954.
8. *Procedure for the Minimum Standard Examination for Drivers*, American Association of Motor Vehicle Administrators. Washington, D. C.: 1939.
9. *The Uniform Vehicle Code, Acts I-V*, U. S. Public Roads Administration. Washington, D. C.: Government Printing Office, 1945.

Additional information may be obtained from booklets, issued by various insurance companies; from local traffic regulations, which may be secured at your local police department; and from the state motor vehicle code, which may be obtained from the Motor Vehicle Department of the state in which you live.

UNIT 6

THE ART OF DRIVING

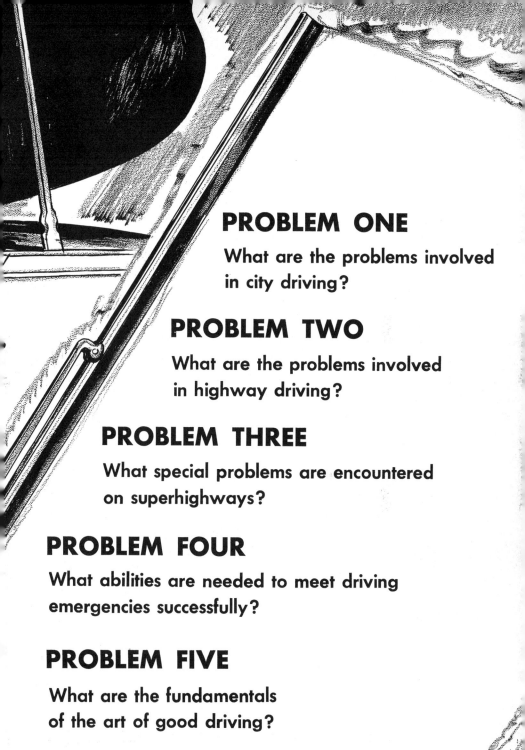

PROBLEM ONE

What are the problems involved in city driving?

PROBLEM TWO

What are the problems involved in highway driving?

PROBLEM THREE

What special problems are encountered on superhighways?

PROBLEM FOUR

What abilities are needed to meet driving emergencies successfully?

PROBLEM FIVE

What are the fundamentals of the art of good driving?

Fig. 6-1. These students have constructed a model of their village, which they use in discussing local traffic problems. (*Courtesy: Wisconsin Department of Motor Vehicles; from Brody and Stack, "Highway Safety and Driver Education," Prentice-Hall.*)

What Are the Problems Involved in City Driving?

In one mile of maneuvering through the kaleidoscopic pattern of vehicles and pedestrians in city traffic you may be called upon to make as many decisions and responses as in 80 miles of driving on the open road. City driving requires constant attention to the actions of others and a readiness for instant responses. It requires drivers to control their speed and position so that they blend smoothly and co-operatively into the stream of traffic.

An experienced driver was about to embark upon a strange ride. He had instructions from the mayor to drive through the center of the city and on to the city limits, and to pay no attention to speed laws or other traffic regulations. The only restriction on his driving was that he was not to injure anybody. Directly behind him, in another car, was another experienced driver with instructions to follow the same course, but to observe all traffic regulations and rules of traffic courtesy. Both cars started out at the same time over the six-mile course. The speeder beat the safe driver by only a little more than three minutes!

This experiment has been duplicated in a number of cities. The results always have been similar—the time gained has been in no case enough to justify endangering life, limb, and property. Speed and right-of-way violations, nevertheless, remain the traffic errors that are reported most frequently in urban districts.

PROBLEMS OF CITY DRIVING 267

DRIVING HAZARDS MULTIPLIED

The hazards and the traffic control devices that the city driver must expect to meet are similar to those encountered on open highways, but they are encountered more frequently. You may drive for miles in the country without coming to an intersection or a traffic signal; in the city you will meet them every few hundred feet. On open highways, pedestrians are few and far between; in the city, the streets swarm with them. City traffic is heavier and more unpredictable in its movement than rural traffic. Masses of buildings, vehicles moving almost bumper to bumper and fender to fender, and trees and hedges growing close to the curb in residential districts reduce visibility in cities far more than is usual in the country. The frequent starting and stopping, the honking of horns, the distractions of advertising signs and shop windows, along with a multitude of other distracting influences combine to produce a confusing and ever-changing kaleidoscope of situations that call for many split-second decisions.

These conditions, plus insufficient attention, errors of judgment, or indecision on the part of both drivers and pedestrians, are contributing causes of practically all traffic accidents that occur in cities. This means that city drivers must be constantly alert and must anticipate what may happen and plan ahead. In other words, a good driver will observe potential dangers and will attempt to prevent them from developing into actual hazards.

DRIVING IN TRAFFIC

Safe Driving Speeds

The stream of city traffic moves with considerable regularity, and it will be necessary for you to become a part of the stream. Speeds on city streets are legally restricted, and there are usually enough signs, signals, and markings to inform the observant driver about the proper speed, when he should slow down or stop, and when he should exercise particular caution. A good driver who conforms to the speed of the majority of cars will experience little annoyance from drivers cutting in ahead of him or from those impatiently honking their horns for him to move on.

Lane Position

If you are going some distance you may find it more satisfactory to keep as close as possible to the center of the street. Usu-

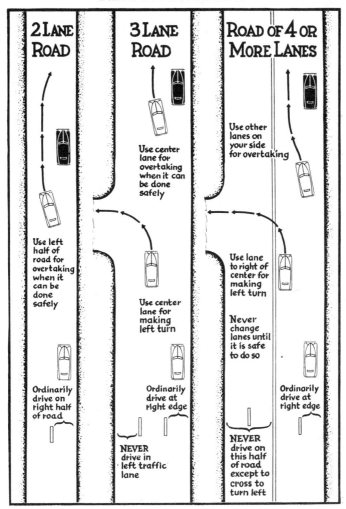

Fig. 6-2. (*Courtesy: American Association of Motor Vehicle Administrators and National Safety Council.*)

ally traffic moves faster and more smoothly here, and there is better visibility and less chance of encountering obstructions to progress. It is important in cities to observe the "one-lane habit," particularly on streets where considerable speed is allowed. Hand, mechanical, and position-signaling should be used in shifting from one lane to another. It is particularly important to be in the proper lane at intersections.

PROBLEMS OF CITY DRIVING 269

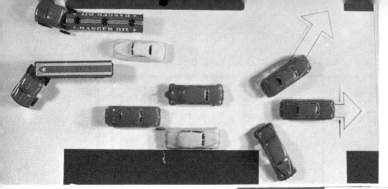

Fig. 6-3. Always get into the proper lane before reaching an intersection.

Fig. 6-4. "A" is driving east on the avenue. Wishing to make a left turn, he gives the signal for the turn and proceeds to make it. "B," who is driving west on the avenue at 20 miles per hour, crashes into "A." Who is at fault? Which laws apply?

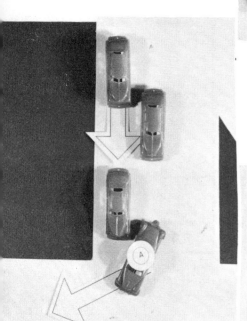

Fig. 6-5. By attempting a right turn from the center lane, "A" sets up an accident situation that may involve several cars.

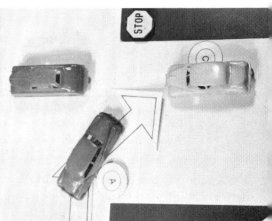

Fig. 6-6. Always begin and complete your turn in the proper lane. In the picture above, "A" has made the turn too wide and is in danger of striking "C."

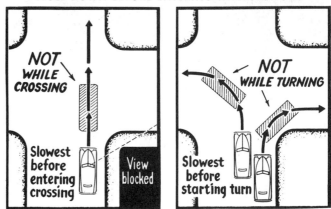

Fig. 6-7. (Courtesy: American Association of Motor Vehicle Administrators and National Safety Council.)

Procedure at Intersections

Most of what has been said about intersections in the section on man-made traffic rules applies particularly to city driving, where there are numerous intersections. Many of these intersections are controlled by traffic lights or by stop signs, but there still remains a considerable problem, partly because of reduced visibility due to buildings, parked cars, and the added distractions of the busy street scene.

Always reduce speed when approaching an intersection. Accidents at city intersections often involve cars going not faster than 25 miles per hour. When you approach an intersection with cars parked on your right, or where hedges, buildings, or other obstructions block your view of a cross street, it is necessary to slow down to less than 25 miles per hour and, in some cases, to stop.

Reduce speed sufficiently when approaching intersections so that you will be able to stop in time to avoid striking any person or vehicle that may enter your path without warning. Be on the alert for cars on your right, which may abruptly turn left across your path from the wrong lane; for vehicles on the intersecting street that may continue to cross even after you have the "go" signal; for those on either side that may cut in ahead of you by "beating the light" or accelerating excessively; and for pedestrians who may cross against the signal, outside the crosswalk lines, or diagonally. Be prepared to avoid accidents that may result from any thoughtless, reckless, or illegal act of any driver, pedestrian, or bicyclist using the intersection.

PROBLEMS OF CITY DRIVING   271

Fig. 6-8. Drivers who enter or leave their cars from the side next to traffic may cause you trouble if you drive too close to parked cars. (Courtesy: Allentown (Pa.) "Call Chronicle.")

Stop Before Crosswalks

When bringing your car to a stop, whether or not there are pedestrian crosswalk lines, stop so that your car does not obstruct the pedestrian crossing space; the front bumper of your car should not enter the crosswalk area. This practice is a courtesy to the pedestrian and is an indication of a good driver.

Passing on the Right

Although the general rule in overtaking another car is to pass on the left, there are occasions when this rule is not applicable. When two or more lanes of traffic are moving in the same direction, there doubtless will be times when the cars in the right-hand lane will move faster than those in the left. When a car is in the act of making a turn left, other vehicles may pass it on the right. Street cars must be passed on the right, except on one-way streets.

Parking Places

Observe parking regulations. Usually, you will find them clearly indicated along city streets. Parking limits often vary; for example, you may find one-hour parking on one street, while on

Fig. 6-9. Because he thoughtlessly pulled away from the curb without looking or signaling, the driver of car "A" has interfered with the flow of traffic and set up a possible accident situation.

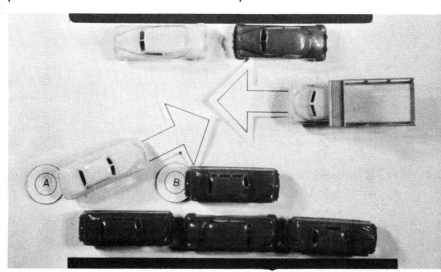

Fig. 6-10. Cars parked at an intersection can seriously reduce a driver's field of vision.

Fig. 6-11. Double parking not only causes congestion but sets up accidents. Car "B" has double parked, blocking the right lane. As a result car "A" is forced to move around it into the path of the oncoming truck. Always be sure the way is clear before you proceed around an obstacle like a double-parked vehicle.

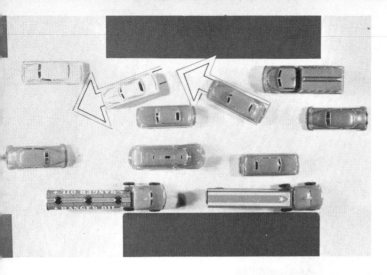

Fig. 6-12. Weaving is a dangerous type of traffic behavior. It interferes with the smooth flow of traffic, sets up possible accident situations, and gains very little for the weaver in terms of time and distance.

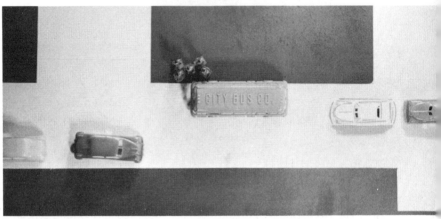

Fig. 6-13. Stop when the school bus stops, and proceed only after the school bus has pulled away and you are sure the road is clear.

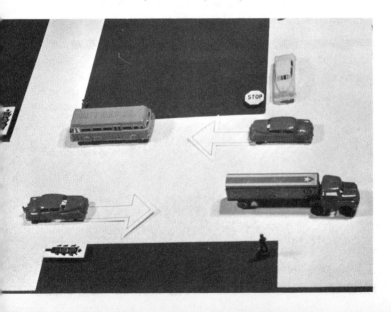

Fig. 6-14. Bus and street car passengers can present a driver with many problems unless he is cautious.

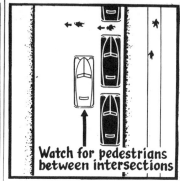

Fig. 6-15. (Courtesy: American Association of Motor Vehicle Administrators and National Safety Council.)

the next street parking may be limited to 15 minutes. Park no closer than the prescribed distances from hydrants, intersections, firehouses, and theater and other public building entrances. Park in the manner called for by the regulations or indicated by the painted markings. Careless drivers sometimes park several feet from the curb. This is not only illegal, but it also constitutes a serious traffic hazard.

Pedestrians

A pedestrian stepping into the street from between parked cars is one of the most serious of city traffic hazards. A good driver, when passing parked cars, is conscious of this potential hazard and meets it in three ways: first, by driving more slowly when in the lane near the curb; second, by increased attention; and third, by driving as much toward the center of the street as traffic will permit. A driver who has taught himself to watch for early clues and signs of danger can often anticipate such movements by pedestrians when they start across the sidewalk and before they have stepped from between the parked cars.

Bicyclists

Bicyclists often constitute a considerable part of the traffic stream. They, too, have their rights and their responsibilities. It is important that the problems of the bicyclist be understood by the motorist. (See Unit VII, Problem Two.)

Children at Play

Always slow down when you see young children playing on the sidewalks or near the street. Children often are impulsive; they act first and think afterwards. If a ball rolls into the street, a child may dart thoughtlessly after it; a child who is being chased by another may, in a similar way, run in front of your

Fig. 6-16. Children are often an over-looked hazard in residential areas.

car. In residential districts, in the vicinity of schools and playgrounds, after school hours and during lunch and recess periods, throughout the vacation days—in fact, wherever and whenever children are likely to be on or near the street, protect them by reducing your speed and by driving with increased vigilance.

Other Aids for City Driving

Starting and stopping consumes more gasoline than driving at a constant speed. In city traffic, it will be necessary for you to start and stop and vary your speed more often than is necessary on the open highway. Nevertheless, try to regulate your driving so that you will reduce the changes in speed to a minimum. In addition to saving gasoline, you will find that it will help you in anticipating traffic situations. Your driving will probably become both smoother and safer.

Ambulances, fire engines, and police cars have the right of way over all traffic, regardless of what the traffic signals may indicate. Pull over to the curb or to the extreme right of the street, and permit them to pass. Funerals also have the right of way. Do not attempt to drive through a funeral procession as it is crossing a street. Also, do not pass or cut into a funeral procession. Parades usually are held under a special permit, which grants them the right of way.

Do not pass a stopped trolley car or a bus that is discharging or loading passengers where there is no safety or loading zone. Before proceeding, wait until passengers have been discharged or taken on, the doors have closed, and the vehicle is in motion. Regulations vary as to the distance you should stop behind the doors of a bus or trolley, but a good rule is to stop far enough behind so that the front bumper of your car is to the rear of the public conveyance. Some municipalities require you to stop farther behind.

Be on the alert for one-way streets. They are always posted, and recognizing them in advance saves the difficulty and humiliation of having to turn around in the street, paying a fine, or having an accident.

SUMMARY

City traffic is heavier and more unpredictable than rural traffic. Consequently, the driver must expect to meet special hazards, which arise with considerable frequency. To be an expert at city driving, one must exercise constant attention and alertness to anticipate city traffic hazards and prevent them from developing into accidents.

DISCUSSION TOPICS

1. What special hazards are peculiar to city driving?
2. How should a driver adjust himself to "allowable" speed and "actual" speed of city traffic?
3. What factors are involved in properly entering a street?
4. How does a good driver enter, drive on, and leave a street that has lane markings?
5. What driving situations exist at intersections? How does a good driver meet each of these?
6. What are the benefits of driving at a smooth, steady pace?
7. What hazards are caused by cars parked along the curb?
8. What passing problems are common in city driving?
9. What problems do pedestrians present in city traffic?
10. What is meant by the phrase "driving according to conditions"?

PROJECTS AND PROBLEMS

1. Draw a rough map of the neighborhood surrounding your home, showing streets, roads, highways, and other pertinent elements. Select several locations, and indicate the hazards at each point. Indicate how you would regulate your speed and position when driving at each of these points. Diagram your maneuver somewhat as you would diagram a basketball play.
2. Draw simple diagrams to illustrate five traffic situations in city driving that demand alertness and skill. Explain how these qualities can insure safety in each situation. Show what you would look for and how you would react in each situation.
3. Draw a diagram of an accident that happened in your community. Describe all of the important factors involved. What laws were broken? What good driving techniques were neglected? What hazards were involved? Who was basically at fault? Who had the last clear chance?

Fig. 6-17. A common fault of many drivers is to follow too closely the vehicle ahead. Tragedies like this one occur all too often on the highway.

THE ART OF DRIVING

What Are the Problems Involved in Highway Driving?

Driving on the open road is not as easy and care-free as it may appear to the inexperienced driver. Highway accidents account for a large percentage of our traffic fatalities. On the highway, making judgments and taking action calls for ready alertness, split-second timing, and precise control. Only experience brings proficiency in highway driving, but knowledge of common highway situations and of the measures that can be taken to meet them will help the beginning driver to establish confidence and skill on the highway.

Accident statistics show us that most rural accidents do not occur on winding or hilly roads, but on *straight* roads! Driving on the open road, simple as it may seem, presents a number of serious hazards. The good driver makes it his business to anticipate and to avoid these whenever possible.

DRIVING ON HIGHWAYS

Safe Following Distances

Open highway driving poses a very difficult problem: How closely should you follow the car in front of you? If you get too close and the car ahead of you stops suddenly, it is probable that not only your car and the car in front of you will collide, but that

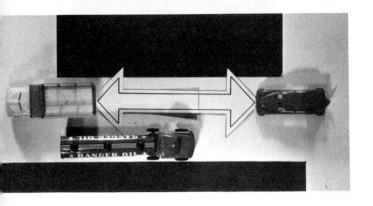

Fig. 6-18. Whenever possible, allow a minimum following distance of one car length for every ten miles per hour of speed.

the cars behind will also be involved in a series of crashes. The cars moving in the opposite direction might also become involved, and a very serious accident could result. On the other hand, if you stay too far behind, you will have cars continually passing and cutting in ahead of you. This means you will have to keep dropping still farther back.

Experience seems to indicate that the following procedure, under normal conditions, provides a satisfactory compromise: allow at least one car length between you and the car ahead for every ten miles per hour of speed; double it if the road is wet, and double it again if the road is icy. When road conditions are favorable, and traffic is moving at 30 miles an hour, keep at least three car lengths (perhaps 60 feet) behind the car in front; at 40 miles an hour, at least four car lengths (about 80 feet); at 50 miles an hour, at least five car lengths (approximately 100 feet). This procedure, however, is no assurance that the distance is sufficient, for under some conditions if the car in front of you were to stop suddenly you would not be able to stop without striking it. If your following distances are too much greater, however, you will undoubtedly find cars cutting in ahead of you.

Passing Other Cars

Ordinarily a driver must adjust his speed to blend with the normal flow of traffic. There are times, however, when it becomes necessary to pass other vehicles, and if passing is not done correctly it can lead to trouble. Most passing is done to the *left* of the vehicle or vehicles ahead. *Never pass on the right unless such passing is specifically permitted, as is the case on some multiple-lane highways.*

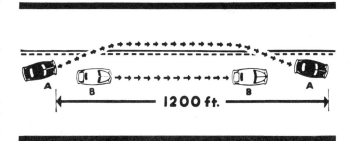

Fig. 6-19. All passing distance figures given here assume a car length of 20 feet, and that the passing car turns out one car length ahead of the slower car for every 10 mph of its speed. Thus a car going 50 mph turns *out* five car lengths behind and *in* five car lengths ahead of the car it is passing. (*Courtesy: American Association of State Highway Officials.*)

A major factor to remember when passing is that your car and the vehicle you wish to pass are moving at a speed that will carry both of them forward a considerable distance before you can complete your maneuver and can return to your proper lane. Thus, on all but multiple-lane highways, where certain lanes are reserved for passing, you will have to drive a considerable distance on the side of the road used by cars that are traveling in the opposite direction.

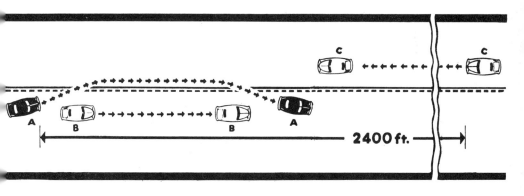

Fig. 6-20. Put an oncoming car in the picture and you need much more clear road to pass. In this situation, car A traveling at 50 mph, car B at 40 mph, and car C at 50 mph. While car A travels the 1200 feet required to pass car B, car C also travels 1200 feet. Therefore, if the passing action is to be completed safely, cars A and C must be 2400 feet apart when the action begins. (*Courtesy: American Association of State Highway Officials.*)

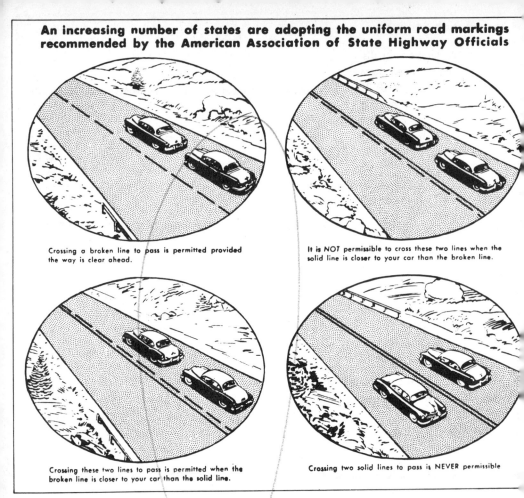

Crossing a broken line to pass is permitted provided the way is clear ahead.

It is NOT permissible to cross these two lines when the solid line is closer to your car than the broken line.

Crossing these two lines to pass is permitted when the broken line is closer to your car than the solid line.

Crossing two solid lines to pass is NEVER permissible

Fig. 6-21. (Courtesy: American Association of State Highway Officials.)

When Passing Is Prohibited

There are four particular situations in which passing is prohibited: at an intersection, on an upgrade just below the crest of a hill, on a curve, and at a railroad crossing. When you attempt to overtake and pass another car at any one of these points you are creating a potential accident situation. The vehicle approaching may not be there *this* time to meet you, but the law of averages says that it *will* be there some day! You are not giving the other driver a fair chance for his life. You are not giving yourself a chance, either. You are gambling with sudden death: you are betting your own life and the lives of two other drivers against fifteen seconds of time!

HILLS

CURVES

Fig. 6-22. Do not overtake and pass at these locations. (Courtesy: American Association of Motor Vehicle Administrators and National Safety Council.)

RAILROADS

INTERSECTIONS

Fig. 6-23. An improper pass on the gridiron may result in an interception. An improper pass on the highway may result in a head-on collision.

PROBLEMS OF HIGHWAY DRIVING   283

Fig. 6-24. The car on the left was passing on a curve.

Courtesy in Passing

Because you will frequently be passed by other drivers, you should remember that the distance a car passing you must travel on the left-hand side of the road is largely determined by the speed of your own car. Guard against being forced off the road or sideswiped by passing cars whose drivers have misjudged distances and speeds for passing. Slow down the instant you see that it is necessary! It makes no difference whether the driver who is attempting to pass is in the wrong, or even if he is a "road hog." *It is to your interest to avoid an accident, no matter who is at fault.* Slow down, and give the other driver room to cut in ahead of you. Or, if he suddenly drops back, increase your speed and give him the opportunity to fall into line behind you. Never race a car that is attempting to pass. Let it pass. Keep well to the right-hand side of the road when other cars are passing. This is neither the time nor the place to try to teach a person a lesson!

Passing a "Slow-Poke"

You will find that some drivers have the impression that the slowest one is always the safest. Some like to drive so slowly that they impede the movement of the majority of drivers who are anxious to get to their destination within a reasonable period of time. A "slow-poke" frequently holds up a long line of cars, and at

284   THE ART OF DRIVING

the first opportunity they crowd past him in an almost continuous stream. This is a particularly dangerous situation, partially because people under these conditions are likely to be irritated, partly because it is difficult in such a situation to get a clear view of the road, and partly because it is difficult to get back into line when necessary. The best procedure is to wait until the cars ahead of you have passed, and then to pass at the first favorable opportunity after your car has become first in line behind the slow-moving car. Do not pass, however, when it is not safe, *no matter how long you have to wait!*

Pointers on Passing

The "eager beaver" driver rides right on the tail of the car he is trying to pass, waiting for a gap in oncoming traffic. As soon as the gap appears, he makes a run for it. But in this position he is at a great disadvantage. He is so close that he cannot see clearly ahead without pulling out dangerously far to the left. He is also in danger of a rear-end collision should the car in front suddenly slow down, and he has insufficient distance to pick up speed and get a running start when the passing opportunity presents itself. The correct way is to hold back at normal following distance where you can see better, then pick up speed when the safe moment arrives.

Fig. 6-25. Skillful passing requires anticipating what "the other driver" is going to do, whether he is in front or in the rear.

Another error that some drivers make is that they fail to signal their intention to pass. If a driver knows that he is about to be passed, he is less likely to pull over in front of you or otherwise interfere with your passing maneuver. Sounding the horn or, at night, blinking the lights serves warning of your intention to pass.

The expert driver is also cautious about moving into a narrow slot between two other vehicles. It is unwise, even on three- or four-lane roads, to pass a vehicle when an oncoming car is opposite. This would put you in the middle, when you can move neither left nor right if either car moves over. If you make a mistake and find yourself in this dangerous situation, speed up and complete the passing maneuver before the oncoming car reaches the passing area, or, if you can do so without interfering with the cars behind you, slow down and wait for the approaching car to pass.

Also beware of a car passing a car coming toward you. Slow down so that, if he is unable to pass successfully, he will not involve you in an accident.

When a driver ahead of you starts to pass, never follow right behind him and pass at the same time. There may be time for only one car to pass successfully, and you will be trapped in the center of the road: you have no time to pass, and it's too late to go back. Always wait until the car ahead completes its pass before you begin.

The good driver always avoids being "trapped" by other vehicles. It has been said that you take your life in your hands when you drive. It is worse when you pass another vehicle—in a sense you put your life and the lives of your passengers in the hands of the drivers of the vehicles in front of you.

One-Lane Habit

Develop the habit of staying in the same lane as far as possible. Weaving in traffic is one of the most disagreeable of all practices, and it is a sign of a poor driver. People will recognize your "rights" if you stay in your lane, but they also, in turn, have a right to expect you to stay in your lane unless you have a good reason for doing otherwise.

Changing Lanes

When it is necessary to change position from one side of the road to the other, or from lane to lane on multiple-lane highways,

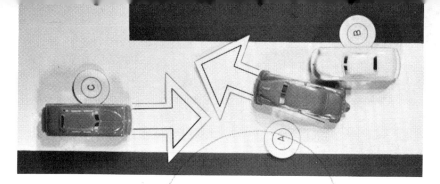

Fig. 6-26. A smart driver allows himself plenty of room in which to pass. When planning to pass, "A" underestimated the distance of oncoming car "C." Now "B" or "C" must make room for him if "A" is to get out of the spot safely.

Fig. 6-27. When driving on the highway, it is unwise to pass a car that is passing a vehicle parked along the roadside. As the diagram at right indicates, if parked car "C" pulls out into the roadway, car "A" will be forced to move to the left, and car "B," which is passing car "A," will be forced into the ditch.

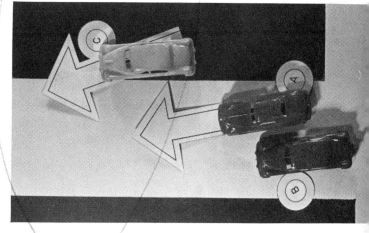

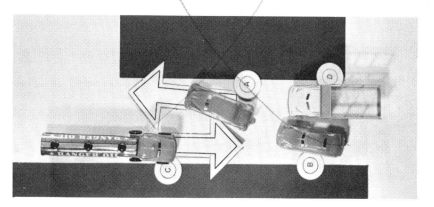

Fig. 6-28. Always allow the car ahead to complete its pass before you begin yours. Here car "B" is trapped because it has followed car "A" too closely. In order to avoid a collision, trucks "C" and "D" must make room for it.

PROBLEMS OF HIGHWAY DRIVING

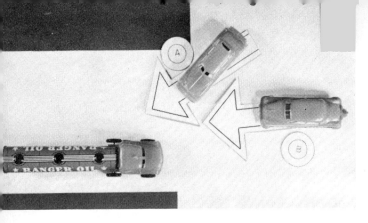

always glance in the rear-view mirror and look quickly from side to side to determine whether you can make the shift in position without interfering with the movement of traffic behind you and to the sides. If you make a sudden shift of position without warning, you may force cars approaching from behind to swerve sharply to avoid striking you. Signal your intention clearly by using hand signals and mechanical signals as well as by the gradual shift of position of the car. By "inching" gradually toward the position you intend to occupy, drivers will recognize your intention and either allow you sufficient space to complete the maneuver or signal to caution you.

Intersections

The procedure at highway intersections is discussed in the problem on Rules of the Road. Most of the accidents at intersections are caused either by failure to grant the right of way or by failure to agree on who has the right of way. *Be prepared to grant the right-of-way to other drivers, even if they are in the wrong.* An intersection is not a good place for demonstrating your rights. If you have an accident, it's little consolation to know that you had the right of way.

Speed should be sufficiently reduced at intersections to provide for all possibilities. When cruising at 40 or 50 miles an hour, you will be in a "tight spot" if a car from a side road pulls out in front of you at a slow speed. If you are too close you may not be able to stop, and you may not be able to pass to the left if an oncoming car is near; you may be forced into the right-hand ditch! When you see a car on a side road, slow down. Do not assume that the driver will wait for you to pass the intersection before entering the highway. Take special care also when approaching and passing cars that have stopped on the side of the highway or on the

THE ART OF DRIVING

shoulder. Cars coming from driveways of gasoline stations, snack bars, motels, and the like can also cause trouble for the faster-moving vehicle on the highway.

Railroad Grade Crossings

It is more difficult to stop a train than it is to stop an automobile. For this reason, the train has the right of way at grade crossings. It is both a legal and a social obligation on the part of the driver to follow the advice that is given on thousands of railroad intersection signs: "STOP–LOOK–LISTEN." The tracks are often visible for a long distance in each direction, and in such cases bringing the car to a halt may not be necessary. Nevertheless, it is so important to be sure that no train is approaching before crossing railroad tracks that many commercial truck and bus companies insist that their drivers come to a stop before crossing. Some states require all motor vehicles to stop before crossing railroad tracks. Even if your state does not, however, always reduce speed to less than 15 miles per hour, look left, then right, and then left, and cross tracks only if you are *sure* that a train is not approaching. If you have to stop while a train is passing, do not drive onto the tracks until it has passed sufficiently far beyond the intersection for you to make certain that another train is not approaching on another track, particularly from the opposite direction. Many fatalities have been caused, not by the first train, but by a second train that was not seen. The sound of a passing train will frequently make it difficult to hear either the noise or the bell or whistle of another train. If there are several parallel tracks, if the track bed is irregular, or if you must drive up a grade to enter upon or cross the tracks, it is advisable to shift into a *lower* gear to ensure a greater margin of pulling power until you get clear of the tracks.

Fig. 6-30. Railroad crossings. Watch for the double track. The train which has just passed may hide one just coming. Railroad crossings are dangerous places. Look both ways.

WATCH FOR THE DOUBLE TRACK

LOOK BOTH WAYS AT GRADE CROSSINGS

Many grade crossings are not adequately provided with warning signs sufficiently in advance of the crossing to permit a car traveling at high speed to stop before reaching the crossing. This is another good reason for not speeding. Remember, a train will seldom leave the tracks to hit you; therefore, it is up to you. Do not set yourself up for an accident.

Never follow a line of cars over a railroad crossing until you have determined that there is sufficient space on the other side of the tracks for your car to stop without projecting onto the tracks. There are instances on record where a motorist was wedged between a line of cars and was unable to move backward or forward when a train approached, thus becoming involved in a serious accident.

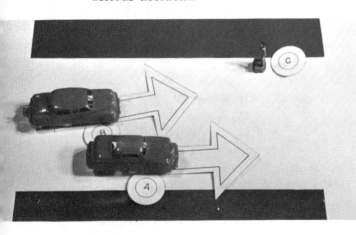

Fig. 6-31. Smart drivers do not pass a vehicle on the highway if there is a pedestrian walking along the roadside. If car "A" moves to the left, or pedestrian "C" walks into the roadway, car "B" will be set up for an accident.

Pedestrians

The pedestrian hazard on highways, especially at night, is particularly important, because there are usually neither sidewalks nor adequate shoulders along country roads. Each day many children walk to and from schools located on open highways. A good driver slows down whenever he sees a small child walking along the shoulder of the highway. He also moves to the left if traffic permits. He knows that he must be ready to stop or swerve should the child run out in front of him unexpectedly.

Good drivers never overtake and pass a vehicle on the open highway if there is a pedestrian on the edge or the shoulder of the road. The pedestrian's presence eliminates the passer's "dodging" area, should the car being passed move toward the left.

THE ART OF DRIVING

Moreover, if the pedestrian steps onto the pavement, the driver often is faced with the problem of hitting him or sideswiping the car being passed.

ROUTE NUMBERS AND MAPS

All of the more modern highways are numbered; they form part of an interrelated system of state and Federal routes. Such routes are marked at frequent intervals; especially at cross roads and corners by distinctive signs. The standard Federal marker is a shield. These Federal routes form the more important interstate highways.

Transferred to maps, these route numbers make it easy for the motorist who is planning a long trip into unfamiliar territory to select the shortest and best roads. When a driver can read and understand a road map, he is in a better position to travel to a desired point over the shortest and best route available under existing conditions. He can also determine easily the distances from place to place by adding the mileage numbers shown along a route. Another aid that the map provides is a classification of highways. Lines shown in various colors or widths usually indicate whether the road is connecting, secondary, or main. Types of roads such as "improved," "all-weather," hard-surfaced or paved, or "under construction" are symbolized in the map legend. A number within a shield is used to show United States, or Federal routes, while state routes, as well as some county roads, are generally indicated by a number within a circle or diamond.

Perhaps the best way in which to become familiar with the makeup and use of maps is to obtain one and study it carefully. State highway departments, civic associations, insurance companies, automobile clubs, oil companies, and other agencies prepare and distribute free road maps. A good technique is to use a map to plan an actual or imaginary trip from one point to another. In so doing, many of the "mysteries" about road maps will disappear. The letters and numbers on the margins of the map are a great help in determining the location of particular places and distances. Most road maps are made so that the top is due north and the right is east.

It is best for you to prepare your road map before starting a trip, by drawing a heavy line over your intended route from point of departure to destination. Towns, mileage and route numbers should be placed on a small card for check points while en route. Never try to look at a road map while driving. The best and safest practice is to stop off the highway and study your road map or ask directions if in doubt.

SUMMARY

Driving on the open highway presents special problems that the new driver will want to master; for example, how to follow safely behind and, at the proper time, pass the car ahead without unnecessary risk. Good observation and foresight are necessary because the widths of highways vary constantly, road intersections present potential hazards, railroad grade crossings are to be expected, and improperly parked cars present a problem. Constant attention to the operation of the car is of first importance. *Good drivers are not taken by surprise.* They "size up" traffic conditions as far ahead as visibility permits, *anticipate* trouble at all times, and drive according to roadway, weather, and traffic conditions.

Fig. 6-32. This boy (inset) was a passenger in the car at the left. He paid the price of a moment's carelessness. (*Courtesy: Allentown (Pa.) "Call-Chronicle."*)

DISCUSSION TOPICS

1. What is meant by "safe following distance?"
2. What are the hazards involved in passing other cars?
3. When is passing prohibited?
4. Describe the typical driving behavior of a motorist who uses good observation and foresight. Why do accidents seldom occur to this type of driver?
5. What problems are involved in driving on curves? What driving practices must be used because of centrifugal force and momentum? Explain.
6. What dangers are created by a car that is moving much more slowly than all other cars on the highway?
7. How should a driver approach railroad crossings? Intersections?
8. What are the conditions that determine safe speed?
9. Why are blow-outs dangerous at high speeds?
10. What problems do pedestrians present for the highway driver?

PROJECTS AND PROBLEMS

1. Prepare a list of the mistakes which drivers commonly make on the highways. Explain the ways in which you may avoid accidents that may result from these mistakes. Illustrate with simple diagrams.
2. Select a highway in your community where traffic is heavy. Observe the driving practices of the motorists. Summarize your findings, noting the type and frequency of sound and unsound practices you observed.
3. Diagram safe and unsafe passing maneuvers common to highway driving. Explain the details of each.
4. Diagram the proper method of entering and leaving a high-speed highway.
5. What special problems are encountered on a highway at night, in rain, snow, and fog, or in icy weather? List these problems, and offer possible solutions.
6. Write an essay explaining the factors a driver should consider in deciding upon a reasonable speed for highway driving. List these factors in order of importance, and show how they influence driving.
7. Determine what proportion of rural traffic fatalities in your state occurs on curves, on straight roads, on hillcrests, and in passing. Summarize your findings. Explain to the class the driving faults or violations that are most often involved in such accidents.

Fig. 6-33. A quick stop on a high-speed highway can involve many drivers in an accident, as evidenced by this scene following a "chain-reaction" smashup on New York's West Side Highway.

THE ART OF DRIVING

What Special Problems Are Encountered on Superhighways?

Driving on superhighways could be one of the most convenient and enjoyable kinds of driving, yet it has become characterized by breakneck speeds, reckless weaving, and hence constant peril. The smooth, straight, seemingly endless highway tempts the driver to push his car at speeds which are beyond his human limitations to control. The knit brow and squinting stare on the face of the typical turnpike driver bears testimony to the fact that the design of the car and the highway are outgrowing the capabilities of their human users. The driver must become aware of this and related problems and develop the restraint and intelligence to use these technological developments in the manner for which they were designed.

Just as aviation authorities are aware of the fact that jet planes are superior to pilots in their ability to perform, traffic authorities are beginning to recognize that superhighways and high-speed roads have outgrown the capabilities of drivers. Modern expressways were designed for convenient, rapid travel between various sections of the country. Although designed to be accident-proof, the fact is that certain kinds of accidents—rear-end collisions, for example—occur more frequently on turnpikes than on other roads. Furthermore, the high speed that characterizes turnpike driving greatly increases the severity of these accidents.

Fig. 6-34. Special abilities are needed for turnpike and superhighway driving. (*Courtesy: General Motors Corporation.*)

REASONS FOR TURNPIKE ACCIDENTS

Unawareness of Potential Accident Situations

One important reason why drivers become involved in turnpike accidents is that many are lulled into a false sense of security when they are operating on a superhighway. They tend to reason that anything "super" must be better than ordinary, and are unaware of the fact that superhighways actually increase the number and seriousness of certain types of accidents.

As he speeds over the straight, flat, divided highway, a driver becomes more convinced that accidents are impossible. He fails to realize that at speeds over 50 miles an hour his total stopping distance may be more than the length of a football field! The two or three seconds it takes him to recognize an emergency in the making may be just enough to make it impossible for him to avoid an accident.

Velocitization and High-Speed Hypnosis

The American Petroleum Institute in New York has coined

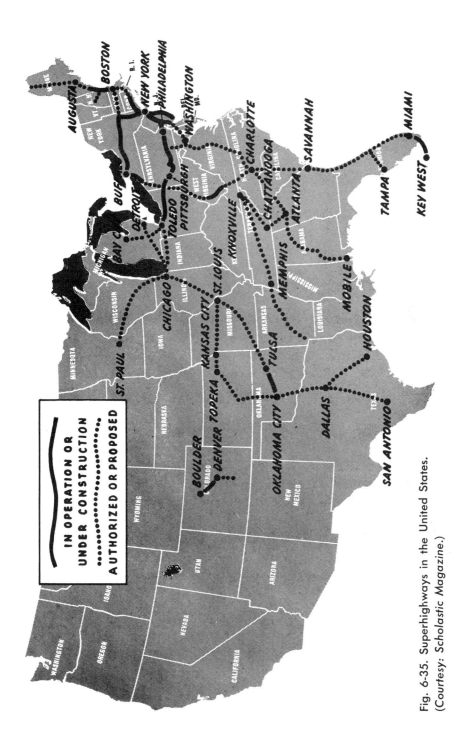

Fig. 6-35. Superhighways in the United States.
(Courtesy: Scholastic Magazine.)

some new words, *velocitization* and *high-speed hypnosis,* to describe the effects of high-speed turnpike driving on the average motorist. Velocitization refers to the deceptive speeds possible on a modern expressway. The roads, trees, buildings, pedestrians and other objects close to the conventional roadside give the driver a frame of reference for estimating his speed; the roadside of the turnpike does not provide these references. Moreover, in a modern, smooth-running, almost sound-proof motor car, there is little noticeable difference between riding at 70 mph and riding at 50 mph. However, after riding at 70 for a short time, "slowing down" to 40 gives the driver a feeling that he is now proceeding at a mere crawl.

High-speed hypnosis is the phenomenon that occurs when the road is straight, flat, and seemingly endless. As the driver focuses his eyes far ahead down the highway, he sees the ever-present "wet spot" glare on the pavement. The steady speed, the hum of the tires on the virtually bump-free road surface, the whine of the wind past the windows, and on rainy days the metronomic tick-tock of the windshield wipers—all these have an effect upon the driver similar to hypnosis. This is often the cause of a serious accident.

TECHNIQUES FOR TURNPIKE DRIVING

Superhighway driving is a relatively new experience, not only for you, but for most other drivers as well. Instead of complacently sitting back and relaxing, you must increase your attention. Look down the road as far as you can see, alertly analyzing all traffic movements. Anticipate difficulties before they develop. One of the keys to effective turnpike driving is defensive driving.

Speed Control

Speed is a leading factor in turnpike accidents. Traffic specialists are agreed that high speed can be disastrous; even at a speed of 40 miles an hour, if a car strikes a solid object its occupants probably will be killed. Remember, when driving on superhighways—maintain a reasonable speed, but do not overdo it. Regardless of the maximum speed limit, hold your speed down to one that you can handle safely.

Be careful when entering or leaving a superhighway. Do not get the illusion that you are going slowly, just because you have reduced your speed to 40 miles an hour.

Following Distances

Allow adequate distance between your car and the car ahead. (See page 280.) If the driver behind you is following you too closely, and if you are traveling at a reasonable speed, slow down slightly. In most cases he will then pass you.

Stopping

It is unwise to stop on the roadway unless traffic conditions force you to do so. For repairs and the like, pull off onto the shoulder or into an authorized space. Never make a quick stop on a turnpike unless there is no better way to avoid a crash. You may be able to stop your car safely, but the drivers of the cars following you may not. Many serious rear-end collisions, some involving dozens of cars, have been caused by sudden stops on turnpikes and superhighways.

Lane Position

The "one-lane habit" is essential in turnpike driving. Keep in the right lane except when passing. When situations necessitate changing lanes, do so only after carefully checking the situation to the rear in the rear view mirrors and giving an appropriate hand and/or mechanical signal. Always change lanes gradually; do not move abruptly from one lane to another.

Fig. 6-36. In adverse weather conditions, speed must be reduced even on the best highways. (*Courtesy: New Jersey Turnpike Commission.*)

Avoiding Hypnosis

To avoid becoming "hypnotized" while driving, it is advisable to glance at the dashboard periodically, and scan the roadside and the rear view mirror. This will tend to break the monotony of constantly gazing directly ahead and will assist you in keeping well informed about the total traffic picture.

When you are overtired, it is best to get off the road and stay off until you are rested. However, if you feel drowsiness coming on, and if for some reason you are unable to stop, the following suggestions may prove of value:

1. Open the windows so that the inrushing air can stimulate your senses.

2. Pull off the road at an authorized place and get out and walk around the car.

A superhighway, like any other highway, is not a place to doze or daydream. Keep alert—your life depends on it.

ADVANTAGES OF TURNPIKE DRIVING

Turnpike driving has many advantages. When used thoughtlessly, the speed factor, which is often thought to be the superhighway's greatest asset, is perhaps its greatest disadvantage. The real advantages of superhighways include such factors as:

1. Smooth, wide, well-maintained, divided highways.

2. Freedom from interference of intersections, bicyclists, pedestrians, and animals.

3. Direct, easy-to-follow routes.

4. Less congestion.

"Super" highways have been built for greater convenience and safety. They are free of most of the hazards that today's traffic engineers can eliminate. In order to enjoy these engineering miracles to the fullest, drivers must learn to use them with restraint and intelligence. In the final analysis, these highways are only as enjoyable and safe as the driver who uses them: whether they are sources of pleasure and convenience or of death and destruction depends entirely on the driver.

DISCUSSION TOPICS

1. What are the leading causes of accidents on superhighways?
2. What could be done to reduce these accidents?
3. What are the real advantages of driving on superhighways?

4. What is "velocitization"? "High speed hypnosis"? How can they be avoided?

PROJECTS AND PROBLEMS

1. Prepare a list of suggestions to guide a driver's behavior on superhighways.
2. Draw a series of posters illustrating the following: turnpike hazards; advantages of turnpike driving; good driving practices and poor driving practice on superhighways.
3. Write a short essay on the question: "Are our superhighways more efficient than our drivers?"

Fig. 6-37. In situations like this, a quick, accurate response may be the difference between life and death. (*Courtesy: "Your Car."*)

What Abilities Are Needed to Meet Driving Emergencies Successfully?

By thinking ahead and driving defensively the good driver avoids most driving emergencies; occasionally, however, a driver finds himself in a tight spot. In such situations his response must be accurate and quick. His life depends upon it. A knowledge of important emergencies, and experience in handling simulated emergency situations, will help a driver to deal more effectively with these problem situations when he meets them in traffic.

Each day, drivers are involved in accidents that result in death and injury. Many of these accidents result from sudden, emergency situations in which the driver, often through no fault of his own, comes face-to-face with a problem that requires split-second thinking and a quick, accurate response. We have emphasized previously the fact that good drivers avoid emergency situations and that most emergencies *can* be avoided; nevertheless, in spite of the skill and caution of the driver, serious emergencies may arise.

Take the instance of a car rounding a curve too fast. The vehicle goes into a skid with the rear wheels sliding to the right side of the road, possibly off the pavement. What would you do? The *natural* tendency might be to steer away from the direction of the skid, to "hit" the brakes, and, if you "lost your head" completely, to step on the clutch. All of these reactions would be *wrong* and probably would result in an accident. An emergency such as this calls one's attention to the many situations in which the *natural* responses are often the *wrong* responses. This illustration highlights the vital need for learning the proper procedures rather than discovering by experience that the most "natural" reaction is not necessarily the correct one.

EMERGENCY DRIVING SITUATIONS

It would be impractical, and probably impossible, to train for every driving emergency. Such training must be limited to the most important emergency situations—importance in this case being based on the frequency of occurrence and the relative severity of the accident resulting from such circumstances. On this basis, a survey of national accident statistics conducted by the Center for Safety Education of New York University has identified 17 important driving emergencies. A panel of authorities, consisting of 100 teachers and experienced drivers, has established recommended responses to these emergency problems. These responses, of course, are not designed to cover every possibility; this would be impossible because of the different conditions that are present in any given situation. Rather, the purpose is to develop certain basic responses and to establish fundamental principles for meeting these common road emergencies successfully. The series of practice drills that follows consists of recommended responses to the most frequent emergency situations, developed as a result of the New York University study.

Fig. 6-38. Mimetic drills help establish habit patterns for meeting driving emergencies.

THE ART OF DRIVING

CITY DRIVING EMERGENCY SITUATIONS

Emergency Situations	Recommended Responses
I. As you are driving on a two-lane road, a car pulls out from a parking space and, without warning, moves directly in front of your vehicle. A car is coming from the opposite direction.	1. Apply brakes. 2. Hold wheel straight. *3. Stop.
II. Your car enters an intersection. Another car enters the intersection from your right at high speed and moves directly in front of your vehicle. There is insufficient time to stop. How can you avoid a collision?	1. Apply brakes. 2. Hold wheel straight. 3. Ease brake pressure slightly. 4. Swerve to right. 5. Recover from swerve.
III. You are driving along a residential street at moderate speed. Suddenly a boy, attempting to catch a ball, dashes out from behind a parked car into your path. Another car is coming from the opposite direction.	1. Apply brakes. 2. Hold wheel straight. 3. Stop.
IV. You are driving behind a bicyclist on a two-lane road. Without warning the cyclist swerves directly in front of you. There is no oncoming traffic.	1. Apply brakes. 2. Blow horn. 3. Steer to the left. 4. Stop.
V. You are driving in the passing lane of a four-lane roadway. As you reach an intersection, a car in the right-hand lane makes a left turn directly in front of your car.	1. Apply brakes. 2. Ease brake pressure slightly. 3. Swerve to the right. 4. Recover from swerve.
VI. You are driving down a steep hill on wet pavement. Without warning, a vehicle backs out of a driveway into your path. You apply brakes, which causes your car to skid to the right.	1. Foot off brake. 2. Turn wheel to right and regain control. 3. Apply brakes gently and intermittently. 4. Pass obstacle slowly.

* Where the recommended response calls for a *stop,* it is recommended in practice situations that a stop signal be given. It is recognized, however, that in an actual emergency situation there may not be time for this procedure.

HIGHWAY DRIVING EMERGENCY SITUATIONS

Emergency Situations	Recommended Responses
I. You are rounding a curve on wet and slippery pavement. Suddenly the rear of your car skids toward the left side of the road.	1. Turn wheel to the left. 2. Apply slight gas pressure. 3. Avoid braking. 4. After gaining control, recover to right side of road.
II. You are the driver of the middle car of three vehicles traveling in the same direction. There is very little distance between cars. All three cars are passed by a fourth vehicle. This car suddenly cuts in front of lead car to avoid oncoming traffic.	1. Reduce speed as car passes. 2. Apply brakes as car cuts into lane. 3. Stop or proceed cautiously.
III. You are passing another car on a two-lane highway when you suddenly encounter a restricted passing zone.	1. Apply brakes. 2. Allow car on right to pull ahead. 3. Return to proper lane.
IV. While driving at 45 mph you encounter a blind curve in the road.	1. Hard jabs of brake pedal. 2. Foot off brake. 3. Slight gas pressure. 4. Keep in proper lane.
V. You are driving on a two-lane highway at moderate speed when a vehicle suddenly backs from a driveway into your path.	1. Apply brakes. 2. Hold wheel straight. 3. Stop.
VI. Your car approaches a stop signal at a main intersection on a wet and slippery highway.	1. Apply brakes gently and intermittently. *2. Keep clutch engaged as long as possible. 3. Stop.
VII. As you are driving on a two-lane highway, an oncoming car forces you to swerve to right side of lane. As a result, your right front wheel drops off the pavement to the road shoulder several inches below.	1. Ease up on gas. †2. Steer so that both right wheels (front and rear) are 3 feet from pavement. †3. Pump brake pedal. 4. After gaining control, turn back to pavement.

* Does not apply to automatic transmission cars.
† In emergency situation VII it is assumed that there are no obstacles present that would interfere with recommended responses 2 and 3.

THE ART OF DRIVING

OTHER EMERGENCY SITUATIONS

Emergency Situations	Recommended Responses
I. You are driving down a steep hill when your brakes fail.	1. Pump brake pedal repeatedly to build up pressure. 2. Pull hand brake full on. *3. Shift into lower gear. 4. Edge toward side of road.
II. You are driving at moderate speed when a tire blows out.	1. Firmly hold wheels straight. 2. Maintain slight gas pressure. 3. Avoid braking (unless necessary). 4. Gradually stop.
III. You are driving at night on an unlighted highway. Suddenly a pedestrian, walking on the right side of the pavement, appears in your headlights.	1. Apply brakes. 2. Blow horn. 3. Ease off brakes. 4. Proceed to left of pedestrian.
IV. You are driving on a two-lane highway at night. An oncoming car refuses to dim his headlights.	1. Reduce speed. 2. Hit dimmer button once or twice. 3. Make sure your headlights are dimmed. 4. Look to right side of road while passing.

LEARNING TECHNIQUES

The basic problem in preparing for driving emergencies is how to obtain experiences from which you can develop the necessary knowledge and skills without involving undue risk to yourself or others. Only through experience can you learn enough to prove valuable in time of need. Manipulative skills are best acquired through physical activity, rather than through reading, writing, or listening. Three general techniques have been devised for use in preparing for emergency situations:

1. Mimetic drill.
2. Exercises with the driving-emergency trainer.
3. Practice driving exercises.

---

* In certain cars this may not be possible. When possible, however, shifting to a lower gear is desirable to secure the additional braking of engine compression.

Mimetic Drill

Essentially, mimetic drill is little different from imitating the motions involved in a given activity under conditions similar to actual participation in such an activity. You may have used this procedure for developing skills in numerous sports, particularly swimming. These drills have proven successful in this respect, it is felt that they are also a good method of teaching drivers to contend with emergency situations that they will probably face on the highway.

The following recommended procedures have been developed for using the technique of mimetic drill in the classroom:

I. Preliminary to classroom session.
   A. Carefully study the commonly known emergency situations.
   B. Memorize the correct responses for each.
II. First drill session.
   A. Select a member of the group as leader.
   B. Leader demonstrates drill procedure to be used.
      1. Explanation of what is meant by "driving position."
         Sitting at desk with hands in position on an imaginary steering wheel; right foot extended as it would normally be in exerting pressure on the accelerator; left foot extended as it normally would be in driving.
      2. Location of imaginary brake pedal, hand brake, dimmer button, horn, etc., are defined.
      3. Demonstration of control action—steering, braking, etc.
   C. Class follows leader through action of all controls.
   D. Using City Driving Emergency II (see Practice Exercises) as an example, the leader demonstrates the correct responses.
   E. Group responds to Emergency II on leader's commands, as follows:
      1. Assume driving position.
      2. Apply brakes—right foot moves to imaginary brake pedal.
      3. Hold wheel straight—no action of hands on wheel.
      4. Ease brake pressure slightly—right foot moves up slightly as in releasing pressure.
      5. Swerve to right—hands move as though turning wheel to right.
      6. Recover from swerve—hands move as though turning wheel to left and then returning wheel to straight-ahead position.
   F. This type of drill should be continued for *all emergencies* until proficiency is developed.

G. Group may divide into pairs with one student (using practice exercise sheet) checking the performance of the other.

Some groups, in an attempt to make these drills more meaningful, have prepared motion pictures of the hazardous situations listed on the practice exercise sheets. To secure realism, these films are usually made with the camera mounted in such a position as to furnish a "driver's eye" view of the situation. These films are so designed that in a few minutes many emergency situations can be shown.

The 17 emergency situations listed on the practice exercise sheet require about 200 feet of film which, to be effective, should be projected continuously. There is an inexpensive device on the market that can be easily attached to an ordinary 16 mm. projector to provide continuous operation of the film.

Where this type of film is available or can be developed, additional drills can be used, following this recommended procedure:

III. Subsequent drill lessons (with motion-picture films)
   A. Conduct warm-up period, using all controls.
   B. Using motion-picture films, drill on responses to emergencies presented.
   C. Divide group into pairs with one student (using practice exercise sheet) checking the performance of the other.

Fig. 6-39. Students practice drills on the classroom trainer. (*Courtesy: Aetna Casualty and Surety Company.*)

Using the Driving-Emergency Trainer

The driving-emergency trainer, which corresponds somewhat to the Link trainer in aviation, is a lightweight, portable model of an automobile driving compartment, including all the essential features—steering wheel, clutch, foot and hand brake, gear shift lever, horn, directional signals, and headlight dimmer button. All these devices are connected by switches so that all control movements register on a master scoring panel. This panel board can be so designed that a scorekeeper sitting at his desk could supervise several of the trainers operating simultaneously. The same general practice technique is followed when using this apparatus as was recommended for mimetic drills. If your school does not have a driving-emergency trainer one could be constructed rather inexpensively, or two students working together could practice these drills in a stationary car.

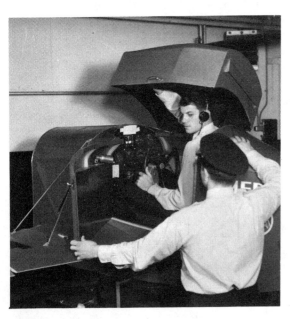

Fig. 6-40. The classroom trainer used in driver education is similar to the Link Trainer used to prepare pilots. (*Courtesy: American Airlines, Inc.*)

Practice Driving Exercises

The mimetic drills and the driving-emergency trainer will prove valuable techniques in preparing you for emergencies you may meet on the highway, but in the final analysis there is no substitute for actual experience behind the wheel of a car. It is, of course, impractical to set up many emergency situations for this purpose, but, if local conditions permit, controlled situations can be set up that will provide experiences similar to actual driving emergencies. It should be obvious, that strict supervision by a qualified instructor in a dual control car is necessary when practicing these "emergency" behind-the-wheel problems.

The following list of practice exercises in meeting emergency situations is designed to give you experience that is as close to reality as practicable. Local conditions will determine the most suitable location of these exercises. The area selected by your instructor should be free of traffic, pedestrians, or obstacles that might result in an accident. Also, these behind-the-wheel drills should be carried on at low speeds. A recommended procedure includes the following steps:

1. Practice each situation, using mimetic drills, until your response is perfect.
2. Study carefully the driving emergency to be simulated and the materials that will be used to simulate it.
3. Review the recommended responses for each emergency.
4. Repeat each emergency drill at least three times.
5. Have your instructor check your responses.
6. Do not attempt these drills unless a qualified instructor is supervising you.

EXERCISE 1

Emergency Simulated: City Driving Emergency I

Procedure: Three large cardboard cartons or some other suitable device to simulate a parked car are used. As student approaches this simulated row of parked cars, the instructor's assistant pushes the cardboard car into the path of the student's vehicle.

EXERCISE 2

Emergency Simulated: City Driving Emergency II

Procedure: Use a large rubber ball about three feet in diameter to simulate "a car entering at high speed from the right." As the student approaches the intersection, assistant rolls the ball rapidly across the path of the car.

EXERCISE 3

Emergency Simulated: City Driving Emergency III

Procedure: A large balloon dummy attached to the end of a long bamboo pole is recommended here to simulate a pedestrian. Assistant thrusts the dummy into the path of the student's car from an obscured position.

EXERCISE 4

Emergency Simulated: City Driving Emergency IV

Procedure: A large balloon dummy attached to the end of a long bamboo pole is used this time to simulate a cyclist. Assistant runs along well in front of the car and well off to the right of its path. Dummy will be directed in a path slightly to the right of the car to simulate the path of a bicycle. As the car nears the bicycle it is thrust or swerved into the path of the car.

EXERCISE 5

Emergency Simulated: City Driving Emergency V

Procedure: In this situation it will be necessary to assume that another car is present and that the car is turning left directly in front of your car. Upon approaching the intersection your instructor will issue the warning, "Car turning left." You will then make the proper response.

EXERCISE 6 AND 7

Emergencies Simulated: City Driving Emergency VI and Highway Driving Emergency I

Procedure: Your instructor may desire to give you experience with skids at very low speeds. This is admittedly hazardous and wherever attempted should be undertaken only after extremely careful planning and preparation.

EXERCISE 8

Emergency Simulated: Highway Driving Emergency II

Procedure: As you are driving on a simulated highway, instructor will say "Car passing" and then "Car cutting in." You are to make necessary response.

EXERCISE 9

Emergency Simulated: Highway Driving Emergency III

Procedure: Two vehicles are used in this exercise. Assistant drives ahead at relatively low speed. You overtake and prepare to pass this car. As you draw abreast, instructor issues warning, "Restricted passing zone." You respond as instructed.

EXERCISE 10

Emergency Simulated: Highway Driving Emergency IV

Procedure: This exercise is best done on a straightaway. This gives the advantage of experiencing results of a high speed without encountering the actual dangers of the curve. You operate car at a speed approaching 45 mph. Instructor issues warning, "Blind curve." You respond as if curve were present even though actually proceeding on a straight-ahead course. A slight curve may be used, at the discretion of the instructor.

EXERCISE 11

Emergency Simulated: Highway Driving Emergency V

Procedure: Again use the three attached cardboard cartons to simulate an automobile. As your car approaches, assistant pushes cardboard "car" into your path.

EXERCISE 12

Emergency Simulated: Highway Driving Emergency VI

Procedure: This drill can be practiced at low speeds under actual wet and slippery conditions, provided there is a location sufficiently free from obstructions and obstacles. If there is no such location, assume that the highway is wet and slippery and stop the car as recommended.

EXERCISE 13

Emergency Simulated: Highway Driving Emergency VII

Procedure: Set up a location where the road has a hard shoulder a few inches below the pavement. Approach at low speed. At the command of the instructor, "Avoid oncoming car," drive right wheels onto shoulder. Then use recommended responses to get out of emergency successfully.

EXERCISE 14

Emergency Simulated: Other Emergency I

Procedure: Find a suitable hill free from traffic or obstructions. As you are driving down hill, instructor issues command, "Foot brakes failed—stop car." You then proceed to use the recommended response for stopping car, with the exception that you simulate pumping the brakes to build pressure.

EXERCISE 15

Emergency Simulated: Other Emergency II

Procedure: You are to assume a tire has blown out when your instructor issues warning. He will say "Blow out" and indicate which tire.

EXERCISE 16

Emergency Simulated: Other Emergency III

Procedure: Where local conditions permit, this exercise may be set up under the following night conditions. Driver approaches balloon dummy; as he approaches, dummy is thrust slightly in front of his path. Driver responds accordingly.

EXERCISE 17

Emergency Simulated: Other Emergency IV

Procedure: Again where local conditions permit, this exercise may be conducted at night. Use two cars. Assistant approaches your car, proceeding in the opposite direction. Assistant does not dim his lights. You respond as recommended.

These exercises will equip you with a knowledge of what to do in an emergency and why to do it, and will also serve as a basis for developing skills to meet emergency driving situations as they arise. The important factor in responding to emergencies is not so much speed as accuracy of response.

No driver can consider himself competent unless he is prepared to meet successfully the common driving emergencies. Remember, an emergency situation exists immediately before each and every accident. It is therefore vitally important that you be able to get out of these situations. But most important, watch for signs of potential emergencies before they develop; a really good driver is very seldom caught in a tight spot.

DISCUSSION TOPICS

1. What are the leading causes of skids? How can they be avoided? What is the proper technique for handling a skidding car?
2. "A good driver is very seldom involved in an emergency situation." Explain the implications of this statement.
3. Are there any emergency situations that occur commonly in your locality? Describe them. How could each be avoided? If you became involved, how would you handle your car in each situation?

THE ART OF DRIVING

4. A philosopher once pointed out, as he saw a workman fall from the roof of a building to the ground, "The accident didn't happen when he hit the ground; it happened when he neglected to walk properly on the roof." What significance has this philosophy for driving?

PROBLEMS AND PROJECTS

1. Draw a series of posters illustrating important driving emergencies. Indicate the driving technique to be used in each.
2. Organize your group as suggested in the text and use mimetic drills to practice the important driving emergencies. If possible, build a driving-emergency trainer similar to the one described.
3. On a map of your community indicate the locations where various types of emergencies are likely to occur. Draw a separate diagram showing how each of these emergencies may be avoided or handled.

Fig. 6-41. There is no such thing as a minor violation. (Courtesy: Northwestern University Traffic Institute.)

THE ART OF DRIVING

What Are the Fundamentals of the Art of Good Driving?

Good driving is an art. It is based upon precise manual skills developed through effective practice. Its finest expression, however, results from the graceful application of these skills to the complex traffic situations that are encountered in everyday driving. The artist at the piano has dexterous skills, developed through intensive practice. The application of these skills through his artistic interpretation of the musical score, however, is the factor that results in beautiful melody and rhythm. In much the same way, the good driver applies his manual skills in terms of his interpretation of the particular pattern of traffic in which he finds himself. As the accomplished driver moves through traffic, he interprets the need for adjusting the position of his car or for accelerating or decelerating. He adapts to conditions created by other motorists and by the various road conditions. The good driver is characterized not only by the smooth manipulative skills that he possesses, but also by the beauty and gracefulness with which he controls and maneuvers his car in traffic.

The art of driving is in reality an application of five fundamental concepts. If you hope to become an accomplished driver, it is important that you understand these fundamentals and reflect them in your traffic performance. The fundamental principles of driving may be summarized as follows:

> Driving is a privilege—not a right.
> Power is useful only when it is controlled.
> Self-enforcement is the basis of all law enforcement.
> Good driving is defensive driving.
> Accidents are evidence of inefficiency and incompetence.

The appreciation and application of these principles is essential to successful driving. Will your driving reflect them?

THE PRIVILEGE OF DRIVING

A driver's license is granted in the belief that an individual is equipped to use a motor vehicle properly and is prepared to share the road with others. When you accept a license you are accepting not only the privilege it grants but also the duties and responsibilities that the use of a car entail. You are free to use a motor vehicle as long as your use of it does not interfere with the rights and privileges of your fellow citizens. This is a basic principle underlying all behavior in a democratic society. The automobile must be used with consideration for the feelings of others, with concern for the rights of others, and with due respect for the welfare of others. These are the things on which good citizenship is based.

Every driver has certain basic responsibilities, which cannot be overlooked:

> 1. To keep physically and mentally fit.
> 2. To acquire essential knowledge and skill.
> 3. To develop efficient habits, sound judgment, and co-operative attitudes.
> 4. To conduct himself in a courteous, sportsmanlike manner in all traffic situations.

The really good driver is never satisfied to merely maintain the minimum standards required for a driver's license. He strives for high standards of personal performance, because he realizes that if he accepts the privilege to drive without also accepting the responsibilities that it entails, he is taking something to which he is not entitled.

CONTROLLED POWER

Most individuals have more power at their direct disposal in driving than in any of their daily activities. This power has a strange effect on some drivers, and they let it get out of control. The good driver knows that power out of control can cause tragedy. The good driver, therefore, keeps a firm rein on his emotions. He realizes that an angry or worried driver is inefficient and dangerous.

Poor car control reflects unfavorably, not only on one's adjustment to driving, but also on one's general emotional and social adjustment. Frequently names like "Roadhog," "Cowboy," "Speed Demon," and the like are used to label drivers whose traffic performance indicates a basic personality problem. The driver who controls his car well has developed the emotional maturity and personal responsibility needed to use the power of the car with pleasure and satisfaction.

SELF-ENFORCEMENT

To a great extent, the improvements that have been made in our traffic record are the result of drivers controlling their own behavior and conforming without exception to traffic·laws. These drivers realize that such laws are designed to aid rather than to hinder them, and that without the observance of laws, traffic would result in chaos.

Law enforcement officials cannot be expected to shoulder the entire responsibility of seeing to it that each of us lives according to the law. Specialists in the field agree that at best they can cope with only a small percentage of traffic violations. Actually, the cost of providing 100 per cent enforcement by present police enforcement measures would be prohibitive. Therefore, officials deal with the most glaring violations but are sometimes forced to overlook so-called minor ones.

"Minor" Violations

The good driver realizes that there is no such thing as a minor violation. An unlawful act in traffic may go almost unnoticed at

FUNDAMENTALS OF GOOD DRIVING 319

one moment, but a few moments later the same act may result in a fatal crash. The only difference between a so-called minor violation and a fatal accident usually is a split second and a lot of luck.

Repeated violations are precursors of an accident. A driver who repeatedly violates traffic rules may find that the law of averages catches up with him before a traffic officer can get around to correcting him. You may not have an accident when you commit the first violation. With repeated violations, however, the chance of an accident increases, and sooner or later you will run into difficulty. A violation is a factor in nearly every traffic accident. If you violate traffic rules you are a poor driver, just as an athlete who violates the rules of the game is a poor player. The good driver does not gamble with the law of averages or count on luck; he manages his driving in a skillful, sportsmanlike manner, according to the rules.

DEFENSIVE DRIVING

The good driver is defensive. He realizes that people have limitations and disabilities and that they make mistakes. He knows that, because of inadequacies in licensing standards, the driver of the car coming toward him may actually be unfit to drive. For example, in states where no vision test is given, a man may collect his pension for the blind, have his "seeing-eye dog" lead him to the motor vehicle bureau, and with that money purchase his driver's license. Fortunately, this rarely happens. Yet a person who is occupationally blind may still have enough vision to move his car down the highway. It is apparent that his actions, however, would be quite dangerous. Moreover, the good driver knows that even people who are normally in sound condition frequently, because of temporary illness or emotional upset, are not functioning at their best. The good driver anticipates and uses defensive driving techniques to compensate for the disabilities, poor judgment, and mistakes of others.

Thinking Ahead

When you are driving in traffic, will you be continually getting into tight spots or emergency situations, or will you take appropriate actions to avoid them? Every hazardous situation has its causes; it was developing for some time before it became an acute danger. *An expert driver develops an ability to think, and feel ahead.* He notices little disturbances in the traffic flow that may develop into serious situations, and he gets into position to meet them some time *before* they actually occur.

Whenever you get behind the wheel, you must be concerned with five drivers: yourself, the one ahead of you, the one behind you, the one approaching, and the one who may dart out of a side street or away from the curb. The good driver has a knack for knowing what other cars are going to do. He observes changes in their speed and position that the average driver might never notice. For example, a thin trail of exhaust smoke coming from a parked car down the road warns him that the car may pull out into traffic at any moment, possibly without warning. Pedestrians hesitating at the curb and engaged in animated conversation are a warning to him that they may step into the road without making sure that the way is clear. A youngster on a bicycle is a definite warning. So is a ball rolling across the road ahead, for a child may suddenly dart out after it. Cars roaring up behind, when traffic is flowing in an unbroken stream, warn the expert that he may have to turn off onto the shoulder of the road to avoid being sideswiped as they cut in. Even the various seasons of the year and hours of the day have their special hazards, for which he is prepared.

The ability to see and think ahead, to *anticipate,* makes it possible to avoid situations that call for quick and desperate action. A driver who has this ability does not need to take chances, for he is always thinking far ahead of what is immediately hap-

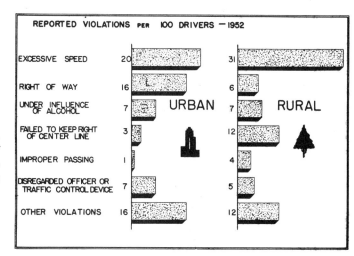

Fig. 6-42. Driver violations in fatal accidents. (*Source: Accident Facts.*)

REPORTED VIOLATIONS PER 100 DRIVERS — 1952

	URBAN	RURAL
EXCESSIVE SPEED	20	31
RIGHT OF WAY	16	6
UNDER INFLUENCE OF ALCOHOL	7	7
FAILED TO KEEP RIGHT OF CENTER LINE	3	12
IMPROPER PASSING	1	4
DISREGARDED OFFICER OR TRAFFIC CONTROL DEVICE	7	5
OTHER VIOLATIONS	16	12

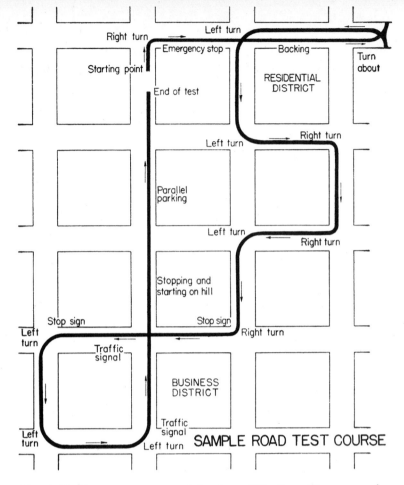

Right turn   Left turn
Emergency stop   Backing   Turn about
Starting point   RESIDENTIAL DISTRICT
End of test

Left turn   Right turn

Parallel parking

Left turn   Right turn

Stopping and starting on hill

Stop sign   Stop sign
Left turn   Right turn
Traffic signal

BUSINESS DISTRICT

Traffic signal
Left turn   Left turn   SAMPLE ROAD TEST COURSE

Fig. 6-43. Plan a test course at least as difficult as this one, and have a competent person check your driving performance.

pening. He therefore has time to avoid dangerous situations, instead of having to meet them. He drives steadily and easily at a fair rate of speed; if he has any doubts about whether or not a maneuver can be completed with safety, he does not attempt it. In reality, his smooth driving is not magic, but the result of foresight. The cultivation of this ability to see and think ahead is very definitely a part of the art of driving.

Correcting a Mistake

In spite of the habit of thinking ahead, there will be times when you suddenly realize that you must, at that very instant, perform some maneuver that you are not prepared to execute properly—for example, a left turn. Instead of making the turn at

322   THE ART OF DRIVING

once without signaling, what you should do is go on and then turn around, if necessary, or in some other way correct your mistake. You cannot afford to make an impulsive, unpremeditated move except in an emergency, when not to do so might be still more hazardous.

INEFFICIENCY BREEDS ACCIDENTS

If you are involved in a traffic accident it means that up to that point at least you have failed to become an efficient driver. It does not make any difference whether it is just a nicked fender or a complete smash-up. The important point is that the damage resulted from inefficiency. The degree of damage is more or less the product of chance. What may have been just a side-swiped fender could easily have been a head-on collision as far as your driving behavior was concerned. You failed to keep power under control.

But, you may ask, what about a situation in which the other driver was primarily at fault? The really skilled driver looks at other peoples' blunders as a challenge to his driving skill. If he fails to meet this challenge, morally at least, he accepts the blame.

EVALUATING YOUR PERFORMANCE

Do *you* have the ability to drive safely? What are *your* strengths and weaknesses? It is possible to evaluate your driving ability. The following test has been designed for this purpose. Have your teacher, parent, or a friend who is thoroughly familiar with the contents of the book use the test to check your driving. If you have two or more people check you, it will be interesting to compare the results.

DRIVING PERFORMANCE TEST

Check the one item which best represents the driving error. If the same error is committed three times, multiply the deduction for the item by two.

Part I—Specific Analysis

	Points Deducted	Number of Violations 1 2 3 or more	Total Deduction
A. Getting ready to drive			
1. Failed to check area surrounding car.	2		
2. Failed to enter vehicle from curb side.	3		
3. Fumbled for key and/or had difficulty in putting it in switch.	2		
4. Failed to adjust seat properly.	3		
5. Failed to adjust mirror(s) properly.	3		
6. Did not check doors.	2		

7. Did not assume an erect, alert driving position. — 3

B. Starting the engine

° 1. Failed to depress clutch. — 3

2. Did not place shift lever in neutral. — 3

3. Did not turn on ignition switch correctly and at the proper time. — 2

4. Did not release starter button as soon as engine started. — 2

5. Failed to use choke properly when needed. — 2

6. Did not allow engine to warm up. — 2

7. Raced engine during warm-up period. — 2

C. Moving the car on level ground

° 1. Failed to depress clutch. — 2

2. Selected wrong gear. — 3

3. Failed to release hand brake properly. — 2

4. Failed to look out of the side window and give proper hand signal before leaving the curb. — 3

5. Raced engine. — 3

6. Stalled engine. — 2

7. Caused car to jerk or buck. — 3

D. Backing the car

1. Failed to maneuver car into correct position to back. — 2

2. Failed to look to the rear of the car properly when backing. — 3

3. Backed too fast or with jerky movement. — 2

4. Raced engine. — 2

5. Stalled engine. — 2

6. Oversteered or zigzagged when backing. — 3

7. Turned in wrong direction when steering. — 3

E. * Shifting techniques

1. Failed to keep eyes on the road while shifting. — 3

2. Stayed in low gear(s) too long. — 2

3. Shifted to high gear too soon. — 2

4. Failed to co-ordinate clutch, accelerator, and gear shift smoothly. — 3

5. Failed to reduce gears when necessary. — 3

6. Stalled engine. — 2

7. Raced engine. — 2

8. Clashed gears. — 2

9. "Rode the clutch." — 2

10. Shifted to wrong gear. — 3

11. Coasted downgrade. — 3

° Does not apply to automatic transmission cars.

F. Stopping

1. Failed to slow down and prepare to stop well in advance. — 3
2. Failed to use brake properly. — 3
* 3. Depressed clutch too soon. — 3
* 4. Did not depress clutch soon enough. — 3
5. Stalled engine. — 2
6. Failed to stop in proper position. — 3
7. Failed to give adequate signal to stop. — 3
8. Did not check traffic conditions to the rear properly before stopping. — 3
9. Failed to stop smoothly. — 2
10. Failed to shift to neutral during stops of 30 seconds or more. — 3

G. Steering

1. Placed hands in an unstable position on the wheel. — 2
2. Failed to steer smoothly. — 2
3. Rested arm on windowsill or held left arm outside window. — 2
4. Used one hand habitually. — 2
5. Turned steering wheel while vehicle was not moving. — 2
6. Attempted to steer using crossbars or with hands on the inside of the wheel. — 3

H. Speed control

1. Too fast for conditions. — 15
2. In excess of marked speed limits. — 10
3. Too slow for conditions. — 5
4. Used brakes while going around curves. — 3

I. Traffic position

1. Failed to drive in proper lane. — 10
2. Straddled lanes (marked or unmarked). — 5
3. Followed other vehicles too closely. — 10
4. Drove too close to other vehicles, objects or pedestrians. — 5
5. Changed lanes at will in an effort to weave around other vehicles, pedestrians, etc. — 4
6. Failed to give proper signal (hand, mechanical, and shift of car position) before changing lanes. — 5

J. Right and left turns

1. Began turn from wrong lane. — 3
2. Maneuvered turn at improper speed (too fast or too slow). — 3
3. Made turn too wide. — 3
4. Struck curb or cut corners too short. — 5
5. Entered wrong lane. — 3
6. Moved toward one direction then turned in other (shied away). — 5

---

* Does not apply to automatic transmission cars.

FUNDAMENTALS OF GOOD DRIVING

* 7. Attempted to shift while turning.   3

* 8. Failed to select proper gear before turning.   3

  9. Hesitated too long before straightening wheels.   3

10. Failed to yield the right of way.   5

11. Failed to give the three necessary signals (hand, mechanical, and shift of position).   5

K. Signaling

1. Failed to signal when leaving curb.   3

2. Failed to look carefully before moving into traffic.   5

3. Failed to give three signals (hand, mechanical, and shift of position).   3

4. Used wrong signal.   3

5. Left mechanical signal on after completing turn.   3

6. Used horn improperly, or failed to use horn when necessary.

L. Passing vehicles going in same direction

1. Did not check whether road ahead and behind was clear.   3

2. Failed to sound horn or give suitable signal before passing.   3

3. Followed too close to car in front.   3

4. Misjudged speed of other vehicles.   3

5. Passed at curve, intersection, or crest of hill.   10

6. Cut back into line too soon after passing.   5

7. Passed on the right in areas where this practice is dangerous.   3

8. Attempted to pass too many cars at once.   5

9. Passed in a manner that blocked the vehicle being passed from steering around parked or slow-moving vehicles or pedestrians.   3

10. Failed to observe indications that a parked vehicle may pull away from the curb.   3

11. Failed to observe proper technique of passing a school bus.   5

12. Failed to reduce speed and observe proper caution in passing double-parked vehicles or large trucks that obstruct vision.   3

13. Stayed in passing lane too long.   5

M. Stopping and starting on upgrades

1. Did not stop smoothly.   3

2. Rolled backward.   5

3. Failed to use hand brake when needed.   3

---

* Does not apply to automatic transmission cars.

	Points Deducted	Number of Violations 1 2 3 or more	Total Deduction

    4. Raced or stalled engine. — 3

  * 5. Selected wrong gears when starting. — 3

    6. Failed to hold car stationary for an instant after releasing hand brake. — 3

    7. Used improper technique. — 3

N. Turning around (Y Turn)

    1. Failed to make a complete stop in a safe location before beginning turning maneuver. — 5

    2. Failed to give hand signal and look out side window to check traffic. — 3

  * 3. Selected wrong gear. — 1

    4. Failed to turn steering wheel properly. — 1

    5. Rolled too fast. — 3

    6. Raced or stalled engine. — 2

    7. Bumped curb. — 3

    8. Failed to look behind properly when backing. — 3

    9. Failed to complete the turn in three movements. — 3

O. Parking

    1. Failed to signal intention to stop. — 3

    2. Selected a space that was too small. — 3

    3. Did not stop in proper position to begin a maneuver. — 3

    4. Parked too far from curb. — 3

    5. Struck curb. — 3

    6. Struck bumpers or other parts of adjacent cars. — 5

    7. Moved car too fast. — 3

    8. Turned wheel improperly. — 3

    9. Raced or stalled engine. — 3

   10. Failed to look to the rear of the car properly when backing. — 5

   11. Failed to center the car in space. — 3

   12. Failed to turn the wheels properly in relation to the curb and grade of the road. — 5

   13. Failed to leave shift lever in proper gear position. — 5

   14. Failed to set hand brake securely. — 10

P. Intersections

    1. Approached too fast. — 10

    2. Entered in wrong lane. — 5

    3. Failed to yield the right of way when necessary. — 10

    4. Failed to check traffic properly before entering. — 5

Q. Traffic control signs and signals

    1. Disregarded traffic signs. — 10

    2. Drove through red light. — 10

    3. Attempted to "beat a light." — 10

    4. Failed to observe a warning signal. — 10

---

* Does not apply to automatic transmission cars.

Part II—General Analysis	Points Deducted (check one)	Total Deduction
A. Attention and anticipation		
1. Excellent	0	
2. Good	5	
3. Fair	10	
4. Poor	20	
B. Confidence		
1. Confident	0	
2. Nervous or hesitant	10	
3. Overconfident or cocky	20	
C. Attitude toward other highway users and/or enforcement officers		
1. Co-operative	0	
2. Neither co-operative nor unco-operative	5	
3. Unco-operative	10	
4. Aggressive	20	

Total Deduction _____

Deductions

Part I _____

Part II _____

Total _____

Check your score; generally speaking, this is what it indicates:

0–10   You have achieved excellent performance; keep it up.

10–20   You have the ability to be a good driver; a little more experience will put you right up there with the best.

20–40   Your driving ability is about average; arrange for a conference with your driver education teacher to discuss plans for getting instruction on some of the finer points you now lack.

40 or over   You are not qualified to drive solo; get more practice, and ask your instructor to let you continue your regular driving lessons. (If you have been driving for some time, you should seek remedial help.)

Study your test results to see your particular strong and weak points. Use these test results to guide your practice. It is a good idea to take this test periodically, perhaps one a month or even more often. You and a member of your family or another friend might enjoy testing each other. Periodic testing will keep you from getting stale and also will show you whether or not your driving is improving. The art of driving, like the art of music, requires constant practice to achieve greatness.

DISCUSSION TOPICS

1. What are the five basic concepts on which good driving is based?
2. What is meant by the statement that the reckless driver is taking a privilege to which he is not entitled?
3. "Controlling power takes all the fun out of it." Defend or attack this statement, supporting your argument with facts.
4. "Police should spend their time catching criminals rather than dealing with minor traffic violators." Do you agree or disagree? Explain, supporting your argument with facts.
5. "Traffic accidents are caused by bad luck." Is this statement true or false?
6. Why is defensive driving important?

PROJECTS AND PROBLEMS

1. Have three qualified people test your driving performance using the "Driving Performance Test." Write a brief analysis of the results.
2. Draw a series of charts illustrating the fundamental principles involved in the art of driving.
3. Prepare a series of 30-second "spot announcements" to be used on your local radio station to acquaint drivers with these basic concepts.

SELECTED REFERENCES FOR UNIT VI

1. *Deft Driving*, Milton Kramer. Dearborn, Michigan: Ford Motor Company, 1953.
2. *How to Drive Better and Avoid Accidents*, Paul W. Kearney. New York: Thomas Y. Crowell Company, 1953.
3. *Model Traffic Ordinances*, U. S. Public Roads Administration. Washington, D. C.: Government Printing Office, 1946.
4. *Sportsmanlike Driving*, American Automobile Association. Washington, D. C.: 1948.
5. *The Fundamental Principles of Driving*, H. James Tysor. Dallas: Banks Upshaw and Company, 1953.
6. *Uniform Act Regulating Traffic on Highways* (*Act* V), U. S. Public Roads Administration. Washington, D. C.: Government Printing Office, 1945.

Additional information may be found in local traffic regulations, obtained from your local police department, and in the state motor vehicle code, obtained from the Motor Vehicle Department of your state.

UNIT 7

COOPERATION AMONG HIGHWAY USERS

PROBLEM ONE

How can drivers and pedestrians
co-operate more effectively?

PROBLEM TWO

What is the role of the cyclist in traffic?

Fig. 7-1. Even if she had been in the wrong when your car hit her, could you ever forget the look on this dying child's face?

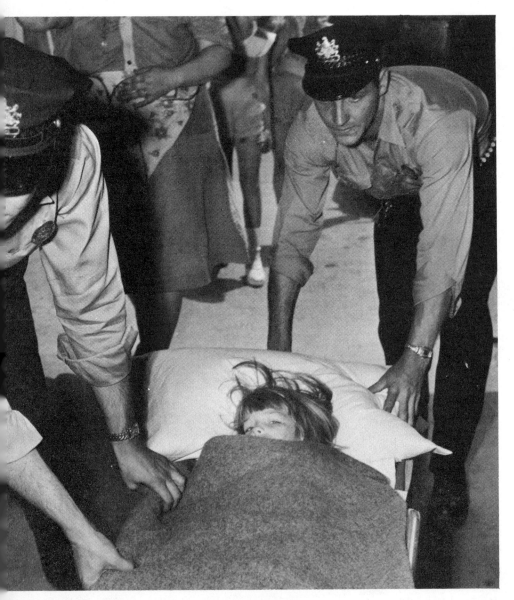

CO-OPERATION AMONG HIGHWAY USERS

How Can Drivers and Pedestrians Co-operate More Effectively?

About two-fifths of all persons killed in traffic accidents are pedestrians. It is apparent that traffic presents a great many dangers for the pedestrian, but these dangers can be conquered with a keener interest, higher skills, and greater co-operation.

The pedestrian is "on the spot." When he crosses a street it may be only after a patient wait, and with the disturbed feeling that a speedy vehicle may suddenly dart at him and run him down! Today's walker is the "underdog" so far as the automobile is concerned—an automobile far outrates him in weight, momentum, striking power, hardness of material, and size.

Here are some pertinent facts regarding accidents to pedestrians:

In the average American city, two-thirds of all traffic fatalities are pedestrians.

In many cities, pedestrian deaths comprise three-quarters of the fatalities.

Four out of five persons killed in traffic in most cities of over 500,000 population are pedestrians.

One out of four car collisions involves an injury; nearly *all* pedestrian accidents result in injuries.

Nearly two out of five pedestrians killed had been drinking.

Twenty per cent of the pedestrians killed are under fifteen years of age. About three-fourths of the children killed in traffic accidents were killed at play.

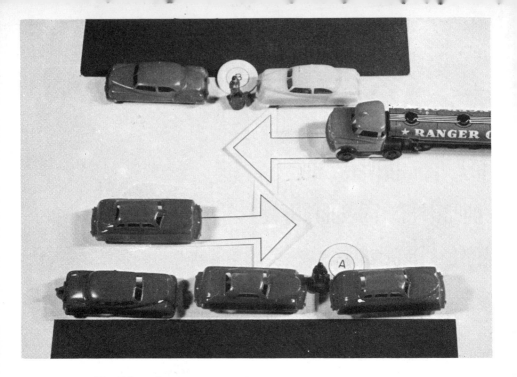

Fig. 7-2. Pedestrians "A" and "B," who are entering the street from between parked cars, may cause trouble unless these drivers are alert.

Only about one-sixth of our population is aged fifty or over, yet about one-half of the pedestrians killed annually are fifty years of age or older.

DRIVERS MUST "THINK FOR THE PEDESTRIAN"

A surprising number of our older pedestrians have never driven a car. They learned to use the streets in the horse-and-buggy days, and they haven't adapted themselves to speed. They are slow and have poor co-ordination, and their sense of timing is poor. They have little understanding of the momentum of heavy motor cars and the distances required to stop them.

We occasionally hear an ignorant or inexperienced driver boast that he can "stop his car on a dime." It is startling to realize, however, that many elderly people feel that same way about a driver's ability to stop for them. They have a confidence in the motorist's magic power to take care of them—the same confidence that is shown by very young children. If we add to this weakness the habit of absent-mindedness in the elderly and the distractions of play in children, it becomes plain that *the driver cannot count on the pedestrian's taking much care of himself.* And even if 99

Fig. 7-3. The pedestrian at intersections. (*Courtesy: American Association of Motor Vehicle Administrators and National Safety Council.*)

out of 100 pedestrians do walk perfectly, the hundredth one who is faulty sets up a hazard probability that the driver must be ready to meet at *any* time.

Darkness

The pedestrian who steps out of deep shadow into the path of a car at night is suddenly splashed with what he feels to be brilliant illumination. He is startled by the vividness of the glare. It is hard for him, no matter how often he himself drives a car at night, not to feel that the headlights make him stand out clearly and boldly.

Fig. 7-4. Light-colored clothes protect you at night. A pedestrian who is wearing light colored clothing is more easily distinguished by the driver at night. Carrying a light handkerchief helps, but it is best to carry a light.

When we are behind the wheel we ·get a very different picture. To us the pedestrian illuminated by our headlamps is just another object in the midst of a thousand other such vague shapes. His dark or neutral clothing merges into a pattern of things that are all equally lighted and equally shadowed. If, however, the pedestrian carries something that reflects light—a white handkerchief or a set of reflector buttons—the driver can instantly catch these spots of reflected light. But the driver must not count on all pedestrians being so wise. He must be ready to meet the worst, not the best conditions. On his part, *the pedestrian must also expect the worst, and not the best, from the driver.* He must say to himself at night: "The chances are that the driver cannot see me. This glare that blinds me is very little help to him." The best rule, then, for walking at night is, "consider yourself invisible to drivers, and walk accordingly."

Alcohol and the Pedestrian

The worst physical handicap to safe walking is alcohol. Nearly two-fifths of the pedestrians killed by motor vehicles have been drinking. *Beware of the intoxicated pedestrian in the roadway.* He is slow-witted and may stagger from side to side or directly into the path of your car. His reactions are poor and his vision is impaired. Slow down, even though he is on the shoulder of the roadway and it appears as though he could never get into the path of your car.

TACTICS FOR SAFE WALKING

Almost all pedestrian accidents involving motor cars are related to one of two acts: crossing streams of traffic, and walking along the highway.

The first rule of pedestrianism might be expressed as "Never interfere with the normal flow of traffic." A walker should be sure that he will not interfere with the progress of any oncoming cars before he steps into the traveled way. A large proportion of our accidents in towns and cities are due to some sudden and unexpected act of the pedestrian. They occur in the first few steps at the edge of car lanes. When the pedestrian suddenly steps into the motorist's way from behind some obstruction, there is little chance of avoiding him.

The following "don't" rules should be particularly observed by all pedestrians:

1. Do not step into a traffic lane from between or behind parked cars.
2. Do not step into a traffic lane suddenly from the screen of any shed, fence, bush, or other object that might obstruct the view of an approaching motorist.

3. After parking, do not step out of your car on the driver side into a busy traffic lane. Step out on the curb under such circumstances.

Crossing the Street

There are a number of positive and practical rules that should be followed to cross the streets safely:

1. Be sure the way is clear before you step into the street. Look first to left, then to right.
2. Cross only on the proper light signal.
3. Cross only at intersections and marked crosswalks.
4. Cross at an even, steady pace. Do not suddenly start to run or reverse your direction. Try to avoid being trapped between traffic lanes.
5. Cross at right angles, and keep a straight course. Do not cross an intersection diagonally (unless this practice is permitted by law in your locality), and do not dodge or weave.
6. Cross within the crosswalk lines, if there are any.
7. Pass oncoming pedestrians to the right on crosswalks as well as on sidewalks.
8. When crossing streets, give your full attention to traffic and do not become distracted.

Walking on the Open Highway

Using the paved surface of the highway for a sidewalk is a serious problem in rural districts. Usually there are no footpaths provided at the side of the road. Modern road construction, however, provides a shoulder, which is used by cars only under emergency conditions. The pedestrian should use this shoulder. Walking so as to face oncoming traffic, that is, on the left of the road, is usually the law and always advisable. When there are no footpaths, the following rules should be observed:

1. Walk on the left side of the road, preferably on the shoulder.
2. Face oncoming cars.
3. Step off the road when cars pass.
4. Walk single file when cars approach.
5. Wear or carry something white at night.

Street Cars and Busses

Many serious pedestrian accidents occur when pedestrians are alighting from or entering street cars and busses. This situation is partly a responsibility of the motorist. Most traffic regulations make it the duty of an approaching driver to slow or stop under such circumstances. The pedestrian, however, should not throw all caution to the winds. Two special rules are useful for his safety under these conditions.

1. After alighting from a bus or street car, wait and cross behind and not in front. Many serious accidents occur when pedestrians try to cut around quickly in front of a bus before it has time to start, and are struck by the bus or by an oncoming car. When a walker does this sort of thing he violates the primary rule of walking. Certainly a motorist deserves sufficient warning of what the pedestrian intends to do.
2. It is best, when using a safety zone or traffic island, to stand facing the oncoming traffic. This discourages you from making absent-minded starts that a nearby driver will be unable to avoid.

Physical Conditions

There are a number of physical conditions that disturb our walking, such as icy pavements and the obstruction of view by umbrellas in rainy weather. Parcels sometimes obstruct the carrier's view as well as his movement. But, to repeat, the worst physical handicap to safe walking is that produced by liquor.

SUMMARY

Increased use of motor vehicles and increased traffic congestion have resulted in dangerous situations for pedestrians and drivers alike. In our motor age, *the man on foot must modernize his attitude and conform to common-sense pedestrianism and to the traffic regulations that have been designed to protect him.* Both he and the driver are obliged, by the nature of modern traffic conditions, to protect one another. Every pedestrian should consider himself invisible to drivers and walk accordingly—planning his course to use safe timing and a safe path to arrive at his destination. Drivers, in turn, should be cautious and accept the responsibility for protecting walkers.

DISCUSSION TOPICS

1. How do foresight and alertness affect walking?
2. What special dangers to pedestrians are introduced by darkness and rainy weather? Explain the precautions that should be taken by drivers and pedestrians under these conditions.
3. What are the physical and mental qualifications of a good pedestrian?
4. What type of pedestrian accidents are most common?

5. Analyze the nature of certain distractions that contribute to the causes of pedestrian injuries.
6. Describe in detail several basic rules for pedestrian safety.
7. How can legislation help protect the pedestrian?
8. How can we educate for improved pedestrian safety?
9. What can drivers do to avoid being involved in pedestrian accidents?

PROJECTS AND PROBLEMS

1. Locate the dangerous intersections on the way from your home to school. Are they guarded in any way? If not, how should they be guarded?
2. As you step off the curb to cross the street, a car 300 feet away is coming toward you at the rate of 25 miles an hour. If you walk at the rate of 4 miles an hour and the street is 40 feet wide, where will the car be when you reach the middle of the street?
3. Observe pedestrian behavior of students on the streets around your school. List the bad practices, and suggest a program that the school should conduct to improve the situation.
4. Hold a debate on the subject: "Resolved, that pedestrians should be arrested and fined for violations of traffic rules."
5. Make a survey of playground or vacant lot areas in your community. How can these places be popularized to reduce the amount of playing in the streets?
6. Utilize police reports and news articles to indicate local pedestrian accidents on a spot map. In the light of accident occurrence, recommend practical engineering, enforcement, and educational measures to reduce the frequency of accidents.
7. Formulate a brief code for sound pedestrian practices. Check the observance of this code at a busy intersection. Report your findings to the class.
8. Using models, develop situations that illustrate the teamwork needed between motorists and pedestrians for safety. How do the limitations of each involve the safety of the other?
9. Find out what pedestrian actions are causing accidents in your community.
10. Make a survey of the things being done by your community for pedestrian safety. Report, with your own recommendations added.

Fig. 7-5. (Courtesy: Luoma Photos, Cove Station, Weirton, W. Va. From "Building Your Life," by Landis and Landis; Prentice-Hall, 1954.)

What Is the Role of the Cyclist in Traffic?

The cyclist is neither driver nor pedestrian, yet he is an important member of the traffic team. Co-operation among these three is essential for safety and efficiency in traffic.

The presence of the bicycle on our highways and streets has become a very definite and important factor in our traffic problem. Difficulties have piled up suddenly in the last few years, with the great increase in the number of bicycles, the increase in the number and speed of automobiles, and the greater density of pedestrian traffic. Today bicycle riders and motorists must know the traffic rules which apply to them and must understand each other's habits and problems.

THE THREE STREAMS OF TRAFFIC

Traffic authorities have divided the streets into three general sections: sidewalks for pedestrians, curb strips for bicyclists, and the central lanes for cars. These divisions are not, of course, fenced off or even marked with painted strips, but it is generally understood that these are the relative positions and places for each. If no one wanted to cross the other fellow's path, this simple division of the street would cure most of the troubles. But the three different groups are constantly crossing one another's path, and this causes a large number of our accidents.

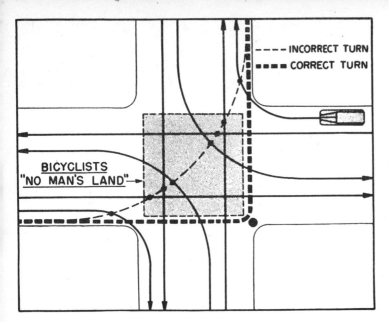

Fig. 7-6. The correct method for turning on a bicycle at a busy intersection.

Accident Analysis

Improper turns cause 25 per cent of the bicycle traffic accidents, and the disregard of a stop sign or signal causes 17 per cent. Now if we add to them the item, "Did Not Have the Right of Way" and "Weaving and Cutting In," we see that cross-interferences cause more than half of the bicycle troubles. (See Figure 7-7.)

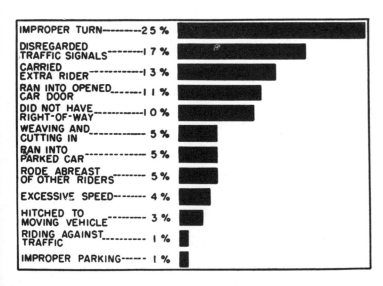

Fig. 7-7. A survey of records in two cities showed these bicycle violations.

Fig. 7-8. When approaching a cyclist, smart drivers slow down and move as far toward the center of the road as traffic conditions permit.

Give the Cyclist a Wide Berth

Expert drivers cut their normal speed in half and move toward the center of the road if traffic permits when they approach a child or a bicycle. This makes it possible for them to stop short should the youngster suddenly lose his balance or thoughtlessly make an unexpected turn. Remember, if you were to run over him, even though he was technically at fault, you would never forget the picture of that youngster lying limp and bleeding under the wheels of your car. Your conscience would hurt you the rest of your life.

Bad Habits of Motorists

The following errors are frequently committed by careless motorists. The bicyclist must be prepared for them if he is to share the road safely (the starred items are particularly dangerous):

1. Neglecting to use hand signals.
2. Opening doors on the left side and stepping out of parked cars into the bicyclist's lane of travel.*
3. Turning right from the center lane and cutting the corner.
4. Turning left from the curb lane and cutting the corner.
5. Not coming to a full stop at a stop sign.
6. Overtaking another car and passing on the right side on narrow streets.*
7. Starting out or backing out suddenly, without looking, from a parking position.*

There are, of course, other faulty motorist's maneuvers, but the above list shows those which are particularly important to the safety of cyclists.

LEFT TURN   RIGHT TURN   SLOW OR STOP

Fig. 7-9. Cyclists can use their hand signals advantageously to make known their intentions to turn, slow down, or stop.

Motor Scooters and Power Cycles

Most of the serious accidents involving a motor scooter or a power cycle probably have been due to either a misuse of the machine itself or to the fact that automobile operators are not accustomed to them in traffic. The major problem in most communities has been the operation of motor scooters by persons under the legal age for motor vehicle operation. Other hazardous conditions include double and triple riding on lightweight machines, inadequate brakes, headlights that furnished very little light, excessively high speeds, inadequate safety equipment on homemade machines, poor compliance with signs, signals, and other traffic laws, and the use of scooters on controlled-access highways and other high-speed, heavily traveled highways. When these vehicles are involved in accidents injuries usually result, owing to the lack of protection to the driver.

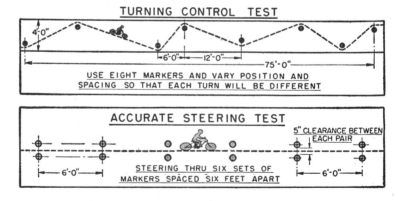

Fig. 7-10. Tests for bicyclists are a measure of their ability to manipulate their vehicles.

CO-OPERATION AMONG HIGHWAY USERS

BICYCLE SAFETY

Avoid riding two or more abreast in traffic.

Always keep bicycle in good mechanical condition.

Ride with traffic. Keep to the right and close to the curb or side of roadway.

Make sure of being safe when leaving a driveway or crossing an intersection.

Obey all traffic signals and rules.

Never stunt—keep hands on handlebars.

Fig. 7-11.

Problems created by the use of motor scooters and power cycles call for the exercise of extreme care by both the motorist and the operators of these vehicles. Operators of motor scooters and power cycles should be of legal age and properly licensed in those states where it is required. They should always know and obey the rules of the road and should be sure that the brakes, lights, and other mechanical devices of their vehicles are in a safe operating condition at all times.

Before undertaking the operation of a motor scooter or power cycle, the novice must first be:

ROLE OF THE CYCLIST IN TRAFFIC 345

1. Thoroughly skilled in the techniques of manipulating the vehicle.

2. Thoroughly acquainted with all of the rules regulating motor vehicle traffic on public highways.

3. Sure that the type and model of vehicle selected is properly constructed (with reference to permissible speed of travel, lights, and brakes) for safe operation.

4. Licensed or have a permit if one is needed.

SUMMARY

The bicyclist is neither pedestrian nor motorist, but he is subject to traffic regulation. What he does in traffic is very important to safety.

Sound bicycling habits include constant attention to the improvement of skills in handling the bicycle, thorough knowledge and proper use of bicycle traffic rules, and care and repair of the bicycle. However, youngsters on bicycles sometimes forget about traffic safety. These are the times when the driver must do their thinking for them. A collision between a motor car and a bicycle almost always results in the injury or death of the cyclist.

Motorized bicycles and motor scooters should be regarded as being *motor vehicles*. Alertness, skill, and obedience to traffic rules by all motor-driven cycle operators are needed for safety.

DISCUSSION TOPICS

1. Why has cycling become a serious problem?
2. What factors should be considered as part of a safe cyclist's behavior?
3. What actions of cycle riders frequently result in accidents?
4. How can cycle riders co-operate with motorists?
5. Describe in detail sound rules for skillful riding.
6. What bad driving practices of some motorists directly affect the cyclist?
7. What are the responsibilities of cyclists toward established traffic regulations?
8. What effect do cycle ordinances have on safe riding?
9. What is the value of examinations and skill tests for cycle riders?

PROJECTS AND PROBLEMS

1. Investigate your city and state traffic laws and ordinances to see what regulations affect the cyclist. Are these regulations adequate for safety? What other regulations could you suggest? Explain.
2. How many cycle accidents, and what kinds, have occurred in your community? How many involved personal injury? Property damage?
3. List mistakes in riding made by cyclists that should be understood by automobile drivers. What should cyclists do to avoid accidents with an automobile?

4. Develop a bicycle safety program for your community. Indicate in detail those skill tests that should be given to the bicyclist.
5. Explain the values of a bicycle inspection program in a school. What mechanical features of the bicycle should be regularly inspected?
6. Explain the similarities and differences in the operation of an automobile and a power cycle or motor scooter.

SELECTED REFERENCES FOR UNIT VII

1. *Accident Facts*, National Safety Council. Chicago: annual publication.
2. *Bicycle Safety*, National Safety Council. Chicago.
3. *Bulletins on Bicycle Skill and Safety*, Obtained from Bicycle Institute of America. New York: 1953.
4. *Pedestrian Safety*, National Safety Council. Chicago.
5. *Sportsmanlike Driving*, American Automobile Association. Washington, D. C.: 1948.

UNIT 8

MEETING THE CHALLENGE

How can you help?

DEATH · INJURY · PROPERTY LOSS

Fig. 8-1. Lest We Forget.

How Can You Help?

 Take an active interest in the traffic problem, support those organizations that are working toward a solution, and set an example that will show that you sincerely practice what you preach. Yes, traffic can be made to flow smoothly and safely, but it is up to you!

You can do your part to make traffic safer and driving more enjoyable in three ways:

1. Take an active interest in the traffic problem in your community.

2. Give your co-operation and support to those public and private agencies that are working toward a solution of the problem.

3. Set an example by your own traffic behavior that will tend to make others in your community want to improve their own driving and walking practice.

TAKE AN ACTIVE INTEREST

What do you know about the traffic problem in your community? What does it cost in lives, injuries, property damage, delay, congestion, and the like? What engineering facilities are being made available to improve conditions? What enforcement activities are being carried on? Are any educational programs being undertaken? What agencies in your community are particularly concerned with the problem? What specific difficulties are facing these groups? What help do these groups need from you? Until you learn the answers to these questions, you have not demonstrated a sincere, active interest in the traffic problem, nor have you begun to take your proper place in the traffic safety movement.

Fig. 8-2. These young people are taking an active interest in their community's traffic problem by helping adult drivers evaluate their psychophysical fitness. (*Courtesy: Porto-Clinic Instruments, Inc.*)

Before we can make any of our dreams a reality, we must understand the various factors involved and carefully devise workable plans. Therefore, if the traffic problem disturbs us and we look forward to solving it, each of us must try to understand it and make our own individual plans. This problem cannot be solved solely by community leaders, state associations, national committees, or even by the President of the United States. These people can lead the way, but alone they can never achieve a solution. Moreover, the traffic problem cannot be solved on a national level. When the final solution comes, it will result from work done on the community level in every city, village, and hamlet in our nation. The traffic problem can only be solved by the active interest and dynamic efforts of each individual citizen in the county.

Fig. 8-3. Services provided by various organizations. (Courtesy: Brody and Stack, "Highway Safety and Driver Education," Prentice-Hall.)

Service	U.S. Office of Education	State departments of education and safety	Highway patrol	Motor vehicle department	Highway departments	Local police departments	National Safety Council	Local safety councils	National Commission on Safety Education (NEA)	American Red Cross	Center for Safety Education (NYU)	Association of Casualty and Surety Companies	Individual insurance companies (and local agents)	American Automobile Association (and local clubs)	Automobile industry	Parent-Teacher Associations	Chambers of commerce (and junior chambers)
Sponsor or help sponsor		•	•				•					•	•	•		•	•
Help obtain instructional cars												•	•	•			
Provide speakers, lecturers		•	•	•	•	•						•	•	•	•		•
Conduct or help conduct — teacher training institutes		•	•					•				•	•	•			
Conduct or help conduct — college workshops	•											•					
Conduct or help conduct — seminars												•					
Provide scholarships for teachers												•		•		•	
Put on safety demonstrations		•	•											•			
Psychophysical testing		•	•											•			
Audio-visual aids		•					•	•	•			•	•	•	•		
Courses of study and lesson outlines		•					•	•			•	•		•			
Textbooks — Publish												•		•			
Textbooks — Provide													•				
Guides for administrators and supervisors of safety		•										•					
Pamphlets and periodicals on driver education and traffic safety	•		•	•	•		•	•	•			•	•	•	•	•	
Testing materials												•	•				
Bicycle and pedestrian safety booklets		•	•			•		•					•	•			
Research studies in traffic safety: Perform												•		•			
Research studies in traffic safety: Publish												•					
Research studies in traffic safety: Assist in												•					
Posters				•			•	•									

CO-OPERATION AND SUPPORT

The agencies at work in your community can provide no better traffic program than we are willing to support. This means that if we want better highways, we must be willing to pay for them. If we want more adequate traffic enforcement, we must ade-

Fig. 8-4. Actions speak louder than words. (*Courtesy: Travelers Insurance Company.*)

quately support and co-operate with our local police departments in their efforts to promote efficiency on our highways. Ticket fixing, for example, will only be eliminated when we, as citizens, are willing to face the fact that it undermines the work of enforcement officers and are willing to pay the penalty for our traffic errors. In the same way, all of the other aspects of a sound traffic program will materialize when each of us wants them badly enough to support them. The community safety council offers every citizen an opportunity to take an active part in the local traffic program. By taking part in the work of safety council committees, by promoting council policies and recommendations, and by contributing to the council's financial support, each person in the community can play a truly active role.

Safety committees in schools, Parent-Teacher Associations, Lions' Clubs, Junior Chambers of Commerce, veterans' organizations, Rotary and Kiwanis Clubs, women's clubs, and the like offer group members an opportunity to advance the cause of traffic safety in their local communities. These are a few of the ways that you can help.

Set an Example

If we expect to convince others that they can have greater adventures and more fun with a car through safe and efficient driving, we must lead the way by showing them how it is done. We must prove that good driving is advantageous to each individual and to society in general. Actions speak louder than words. We must practice what we preach. Why not decide right now that you will be one of the people who *does* something about the traffic problem, instead of just talking about it! A student of driver education is well aware of the various factors involved in good driving. With sufficient practice, he can easily develop the skill necessary to handle his car safely and efficiently. However, to be truly effective in the traffic safety movement an individual must *apply* this knowledge and skill to his driving behavior.

Fig. 8-5. It can be done. This driver, who works for one of the nation's largest motor carriers, has driven well over a million miles without an accident or violation. (*Courtesy: David B. Hecht.*)

Resolve to Do Your Part

Ability is of vital importance, but you will never be a truly competent driver unless you really want to. In sports we call this "will to win." You must develop the desire and determination to achieve quality performance. Resolve now, as so many other top-notch drivers have done, always to behave like a good sport behind the wheel. Join those drivers who are pioneering in the development of a new code of driving behavior.

This is a resolution that you might consider to guide your future driving behavior.

> I firmly resolve that I shall attempt to conduct myself as a driver and as a pedestrian in a manner that will tend to raise present driving standards and will bring honor to my family, my school, and my community.

1. I shall obey all signs, street and highway markings, signal lights, and other traffic regulations.
2. I fully realize that the motor car is not a plaything, but a machine that has the power to injure and kill; I will not try to show off with it.
3. I shall drive at all times at a speed that is reasonable and proper under existing conditions; I shall never exceed the maximum speed permitted in the state in which I am driving.
4. I shall reduce speed and observe traffic conditions carefully at all intersections, even though I may have the right of way; I shall not hesitate to yield the right of way when it is in the interest of safety to do so.
5. I shall not attempt to pass other cars, unless there is plenty of room to pass with safety.
6. I shall give pedestrians and cyclists the right of way, even though they may be violating the rules of traffic safety.
7. I shall never drink any form of intoxicating liquor before driving or while a car is in my charge, nor will I ride with a driver who has been drinking.
8. I shall not attempt to drive if I am over-tired or sleepy.
9. I shall attempt to keep myself and my car in efficient operating condition at all times.
10. I shall take pride in my driving ability and constantly strive to become a better driver.

Behavior of this type will show that you are meeting the challenge. It will indicate that you are mature enough to maintain your privilege to drive. It will indicate that you have embarked upon one of the most worthwhile of all human endeavors—the task of prolonging human life and making life more enjoyable.

SUMMARY

Yes, you and only you can solve your traffic problem. In fact, if your car were able to communicate with you this is the message it would bring:

I'm just a wheel — a steering wheel — and you're my captain.

Behind me you're the lord and master of a miracle.

You can make me take the kids to school.

You can turn me down the sunny road toward town.

With me you can guide your goods to the market place . . . you can rush the sick to be healed . . . you can go in minutes to places hours away.

You can do magic.

Yet, in the blink of an eye, in the tick of your watch, I can turn deadly killer.

I can snuff out the life of a kid still full of life — maybe your kid.

I can twist a smile into tears . . . I can wreck and cripple and destroy.

I can deal out death like the plague.

And I'm no respecter of persons . . . a child, a grandmother, even you, my friend . . . it's all the same to me.

I'm sensitive. I respond instantly to the hands you give me.

Give me calm hands, steady hands, careful hands . . . and I'm your friend.

But give me unsteady hands, fuzzy-minded hands, reckless hands . . . then I'm your enemy, a menace to the life, the happiness, the future of every person, every youngster riding, walking, playing.

I was made for pleasure and usefulness.

Keep me that way.

I'm in your hands.

I'm just a steering wheel, and you're my captain.

Behind me you're the lord and master of a miracle . . . or a tragedy.

It's up to you.

(From I'm Just a Steering Wheel, American Oil Company.)

DISCUSSION TOPICS

1. What are the three important ways that you can help fight the traffic problem?
2. What indications are there that traffic safety work is worthwhile?
3. What is meant by the "will to win"? How does it apply to traffic safety?
4. What are some of the important values of the resolution suggested in the text? If everyone followed this code, what might be the effect on traffic?

PROJECTS AND PROBLEMS

1. Conduct a survey, and draw up a fact sheet describing the traffic situation in your community. This should include accident facts, the function of public and private agencies, important local problems, and needs and concrete suggestions to guide the action of individual citizens.
2. Write a letter to the editor of the local newspaper explaining the findings of your survey and explaining your recommendations. Request him to invite others to express their opinions on this problem.

SELECTED REFERENCES FOR UNIT VIII

1. *Inventory and Guide for Action,* President's Conference on Highway Safety. Washington, D. C.: U. S. Government Printing Office, 1951.
2. *Why We Have Automobile Accidents,* Harry R. De Silva. New York: John Wiley and Sons, Inc., 1942.

A

Accelerator, 62
  motion point, 83
Accelerator pedal, 76
Accident Facts, 214-15
Accident-repeater driver, 142-43
Accidents:
  alcohol, effects, 132
  behavior in case of, 252-54
  bicyclists, 342
  contributory negligence, 249
  impact, forces, 217
  inefficiency breeds, 323
  insurance, *see* Insurance
  liability, 248-49
  motor scooters, 344-46
  paying for, 249-50
  potential situations, unawareness of,
    246
  power cycles, 344-46
  reporting, 254
  responsibility in, 248
  speed invites sudden death, 218
  traffic toll, 15-17
  turnpike, reasons for, 296-97
Adjustment, *see* Maintenance
Agencies, enforcement, 258-60
  courts, 260
  motor vehicle departments, 260
  police, 258-60
Age of driver, 134
Alcohol:
  effects, 132-33
  pedestrian and, 336
American Petroleum Institute, 296
Ammeter, 54-55
Angle parking, 105-07
Art of driving and living, 146
Automatic transmission cars:
  fluid coupling principle, 168-69
  leaving the car, 78
  motion point of accelerator, 83
  moving the car, 81
  selector lever for, 63-66
  shifting gears, 91
  slowing down and stopping, 83
  starting cars with, 76
    on upgrade, 103-104
  stopping the engine, 78

Automatic transmission cars (*Cont.*):
  turns, right and left, 97
Automobile:
  advantages, 19-26
  automatic transmission, *see* Automatic
    transmission cars
  benefits, 19-26
  development, 33-40
  early faith in, 40-42
  educational opportunities, extended,
    20
  insurance, *see* Insurance
  job maker, as, 20-21
  numbers, increase in, 43
  parts, basic, 151-52
  recreational advantages, 19-20
  speed, increase in, 43
  streamlined, 38-40
  used, *see* Used cars
Automotive engineering, 235
Axle, rear, *see* Rear axle

B

Backing the car, 84-86
Barnum and Bailey, 33
Battery, 154
  maintenance, 180-81
Beam indicator, 58
Bicyclists:
  accident analysis, 342
  bad habits of motorists, 343
  city driving, 275
  role in traffic, 341-46
  wide berth to, giving, 343
Body, 174
  maintenance, 186-87
Brake drum, 171, 172
Brakes, 171-73
  care of, 183
  hand and foot, 62
  hydraulic system, 171-73
  parking, 173
  power, 173
Braking distance, stopping distance de-
    termined by, 211-13
Busses:
  pedestrian accidents, 337-38
  school, passing, 232
  transportation, 23

C

Cadillac, self-starting sedan, 38
Cams, 160
Camshaft, 160
Carbon monoxide poisoning, 133-34, 181
Carburetor, 152-53
Caution habit, 93
Centrifugal force, 205-208
Chains, friction, 205
Chassis and running gear, 170-74
  brakes, 171-73
  frame, 170
  lubrication, 178-79
  parking brake, 173
  shock absorbers, 171
  springs, 171
  steering mechanism, 173-74
Check-up, periodic, 186-87
Children at play, city driving, 275-76
Choke, 59-60, 75
Choke value, 153
Cigarette lighter, 62
City driving, problems, 267-77
  aids for, other, 276-77
  bicyclists, 275
  children at play, 275-76
  crosswalks, stopping before, 272
  hazards, 268
  intersections, procedure at, 271
  in traffic, 268-77
  lane position, 268-70
  parking places, 272-75
  passing on right, 272
  pedestrians, 275
  speeds, safe driving, 268
Climbing hills, 214
Close-quarters maneuvering, 101
Clutch, 164-65
  adjustment, 181
  friction point, 82
Clutch pedal, 62-63, 75
Coasting, 214
Coefficient of friction, 201-202
Collision insurance, 189
Color blindness, 125-26
Compensable disabilities, 118
Complex reaction time, 127, 216-17
Comprehensive coverage, insurance, 189
Compression rings, 158
Compression stroke, 157-58
Connections, electrical, checking, 181
Contributory negligence, 249
Controls, driving, see Driving controls
Cooling system, 161-62
  maintenance, 180
Correctable disabilities, 118
Courtesy in passing, 284
Courts, enforcement agencies, 260

Crankshaft, 156
Crossing the street, 337
Crossing traffic, basic rules, 226-27
Crosswalks, stopping before, 272
Cylinder head, 153
Cylinders, 153

D

Decreasing speed, see Stopping the car
Defensive driving, 320-23
  correcting a mistake, 322-23
  thinking ahead, 320-22
Depth perception, 122-23
Descending hills, 213-14
Differential, 170
  maintenance, 182
Dimmer switch, 61
Disabilities, compensable or correctable, 118
Distributor, 155
  points, checking, 181
Drivers:
  accident-repeater, 142-43
  age, 134
  challenge to, 10, 48
  characteristics of good, 143-46
  concept of own abilities, 145
  emotional fitness, 145-46
  experienced, retraining, 8-9
  inattentive, 141-42
  irresponsible, 141
  obstacle to traffic control, 45-47
  pedestrian co-operation with, 333-38
  personality traits, 137-46
  physical condition, 117-35
  physical fitness, 145-46
  practice makes perfect, 7-8
  preparing to drive, 6
  problem, 138-43
  self-centered, 138-40
  self-improvement, interest in, 146
  show-off, the, 140
  skillful, advantages, 10-11
  social responsibility, sense of, 145
  temperamental, 141
Driving:
  art of, 146
  city, see City driving
  defensive, 320-23
  drills, fundamental, 69-111
    driving speed, adjusting, 89-95
    lower gears, using, 86-88
    maneuvering on grades, 101-105
    moving the car, 80-86
    parking, angle and parallel, 106-111
    preparing to drive, 73-79
    purpose, 70
    turns, right and left, 95-99

Driving (*Cont.*):
drills, fundamental (*Cont.*):
  using, 72-73
  Y turn, 99-101
economically, 188-89
emergency, *see* Emergency driving
fundamentals, 317-28
good form in, 69-112
habits, forming, 69-70
hazards, *see* Hazards
highway, *see* Roads and highways
lower gears, in, 86-88
maneuvering:
  close-quarters, 101
  on grades, 101-105
natural laws affecting, 199-218
performance, evaluating, 323-28
preparation for, 73-74
privilege of, 318-19
psychological factors, 129
speed:
  adjusting, 89-95
  stopping when operating at, 91-93
superhighway, *see* Turnpike driving
turning:
  right and left, 95-99
  Y turn, 99-101
turnpike, *see* Turnpike driving
Driving controls, 62-65
accelerator, 62
adjustment to, 66-67
brakes, hand and foot, 62
clutch pedal, 62-63
selector lever, automatic transmissions, 63-66
shifting lever, 63-64
  older cars, on, 64
steering wheel, 66
Driving-emergency trainer, using, 310
Duryea, Charles and Frank, 32, 33, 34

E

Economic influence of trucking, 23
Educational opportunities, extended, 20
Edwards, Gus, 35
Electrical connections, checking, 181
Emergency driving, 303-14
driving-emergency trainer, using, 310
mimetic drill, 308-309
practice exercises, 310-14
situations, 304-307
techniques, learning, 307-14
Emergency repairs, insurance coverage, 189-90
Emergency vehicles:
city driving, 276
making way for, basic rules, 232
Emotional fitness, 145-46
Enforcement of traffic laws, 257-61

Enforcement of traffic laws (*Cont.*):
agencies, 258-60
  courts, 260
  motor vehicle departments, 260
  police, 258-60
co-operation with officers, 257-58
self-enforcement, 319
Engine, 152-63
camshaft, 160
carburetor, 152-53
cooling, 161-62
crankshaft, 156
cylinders, 153
flywheel, 156
four-stroke cycle, 157-59
  compression stroke, 157-58
  exhaust stroke, 159
  intake stroke, 157
  power stroke, 158-59
fuel pump, 152
functions, basic, 152
ignition system, 154-55
intake manifold, 153
lubricating, 162-63, 177-78
piston, 153, 156
power, harnessing, 156
"racing," 76
spark plugs, 153
speed:
  changing, 76
  regulating, 159-60
starting, 74-76, 163
stopping, 76-78
timing, 160-61
Engineering, effects of, 235-45
traffic engineering, 235, 237
Engine temperature gauge, 56-57
Exhaust:
leaks, 181
stroke, 159
value, 153
Existing facilities, effective use, 238

F

False signals, 224
Fan, 162
Fatigue, 131-32
Field of vision, 121-22
Filter, 152
oil, 163
Financial responsibility laws, 250
First gear (low), 166-67
Fisher brothers, 38
Fluid coupling principle, automatic drive, 168-69
Flywheel, 156, 165
Following distances, safe, 279-80
turnpike driving, 299
Foot brake, 62

Ford, Model T, 35-38
Ford, Henry, 31, 32, 35-38
Forward gears, shifting through, 89-91
Four-stroke cycle, 157-59
  compression stroke, 157-58
  exhaust stroke, 159
  intake stroke, 157
  power stroke, 158-59
  sealing in the power, 158
Frame, 170
Friction, 199-205
  chains, 205
  coefficient of, 201-202
  skidding, 203
  slippery roads:
    slowing and stopping on, 203-204
    stopping distances on, 204
  starting on ice, snow, mud, or sand, 200-201
  stopping the car, 201
  tires, 205
Friction point of clutch, 82
Fuel gauge, 54
Fuel pump, 152
Furnas, J. C., 218

G

Gauges:
  ammeter, 54-55
  beam indicator, 58
  engine temperature, 56-57
  fuel, 54
  odometer, 57-58
  oil pressure, 55-56
  reading, 76
  speedometer, 57
Gear box, 165-68
Gears:
  arrangement options, 166
  lower, driving in, 86-88
  second, speed in, controlling, 87
  shifting, 86-87
    reducing, 93-95
    through the forward gears, 89-91
  transmission, 165-68
Generator, 154
Grades, maneuvering on, 101-105
Gravity, 213-14
  climbing hills, 214
  coasting, 214
  descending hills, 213-14

H

Habits, driving:
  bad, of motorists, 343
  caution habit, 93
  forming, 69-70
  one-lane habit, 286

Hand brake, 62
Hand signals, 223-25
Hand throttle, 60
Hazards, city driving, 268
Hearing, 131
Heater switch, 61
Heise, Herman A., 132
High-speed hypnosis, 296-97
  avoiding, 300
Highway engineering, 235
Highways, see Roads and highways
Hills:
  climbing, 214
  descending, 213-14
  maneuvering on, 101-105
Horn, 61
Horse and buggy transportation, 29-32
Hydraulic braking system, 171-73
  maintenance, 183
Hypnosis, high-speed, 296-97
  avoiding, 300

I

Ice, starting on, 200-201
Ignition switch, 58-59
Ignition system, 154-55
  maintenance, 180-81
Impact, forces of, 217
Inattentive driver, 141-42
Information instruments, 53-58
Inspection, 179-86
Instruments, information, 53-58
  ammeter, 54-55
  beam indicator, 58
  engine temperature gauge, 56-57
  fuel gauge, 54
  odometer, 57-58
  oil pressure gauge, 55-56
  speedometer, 57
Insurance, 189-90, 250-52
  automobile owners, for, 250
  collision, 189
  comprehensive coverage, 189
  financial responsibility laws, 251
  liability or "third party," 250-51
  prevention, as, 251-52
  rates, 252
  towing and emergency repairs, 189-90
Intake:
  manifold, 153
  stroke, 157
  value, 153
Intersections:
  highway driving, 288-89
  procedure at, 271
Irresponsible driver, 141

J

Jobs, automobile as maker of, 20-21

K

Kettering, Charles, 38
Kinetic energy, *see* Momentum

L

Lacerated tread tires, 205
Lanes:
    changing, 286-88
    one-lane habit, 286
    position:
        city driving, 268-70
        turnpike driving, 299
Law enforcement, traffic, problem, 45
Laws, *see* Natural laws; Traffic laws
Leaks, exhaust, 181
Leaving the car, 76-78
Left turns, 95-99
    hand signal, 223
Liability, 248-50
    accidents, 248-49
    contributory negligence, 249
    insurance, 250-51
Licensing, laws concerning, 247-48
Lighting system, maintenance, 186
Light switches, 61
Living, art of, 146
Lower gears, driving in, 86-88
Lubrication, 177-79
    amount, 179
    chassis, 178-79
    engine, 162-63, 177-78
    type, right, 179

M

Magnetic field, 154
Maintenance:
    battery, 180-81
    body, 186-87
    brakes, 183
    check-up, periodic, 187
    clutch adjustment, 181
    connections, electrical, 181
    cooling system, 180
    differential, 182
    distributor points, 181
    economic driving, 188-89
    exhaust leaks, 181
    ignition system, 180-81
    lighting system, 186
    power train, 181-82
    rear axle, 182
    repair shops, 187
    shock absorbers, 182
    spark plugs, 181
    springs, 182
    steering system, 182-83
    tires, 184-85

Maintenance (*Cont.*):
    transmission, 182
    universal joint, 182
Maneuvering:
    close-quarters, 101
    on grades, 101-105
Maps, road and highway, 291-92
Master cylinder, 172
Mimetic drill, emergency driving, 308-309
"Minor" violations, 319-20
Mistakes, correcting, 322-23
Model T Ford, 35-38
Momentum, 208-13
    economic use of, 188-89
    force of impact, 217
Motion point of accelerator, 83
Motor car, *see* Automobile
Motor scooters, 344-46
Motor vehicle departments, enforcement agencies, 260
Moving the car, 80-86
    backing, 84-86
    slowing down, 83
    slow speeds, 81-83
    steering, 84
    stopping, 83
Mud, starting on, 200-201
Mud-snow tires, 205
Muffler leaks, 181

N

National defense, motor transportation in, 23
Natural laws affecting driving, 199-218
    centrifugal force, 205-208
    friction, 199-205
    gravity, 213-14
    momentum, 208-13
    regulating speed in accordance with, 217-18
    speed, influence on traffic safety, 214-18
Neutral gear, 166, 168
Newton's Law, 205
Night vision, 123-25
Numbers of vehicles, obstacle to traffic control, 43

O

Odometer, 57-58
Officers, traffic:
    co-operation with, 257-58
    enforcement agency, 258-60
Oil-control rings, 158
Oil filters, 163
Oil pressure gauge, 55-56
Olds, R. E., 32, 35

Oldsmobile, 1901, 35
One-lane habit, 286
One-way streets, 240, 277

P

Parallel parking, 107-111
Parking:
  angle, 105-107
  on a hill, 104-105
  parallel, 107-111
  regulations, 241-42
  rules, basic, 227-28
Parking brake, 173
  maintenance, 183
Parking places, 272-75
Passing other cars:
  courtesy in, 284
  highway driving, 280-81
  on the right, 272
  pointers on, 285-86
  prohibited, when, 282
  rules, 225-26
  slowly driven car, 284-85
Paying for accidents, 249-50
Pedestrians:
  alcohol and, 336
  city driving, 275
  crossing the street, 337
  darkness, in, 335-36
  driver co-operation with, 333-38
  highway driving, 290-91
  street cars and busses, 337-38
  walking, safe:
    on open highway, 337
    physical conditions, 338
    tactics for, 336-38
Perception, 215
Performance, driving, evaluating, 323-28
Periodic check-up, 187
Personality traits, 137-46
  accident-repeater driver, 142-43
  concept of own abilities, 145
  emotional fitness, 145-46
  good driver, characteristics, 143-46
  inattentive driver, 141-42
  irresponsible drivers, 141
  physical fitness, 145-46
  problem drivers, 138-43
  self-centered driver, 138-40
  self-improvement, interest in, 146
  show-off, the, 140
  social responsibility, sense of, 145
  temperamental driver, 141
Physical condition, 117-35
  age, 134
  alcohol, effects, 132-33
  carbon monoxide poisoning, 133-34
  color blindness, 125-26

Physical condition (*Cont.*):
  depth perception, 122-23
  disabilities, compensable or correctable, 118
  fatigue, 131-32
  field of vision, 121-22
  hearing, 131
  night vision, 123-25
  reaction time, 126-29
  visual acuity, 119-21
Physical fitness, 145-46
Piston, 153, 156
Pitman arm, 173
Poisoning, carbon monoxide, 133-34, 181
Police, *see* Officers, traffic
Power:
  controlled, 319
  cycles, 344-46
  servant or master, 26
  stroke, 158-59
Power brakes, 173
Power train, 151, 164-70
  automatic drive, 168-69
  clutch, 164-65
  differential, 170
  maintenance, 181-82
  propeller shaft, 170
  rear axle, 170
  transmission, 165-68
  universal joint, 170
Preparation for driving, 73-74
Problem drivers, 138-43
Propeller shaft, 170
Public apathy, obstacle to traffic control, 45-46
Public welfare, furtherance of, 23-24

R

Radio switch, 61
Railroad grade crossings, 289-90
Reaction time, 126-29, 215-17
  complex, 216-17
  stopping distance determined by, 211-13
Rear axle, 170
  maintenance, 182
Recreation advantages for, 19-20
Reducing gears, 93-95
Regulating switches, 58-61
Regulations:
  parking, 241-42
  speed, 240
  stop, 239
  turning, 239
  uniform, need for, 44
Repairs, *see* Maintenance
Repair shops, 187

Responsibility for others, rules, basic, 230-31
Reverse gear, 166, 168
Right turns, 95-99
  hand signal, 223
Road construction, lag in, 44
Road markings, 245
Roads and highways:
  driving on, 279-91
    changing lanes, 286-88
    courtesy in passing, 284
    emergency situations, 306
    following distances, safe, 279-80
    intersections, 288-89
    one-lane habit, 286
    passing other cars, 280-81
    passing prohibited, when, 282
    passing slow drivers, 284-85
    pedestrians, 290-91
    pointers on passing, 285-86
    railroad grade crossings, 289-90
  existing facilities, effective use, 238
  maps, 291-92
  one-way streets, 240
  route numbers, 291-92
  slippery:
    slowing and stopping on, 203-204
    stopping distances on, 204
  structural changes, 245
  superhighways, see Turnpike driving
  turnpikes, see Turnpike driving
Rocker arms, 160
Route numbers, highway, 291-92
Rules, traffic, see Traffic laws
Running gear, see Chassis and running gear

S

Safety, traffic:
  benefits, 11-12
  driving speeds, city traffic, 268
  following distances, 279-80
    turnpike driving, 299
  significance for youth, 4-5
  speed on, influence, 214-18
  walking, tactics for safe, 336-37
Sand, starting on, 200-201
School busses, passing, basic rules, 232
Second gear (intermediate), 166, 167
  speed in, controlling, 87
Second-hand cars, see Used cars
Selector lever, automatic transmissions, for, 63-66
Self-centered driver, 138-40
Self-enforcement, 319
Self-improvement, interest in, 146
Self-starter, 163
Selling, Lowell S., 137
Shifting gears, 86-87

Shifting gears (Cont.):
  reducing gears, 93-95
  through the forward gears, 89-91
Shifting lever, 63-64
  older cars, on, 64
Shift-of-position signals, 224
Shock absorbers, 171
  maintenance, 182
Show-off, the, 140
Side-vision testing device, 121-22
Signaling:
  basic rules, 222-23
  devices, 224-25
Signals:
  false, 224
  hand, 223-25
  left turn, 223
  right turn, 223
  shift-of-position, 224
  stop or decrease speed, 223
  traffic control, 242-45
Signal switches, 61
Signs, traffic control, 242
Skidding, 203
Slip-joint, 170
Slippery roads:
  slowing and stopping on, 203-204
  stopping distances on, 204
Slowing down, 83
Smith, Uriah, 33, 34
Snellen Chart, 119-21
Snow, starting on, 200-201
Social responsibility, sense of, 145
Spark coil, 154
Spark plugs, 153
  maintenance, 181
Speed:
  control, turnpike driving, 298
  controlling, in second gear, 87
  death invited by, 218
  decreasing, see Stopping the car
  driving, safe, 268
    adjusting, 89-95
    stopping when operating at, 91-93
  engine:
    changing, 76
    regulating, 159-60
  high-speed hypnosis, 296-97
    avoiding, 300
  influence on traffic safety, 214-18
    impact, forces of, 217
    perception, 215
    reaction time, 215-17
  obstacle to traffic control, 43
  regulating in accordance with nature's laws, 217-18
  regulations, 240
    basic rules, 228-30
  safe headlight, 125
  velocitization, 296-97

Speedometer, 57
Spotlight switch, 61-62
Springs, 171
  maintenance, 182
Starter switch, 59
Starting the car:
  on ice, snow, mud, or sand, 200-201
  on upgrade, 102-103
Starting the engine, 74-76, 163
Steering the car, 84
  around corners, 97-99
Steering mechanism, 173-74
  maintenance, 182-83
Steering wheel, 66, 173
Stopping distance:
  on slippery surfaces, 204
  reaction and braking distance deter-
    mine, 211-13
Stopping the car, 83
  friction in, 201
  hand signal, 223
  on slippery roads, 203-204
    stopping distances on, 204
  operating at driving speed, when, 91-
    93
  turnpike driving, 299
Stopping the engine, 76-78
Stop regulations, 239
Street cars, pedestrian accidents, 337-
  38
Structural roadway changes, 245
"Sudden Death," Furnas, 218
Superhighways, see Turnpike driving
Switches, regulating, 58-61
  accessory, 61-62
  choke, 59-60
  cigarette lighter, 62
  dimmer, 61
  hand throttle, 60
  heater, 61
  horn, 61
  ignition, 58-59
  light, 61
  radio, 61
  signal, 61
  spotlight, 61-62
  starter, 59
  windshield wiper, 60-61

                    T

Tail pipe, 159
Temperamental driver, 141
Thermostat, 162
Thinking ahead, 320-22
Third gear (high), 166, 167-68
"Third Party" insurance, 250-51
Throttle:
  hand, 60
  value, 153, 159-60

Ticket "fixing," 259
Timing, engine, 160-61
Tires:
  care of, 184-85
  flat, changing, 185
  friction, 205
  lacerated tread, 205
  mud-snow, 205
  winterized, 205
  winterized mud-snow, 205
Towing, insurance coverage, 189-90
Traffic:
  bicyclist in, role, 341-46
  complexity of scene, 3-4
  crossing, basic rules, 226-27
  driving in, 268-77
  regulations, see Regulations
  streams of, 341-45
Traffic control:
  devices, 242-44
  law enforcement, effective, problem,
    45
  measures, 238-39
  obstacles to, 42-48
    driver, 45-47
    numbers of vehicles, 43
    public apathy, 45-46
    regulations, uniform need for, 44
    road construction and design, lag
      in, 44
    speed, increased, 43
Traffic engineering, 235, 239
Traffic laws:
  basic rules, 222-31
  crossing traffic, 226-27
  enforcement, 257-61
    agencies, 258-60
    officers, co-operation with, 257-58
  engineering, effects of, 235-45
  emergency vehicles, making way for,
    232
  financial responsibility, 250
  hand signals, 223-25
  liability, concerning, 248-50
  licensing, concerning, 247-48
  man-made, basic, 221-31
  natural laws affecting, 199-217
  parking, 227-28
  passing rules, 225-26
  passing school busses, 232
  regulations, see Regulations
  responsibility for others, 230-31
  signaling, 222-23
  speed regulation, 228-30
  turning, 227
  development, 29-48
  national concern, 15-26
  need, 26
  personal concern, 3-12
Traffic toll, 15-16

INDEX

Traffic toll (*Cont.*):
  common concern, 17-18
  worse than war, 16-17
Transmission, 165-68
  automatic, *see* Automatic transmission
  maintenance, 182
Trucking, economic influence, 23
Turning:
  basic rules, 227
  corners, 95-97
  hand signals, 223
  regulations, 239
  right and left, 95-99
  Y turn, 99-101
Turnpike driving:
  accidents, reasons for, 296-97
    high-speed hypnosis, 296-97, 300
    potential situations, unawareness of, 296
    velocitization, 296-97
  advantages, 300
  following distances, 299
  lane position, 299
  speed control, 298
  stopping, 299
  techniques, 298-300

U

Universal joint, 170
  maintenance, 182
Upgrade, starting on, 102-103
Used cars, buying, 190

V

Valves:
  choke, 153
  exhaust, 153
  intake, 153
  throttle, 153, 159-60
Velocitization, 296-97
Violations, "minor," 319-20
Vision:
  field of, 121-22
  night, 123-25
  visual acuity, 119-21
Voltage-regulator, 154

W

Walking, safe:
  on open highway, 337
  physical conditions, 338
  tactics for, 336-38
Winterized mud-snow tires, 205
Winterized tires, 205
Windshield wiper, 60-61

Y

Young drivers, traffic safety, significance for, 4-5
Y turn, 99-101

Mr. Palmer

It has been with great interest that I have observed your behavior and I have reached the unavoidable conclusion that you are not mentally developed enough to attend an institution of this nature, although your decidedly rotund physical stature has sadly surpassed your mind in its developement. I would suggest that you investigate a school more suited to your aptitude such

as N.T.S. or National
School for Obedience
Training for Dogs

Love and Kisses
Harry P Raunch

2 times a year safty inspection
chackes lubraced 1000

.12